DEER HUNTERS'
ALMANAC

FROM THE PUBLISHERS OF DEER & DEER HUNTING®

2001
EDITION

© 2000 by
Krause Publications

W9-AVZ-101

Deer & Deer Hunting is a registered trademark of Krause Publications Inc.

Published by

Krause Publications
700 E. State St. • Iola, WI 54990-0001
Telephone: 715/445-2214   fax: 715/445-4087
World Wide Web: www.deeranddeerhunting.com

Please call or write for our free catalog of outdoor publications. Our toll-free number to
place an order or obtain a free catalog is 800-258-0929. Please use our regular
business telephone, 715-445-2214, for editorial comment or further information.

Library of Congress Catalog Number: 92-74255

ISBN: 0-87341-956-1
Printed in the United States of America

CONTENTS

4

Editor's Note

By Daniel E. Schmidt

Y ou might not realize it, but
you're holding a century's
worth of deer hunting information in this little book. And,
although your 2001 *Deer Hunter's
Almanac* includes thought-provoking
sketches of deer hunting's past, it
documents the sport's present and
future.

Either time really does fly, or we're
all getting older. This is the
Almanac's 10th edition. Each year,
we redesign the book's contents to
include more easy-to-access information. We rely on you — a valued *Deer
& Deer Hunting* reader — for input
when developing these new themes
and sections. In fact, with your help,
last year's collector's edition went
over so well that we expanded the
book's scope in 2001 to include something for everyone — young and old
hunters alike.

Tech-heads will appreciate the
bow- and gun-hunting tips. Big-buck
hunters will marvel at the stories and
photos of some of the biggest whitetails taken in North America over the
past few years. Landowners will learn
how to better manage their land for
bigger and healthier deer. And do-it-
yourselfers will enjoy the meat-
processing insights.

There's even crossword and word-
search puzzles for the younger (and
maybe not-so-young) members of
your deer camp. Regardless of your
deer hunting experience, I'm sure
you'll find the all-new "Deer Hunter's
Quiz" challenging, educational and
entertaining.

So, sit back and enjoy. When you're
finished, let me know what you think!

Daniel E. Schmidt

schmidtd@krause.com

DEER HUNTERS'
ALMANAC

FROM THE PUBLISHERS OF DEER & DEER HUNTING®

Publisher Hugh McAloon

EDITORIAL
Editorial Director Patrick Durkin
Managing Editor Daniel E. Schmidt
Associate Editor Jennifer Pillath
Editorial Intern Ryan Gilligan

ADVERTISING
Advertising Manager Brad Rucks

Sales
Mark Beauchaine • Kathy Quinlan
Kyle Franson • Pat Boyle

Sales Assistant Susie Melum
Sales/Editorial Assistant Renae Murphy

SUBSCRIPTION SERVICES
715/445-3775, ext. 257

Published by
Krause Publications Inc.
700 E. State St., Iola, WI 54990-0001
715/445-2214 FAX 715/445-4087
http://www.deeranddeerhunting.com

This book is published solely for information to the reader.
The publisher is not liable for authors' or advertisers claims,
or any negligence by manufacturers who advertise.
Advertising rates are available upon request.
Address all correspondence to Deer & Deer Hunting,
700 E. State St., Iola, WI 54990-0001.
Allow six weeks for address change, and include old and
new address with your request.

Contact Krause Publications about these
quality magazines:

*Deer & Deer Hunting • Turkey & Turkey Hunting
Trapper & Predator Caller • Whitetail Business
Wisconsin Outdoor Journal*

 Krause Publications
700 E. State St.
Iola, WI 54990-0001

5

Where Do We Go From Here?

Silently, I waited for my heart rate to return to normal.

It was a good shot, well within my range, and I heard the deer fall soon after the shot. Still, I fought the urge to excitedly descend from my stand. Instead, I wanted to take a moment to calm down and descend carefully.

As I sat, my mind wandered back to my first deer hunt almost 20 years ago, and I thought how deer hunting has changed for me. Back then, gun-hunting was deer hunting for me, and it was done five hours away on public land in the North Woods. We hunted from the ground in freezing temperatures till noon, went back to the van for lunch, and returned to the woods until dark. Bucks were legal to shoot and does were not, unless you were lucky and drew the rare antlerless permit. I wore a borrowed one-piece suit, two sizes too large, and I rarely saw a deer.

What would those old men in deer camp think about this kind of deer hunting? I lowered my bow to the ground and smiled. Here I am, a scant five minutes' drive from my suburban home, and I'm hunting deer within the village limits. I'm wearing the latest camouflage and shooting a bow and arrows made from space-age materials. I'm also hunting from a commercially made tree stand, I use rattling antlers and grunt calls, and I de-scent everything from my hair to my socks. Beyond that, I scout deer year-round instead of the day before the opener.

Yes, deer hunting has changed, but why? *Deer & Deer Hunting* recently asked six prominent figures in outdoor communications and wildlife management to help answer that question. We asked them to look back over the past 100 years and identify significant accomplishments and events that shaped the deer hunting landscape. In addition, we asked them to forecast the future. What will deer hunting be like in the next 100 years?

Valerius Geist, wildlife researcher, lecturer from the University of Calgary: The greatest accomplishment in the past century is that the U.S. and Canada got together continentally and generated a system of wildlife conservation the likes of which has no peer. The greatest environmental success of the century is the return of wildlife to North America. Whitetails were virtually non-existent at the turn of the century, having been shot down to numbers in total of about 300,000. What are they now, somewhere around 20 million, 30 million?

The significance is that we have had a "populace system" of wildlife conservation and management in

Daniel E. Schmidt

Is deer hunting becoming a rich man's sport? With today's big-buck craze, many think the answer is a resounding "yes." If hunting becomes the domain of the wealthy, it could force thousands of hunters to abandon their favorite pastime.

which Joe Blow could participate. And Joe Blow did participate — enthusiastically.

All the fancy environmental laws of today, like the Endangered Species Act, wouldn't be worth the paper they're written on without that great architecture of conservation that supports all wildlife.

D&DH: How did deer hunting contribute to the success of this management system?

Geist: It played a very important part in the thinking of the fathers of wildlife conservation. They spoke specifically about deer in their speeches. They were making a point by saying, "Wouldn't it be wonderful if deer were abundant again?" Deer were one of the primary concerns in the mentality of those that started the conservation movement.

D&DH: What do you foresee for deer hunting in the next century?

Geist: It will be grim, I'm afraid. The reason why is we are losing the populace infrastructure that politically supports deer hunting. At the same time, we are seeing a growing trend by landowners to privatize and exploit deer for money. This, of course, leads to hunting by only the elite and wealthy — something we are seeing already.

In addition, the anti-hunting and animal-rights movements are really bamboozling the urban population with philosophies — if one can call them such — which have little merit but nevertheless are attractive enough to have emotional appeal. All this stands to reduce the number of hunters, thus reducing the political clout that wildlife has.

The reason we have turkeys is because we have a lot of turkey hunters and the National Wild Turkey Federation with 150,000 paid members, which raises millions of dollars. There are no such conventions to celebrate white-crowned sparrows or bobolinks — they have no clientele — and they are declining.

Al Hofacker, co-founder of D&DH: At the top of the list is the reintroduction of deer and the development of deer-management principles and practices. At the beginning of the century, sportsman and conservation agencies worked together to reintroduce deer to areas where they were basically extinct. In the 1930s and '40s, Aldo Leopold led the way in the development of (wildlife) management. Without these events, there would be no deer hunting today.

The amount of information now available is also important. Several national magazines, shows, seminars, and innumerable books and published materials are available that were written not just by hunters, but by scientists like John Ozoga. I think this has really helped hunters understand their quarry better — its biology, habits and, of course, methods to hunt it.

Along those lines, I think hunter education greatly improved. Most states made it mandatory for first-time hunters, and it's made the sport much safer. Deer hunters were in the forefront in developing these programs and eventually making them mandatory.

I also believe the compound bow radically changed bow-hunting for the better. It spurred an interest in archery. It really came into existence in the early 1970s, and interest in bow-hunting skyrocketed. When I started hunting in 1969, Wisconsin had about 10,000 archers. Today the state has more than 250,000.

D&DH: What do you foresee for deer hunting in the next century?

Hofacker: I'm not optimistic. Privatization of deer hunting land is a problem now and it's going to get worse. This will force many hunters to public land. I believe the day will come in the next century when you'll still have the opportunity to deer hunt, but not when or where you want. We'll see a lottery system for when and where to hunt on public land, but I hope I'm wrong.

I'm also concerned about who will manage deer in the next century. I say that because after 50 years of developing sound deer-management principles, we still have trouble implementing them as effective practices for management.

In Wisconsin, more than 80 percent of our deer management units are overpopulated, and it's not just a one- or two-year phenomenon. In fact, the

Daniel E. Schmidt

If the outdoor industry learns to reach out to minority groups for participation, then the future of hunting looks good. If they ignore women and minorities, then it's not so good because the racial makeup of the population is changing.

statewide deer population has been over the fall population goal since 1981 — almost 20 years. I don't know how long that can persist.

If deer hunters don't cooperate with wildlife managers to manage deer herds, someone else will step in. In Michigan, there was a case where the Michigan Farm Bureau filed a lawsuit against the state because Michigan's deer herd was far beyond the population goals and only getting worse. Essentially, they were filing a lawsuit to take control out of the hands of the Michigan Department of Natural Resources. They were making the argument, and perhaps rightfully so, that deer weren't being managed.

The days of going into the woods and being away from everything are over. Increasingly, deer hunters are going to be in situations where they're going to hear cars and people.

Charles Alsheimer, *D&DH* **Northern Field Editor:** Obviously, the recovery of the whitetail is number one. But what strikes me most is the specialization of the whitetail industry. There used to be three outdoor magazines: *Sports Afield*, *Outdoor Life* and *Field & Stream*. When *D&DH* hit the street in 1977, it was the first specialized outdoor magazine. After that, other specialized magazines, including other deer-specific magazines began to appear.

Other advancements are the introduction of the compound bow by Allen, which prompted the archery world to explode; the urbanization of America, which caused many farms to return to brush and woodlots; and

the introduction of camouflage specifically for deer hunters, which made hunting a designer sport. In addition, we saw a technological explosion: Gore-Tex, carbon arrows, fast-flight strings, glass limbs and single-cam bows, and stainless steel rifles with Kevlar stocks.

Another significant factor is that the 1980s were probably the greatest single decade from a financial standpoint. People had disposable income for guns, bows, magazines and hunting trips.

The economy drove the whitetail industry. Baby boomers like myself had money to spend on the sport. The magazines helped fuel it, and *D&DH* was the foundation of that — it was the first one on the block.

D&DH: What do you foresee for deer hunting in the next century?

Alsheimer: Roy Rogers said "Buy land — they don't make it any more." We can laugh about that, but it paints a less-than-glowing picture for the future of the hunting world. People are buying land and putting up posted signs — I happen to be one of them — and limiting the utilization of the land. There simply won't be more places to hunt. Combine that with fractured family structure, divorced parents and single mothers — there's nobody to take kids hunting.

I believe we have seen the mountain top. I believe it was reached in the late 1980s. We're now on the down side of that hill. Because of animal-rights groups and a changing social structure, hunting isn't as attractive or accessible to kids.

I see us going the way of Europe, but maybe not in my lifetime. You will have to have money or land to hunt, and you will have heavy regulations.

D&DH: Anything bright ahead?

Alsheimer: Hunters will be more concerned with the quality of deer on their land, and they'll be more concerned with what they can give back to the sport. They'll be better stewards of the land.

John Ozoga, whitetail researcher and wildlife biologist: The past 100 years brings us from less than a half-million deer to the current estimates, which I think are almost 30 million. So in essence, the country went from zero deer hunting — although some places like Michigan still had some hunting — to abundance. That whole process was complex, and it is difficult to pick out specific accomplishments relative to deer hunting. Unfortunately, the animal has become a pest in a lot of areas that are out of the hands of hunters.

D&DH: What do you foresee for deer hunting in the next century?

Ozoga: I'm somewhat pessimistic. We will continue to see a trend toward privatization. The deer-as-pest problem is not going away. It's going to be an enormous challenge to manage deer on small private and suburban parcels. On the other hand, the farmland situation — crop damage and high deer densities — stands a better chance of being solved. I think farmers and deer hunters are more compatible in this situation. We might even see quality deer management in these areas.

On public lands — especially federal — we'll see a trend toward biodiversity and probably less tree cutting, and I think deer populations will be affected by that change. I think state lands will follow that trend eventually, but it's going to take

The Ultimate Deer Hunter's Quiz
Part 1, Deer and Deer Hunting

How much do you enjoy white-tailed deer and deer hunting? Are you an "enthusiast" or certified deer nut? This quiz should answer those questions. Within this book, we have compiled some of the most thought-provoking questions on deer and deer hunting. Each chapter contains questions pertaining to its theme. Grab a pencil and circle the responses you think are correct, then grade yourself by turning to Page 194. Good luck!

1. According to a reader's survey conducted by *Deer & Deer Hunting* magazine, which of the following tree stands is the safest?
A. Commercial ladder stand
B. Homemade ladder stand
C. Commercial tripod stand
D. Commercial climbing stand

2. Which organization agrees that hunting is acceptable if it is done ethically and in accordance with laws and regulations?
A. Friends of Animals
B. The National Audubon Society
C. The Humane Society
D. People for the Ethical Treatment of Animals

3. What is the oldest deer species?
A. Moose
B. White-tailed deer
C. Mule deer
D. Roe deer

4. What is the youngest deer species?
A. Moose
B. Roe deer
C. Mule deer
D. Red deer

Continued on Page 13

Daniel E. Schmidt

The compound bow radically changed bow-hunting for the better. It spurred an interest in archery in the early 1970s, and interest in bow-hunting skyrocketed.

a lot longer.

Dick Lattimer, president, Archery Manufactures and Merchants Organization (AMO): The establishment of the Pittman-Robertson fund in 1937 was probably the most important thing that has happened in the history of conservation. It established a federal excise tax on sporting equipment and provides a lot of money every year for some 3,500 wildlife-management projects in 50 states.

The archery excise tax went into effect in 1975 as part of the Pittman-Robertson Act. Since that time, we've sent $288 million into this fund. The federal government gives each state Pittman-Robertson dollars based on a formula so all states are treated fairly regardless of their size and population.

My point is that this is the hunter's money, not federal money or money collected from the American citizens' income tax. This is money the hunters of America agreed to pool to support the fish and game departments' work, not only to benefit deer and game species, but also nongame species.

D&DH: What do you foresee for deer hunting in the next century?

If the outdoor industry learns to reach out to minority groups for participation, then the future of our sport looks good. If they ignore minorities, then it's not so good because the racial make-up of the population is changing.

D&DH: Have these groups been ignored by the hunting industry?

Yes. I've been attending national meetings in this field for 33 years and seldom do I see blacks or Hispanics. We have to sell our sport to these folks to be successful. If not enough people participate in hunting and not enough hunters buy equipment, we lose Pittman-Robertson dollars, and the states will not be able to run their fish and wildlife agencies. The states get large percentages of their operating budgets from the Pittman-Robertson fund. The keystone of the whole conservation movement is the Pittman-Robertson Act.

Jay McAninch, executive director, Congressional Sportsman's Foundation: As an avid reader of history and a professional biologist, one thing that strikes me is how the white-tailed deer provided for people in the beginning and end of the 20th century.

In 1900, North America was finishing its settlement phase, and deer were a substantial part of the diet for those settlers. Now, skip through the recovery phase and the evolution of wildlife management to the present day. Deer are still providing for us, only they have gone into a broader set of niches where they are providing an up-close-and-personal big-game animal on the doorstep. People can go into urban parks and enjoy watching them. They're common in suburbia, farmlands and most forested areas. Although they began as an important food source, now, in addition to providing some sustenance, deer are probably far more important to the recreational, social and cultural well-being of people in the areas where they exist.

As far as events in the past 100 years, the most significant event was something whitetails did on their own and under the protection of hunters and conservation: they multiplied and filled every niche in the U.S. with unprecedented numbers. In doing that, they made themselves the premier hunting species for the hunter/conservationist.

As we turn into the next century, deer are the animal most young and new hunters are taught to hunt. When I look back to my beginnings, every person I knew learned to hunt squirrels, rabbits and perhaps pheasant and grouse. Deer weren't on our plate. We went deer hunting after we became more experienced. Today, a generation of hunters learned to hunt by hunting the whitetail.

D&DH: Is that a positive thing?

I think it is. Without the whitetail,

The Ultimate Deer Hunter's Quiz
Part 2, Deer and Deer Hunting

5. What is the average weight of a fawn born to a healthy doe?
A. 2 to 4 pounds
B. 4 to 6 pounds
C. 6 to 8 pounds
D. 8 to 10 pounds

6. Buck-hunters often look at a buck's ears to estimate the length of its tines. A whitetail's ear, on average, is how long?
A. 6 inches
B. 7 inches
C. 7½ inches
D. 8 inches

7. On what part of a deer are the preorbital glands found?

A. In front of the eyes.
B. On the forehead.
C. On the hocks of the hind legs.
D. Behind the ears.

8. A white-tailed deer is different from cows and sheep in which way?
A. Deer do not chew their cud.
B. Deer do not have small intestines.
C. Deer do not have chambered stomachs.
D. Deer do not have gall bladders.

9. When standing on its hind legs, how high can an adult buck reach when browsing?
A. 6 feet
B. 7 feet
C. 8 feet
D. 9 feet

10. A 112-pound deer at rest needs how many calories in a 24-hour period?
A. About 1,200 calories
B. About 1,300 calories
C. About 1,400 calories
D. About 1,500 calories

Continued on Page 15

Library of Congress: Detroit Publishing Co. Collection

Deer aren't just a huntable species. They're big and exciting and they do to people today what they did to people centuries ago. In fact, with the exception of the landscape, today's hunters are dealing with the exact same hunting situations as the hunters shown here. These Eastern whitetail hunters tagged this buck in 1903 in the Adirondack Mountains.

hunter numbers would be extremely low. Deer aren't just a huntable species. They're big and exciting and they do to people today what they did to people 300 years ago. It is the abundance and allure of the whitetail that has probably kept hunter numbers up in many states. There's no other species that attracts the number of hunters that deer do.

A lot of people don't realize that virtually every state (conservation) agency runs on two types of income: license sales and federal excise tax on hunting equipment. When you look at license sales and excise tax money, and you look at what portion of that comes from deer hunters, you see that deer put the economic fuel into the system.

So really, not only are whitetails recruiting and maintaining hunter numbers, economically, they're putting the bread and butter into state agencies. This money goes way beyond deer. It supports all kinds of wildlife and land management. You take deer out of the picture, and state agencies wouldn't be able to operate, and they wouldn't have much of a budget.

D&DH: What do you foresee for deer hunting in the next century?

Change is inevitable, and many of us hunt with the memory of how it was when we first started hunting. We have a lot more hunters out there and I don't see that changing. We'll see a more crowded landscape with smaller hunting parcels. We'll see demands on deer hunters — because of this crowding — to behave more responsibly, behavior that's more compatible with the landscape.

The days of going into the woods and being away from everything are over. Increasingly, deer hunters are

Privatization of deer hunting land is a problem now and it's going to get worse. This will force many hunters to public land. That might cause many hunters to quit, especially in states like Texas where most deer habitat is found on private land.

going to be in situations where they're going to hear cars and people. If you accept that kind of change — which is going to happen no matter what we do — and adapt to it, deer hunting will not only remain important, it will grow in importance as we find ways for deer to coexist with human populations.

There's no question deer can do it, they've shown that. The question is, can we adapt to it as hunters? If we do, we can demonstrate that hunting can be a public service, provide recreation and be an effective management tool.

If we look at the growing urban and suburban hunting landscape as an opportunity instead of a detriment, deer hunting's future looks good, and it will be a critical component to whitetail survival.

The Ultimate Deer Hunter's Quiz
Part 1, Deer and Deer Hunting

11. During the rut, a buck might travel how far in search of does?
   A. 2 square miles
   B. 8 square miles
   C. 10 square miles
   D. More than 10 square miles

12. How long would it take, without pressure from predators and hunters, for a deer herd to double in size?
   A. Two years
   B. Three years
   C. Four years
   D. Five years

13. The acorn from which oak provides the most crude protein?
   A. Black oak
   B. Scrub oak
   C. Water oak
   D. Blue oak

14. If a heart-shot deer lived 80 seconds, how far could it run?
   A. 100 yards
   B. 500 yards
   C. 1,000 yards
   D. A deer cannot live longer than 80 seconds without the use of its heart.

15. How many years did the oldest captive whitetail on record live?
   A. 20 years
   B. 22 years
   C. 24 years
   D. 26 years

16. When there is ½-inch or more snow on the ground, which deer leave drag marks when walking?
   A. All bucks
   B. Mature bucks
   C. Deer weighing more than 200 pounds.
   D. Bucks, does and fawns

This is the end of the quiz for Chapter 1. The quiz continues on Page 27. Answers listed on Page 194.

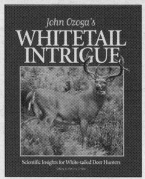

WHITETAIL HUNTING

Rattling, Calling & Decoying Whitetails
How to Consistently Coax Big Bucks into Range
by Gary Clancy, Edited by Patrick Durkin
Deer hunting veteran Gary Clancy explains how deer hunters can coax white-tailed bucks into heart-pounding range with calls, decoys and rattling horns. This book is crammed with anecdotes, diagrams and photos to teach you time-tested decoy techniques to lure bucks out of hiding. Also included is a look at the whitetail's many vocalizations and how you can talk the deer's language. Whether you're a novice or seasoned hunter, you'll quickly grasp Clancy's easy-to-understand hunting techniques.

Softcover • 6 x 9 • 208 pages
100 b&w photos
Item# RCDW • $19.95

Hunting Whitetails by the Moon
by Charles J. Alsheimer, Edited by Patrick Durkin
Charles J. Alsheimer, Deer & Deer Hunting magazine's Northern field editor, explains how deer hunters can use autumn moon cycles to predict peak times in the North and South to hunt rutting white-tailed bucks. He details the ground-breaking research conducted that unlocked the mysteries of the moon's influence on deer activity and behavior.

Softcover • 6 x 9 • 256 pages
100 b&w photos
Item# LUNAR • $19.95

Shots at Whitetails
A Deer Hunting Classic
by Lawrence R. Koller, Revised and Edited by Patrick Durkin
Deer & Deer Hunting reintroduces the hunting classic Shots at Whitetails by legendary Adirondacks deer hunter Larry Koller. While guns and bows have changed since Shots at Whitetails was written in 1948, the deer remains the same elusive, majestic animal, thus keeping this oft-quoted book keenly relevant for today's deer hunters.

Hardcover • 8-1/4 x 10-7/8 • 304 pages
20 illustrations • 30 color photos
Item# SWTT • $29.95

Shipping and Handling: $3.25 1st book; $2 ea. add'l. Foreign orders $15 per shipment plus $5.95 per book.

Sales tax: CA, IA, IL, PA, TN, VA, WA, WI residents please add appropriate sales tax.

Satisfaction Guarantee: If for any reason you are not completely satisfied with your purchase, simply return it within 14 days and receive a full refund, less shipping.

Retailers call toll-free 888-457-2873 ext 880, M-F, 8 am - 5 pm

Deer Hunting's Top 5 Inspirational Leaders

In the January 2000 issue of *Deer & Deer Hunting*, we asked our readers to vote on deer hunting's most inspirational leaders of the 1900s. The ballot contained the names of 57 scientists, manufacturers, politicians, celebrities, communicators and hunters whose names are intertwined with the sport and science of deer hunting. Each had in some way increased our understanding of the white-tailed deer, whether through the invention of camouflage patterns, the establishment of national forests or the writing of internationally known books.

Our ballot allowed five votes per category. Ballots were collected at our Iola, Wis., office and through our Web site until April 1. We also received write-in ballots, which included hunter education instructors, game wardens, fathers and grandfathers, to name a few.

What follows are the top five vote-getters and answers to the question: Who is the most inspirational leader in deer and deer hunting?

Fred Bear, hands down. Bear garnered 54 percent of the vote, followed by Aldo Leopold, 42 percent; Charles Alsheimer, 40 percent; and Theodore Roosevelt and Bill Jordan, each with 30 percent.

Rounding out the Top 10 were John Ozoga, 29 percent; Ted Nugent, 28 percent; Leonard Lee Rue III, 25 percent; James Easton, 24 percent; and H.W. Allen, 20 percent.

What follows are short biographies on the Top 5 vote-getters. We hope you enjoy this glimpse of deer hunting's heritage.

Illustrations by Ruth Pillath

JENNIFER PILLATH

Fred Bear
Father of Modern Bow-Hunting

As ballots rolled in, a pattern emerged. "It was hard nominating just five," read one entry. "I had to go with the people who did it for me when I started to bow-hunt."

"Fred Bear was an inspiration through my teens when I sought the knowledge and love of archery," read another ballot. "I'll never forget my first Bear Whitetail bow."

"My first bow was a Bear Kodiak, which I still have," wrote another reader. "I have been in archery since 1947, and I now have a Bear compound and I still love the sport."

The pattern continued this way, sketching the picture of a man whose influence runs deep. Fred Bear

AT A GLANCE

NAME: Fred Bear

HISTORICAL IMPORTANCE:
Considered by many as the father of modern archery. He started bow-hunting in 1929 and later started his own company, Bear Archery.

QUOTE:
"I hunt deer because I love the entire process; the preparations, the excitement, and sustained suspense of trying to match my woodlore against the finely honed instincts of these creatures. On most days spent in the woods, I come home with an honestly earned feeling that something good has taken place. It makes no difference whether I got anything; it has to do with how the day was spent."

humbly and quietly elevated the sport of archery and established credibility where there once was none. His name is so intertwined with the sport that the two are almost indistinguishable.

Bear's intrigue with archery began in 1927 after viewing Art Young's film, *Alaskan Adventures*. Bear was entranced. He soon met Young, and together the two practiced shooting and toyed with archery designs. In 1929, Bear ventured off on his first whitetail hunt with a bow in a Michigan cedar swamp.

In 1935, Bear finally arrowed a small spike buck, which began a successful hunting career. In the years to come, he took six world records with his bow, including elk, barren ground caribou, mountain caribou, stone sheep, Canada moose and Alaskan brown bear. He also achieved the seemingly impossible — killing elephant, lion, tiger, Asiatic buffalo, grizzly bear and Cape buffalo. Each kill attested to the potential strength and precision of the bow and arrow, and raised the public's confidence in the sport even higher.

But Bear was not just a shooting celebrity. His hands built numerous bows and archery accessories. He held 13 patents on archery equipment, including arrows with interchangeable point systems and the first quiver to attach to the bow. Of all the patents and ingenuity he brought to the industry, Bear never sought royalties or enforced his copyrights. He consciously allowed his ideas to spread to other companies, which in turn built the archery world into what it is.

Fred Bear died in 1988. However, he had already created a fault line deep beneath the industry.

Theodore Roosevelt
Father of Fair Chase

In the late 1800s, Americans did not yet understand the importance of preserving natural resources. Civilization and unrestricted market hunting had decreased wildlife in the West, and the clash between American Indians and the government had harmed big game on the frontier. Game management and conservation were foreign concepts to many people, and a national conscience toward preserving natural resources had yet to be born.

These concepts, still in their infancy, needed a strong and powerful leader. If conservation were to become a driving force in American politics, it would have to be passionately brought to the forefront of the American mind. That task was taken on by Theodore Roosevelt, the 24th president of the United States.

Roosevelt headed numerous pro-conservation initiatives. From 1901 to 1909, he designated 150 national forests, 51 federal bird reservations, five national parks, 18 national monuments, the first four national game preserves and the first 21 reclamation projects. In his 7½ years as president, he provided federal protection for 230 million acres.

It was during this time of rapid growth in conservation awareness that Roosevelt taught Americans about the legacy of natural resources. He defined preservation and wisely used natural resources as an astounding mark of a wealthy nation. "Every step of progress of mankind is marked by the discovery and use of resources previously unused," he said.

Roosevelt's enjoyment of hunting and the outdoors in general shaped his policies. In 1887, he established the Boone and Crockett Club not as a trophy club, but as a way to track the success of game-management programs. Roosevelt worked with George Bird Grinnell, General Tecumseh Sherman, Gifford Pinchot and 21 other outdoor enthusiasts to establish a foundation that would herald the effects of conservation.

In 1895, Roosevelt and Grinnell published the club's first book. But it wasn't until the 1920s that an official measurement system was established. It was used to record species that were vanishing off the landscape. In time, the scientific community recognized the system as a way to track the success of conservation programs. It wasn't until 1950 that the current scoring system was devised.

AT A GLANCE

NAME: Theodore Roosevelt

HISTORICAL IMPORTANCE:
Founded the Boone and Crockett Club in 1887. Its mission: to promote wildlife conservation and the principle of fair-chase hunting practices.

QUOTE:
"In a civilized and cultivated country, wild animals only continue to exist at all when preserved by sportsmen. The excellent people who protest against all hunting and consider sportsmen as enemies of wildlife (do not understand) the fact that in reality the genuine Sports man is, by all odds, the most important factor in keeping the larger and more valuable wild creatures from total extermination."

Aldo Leopold
Father of Wildlife Conservation

Author and theologian C.S. Lewis once stated: "We read to know we are not alone," He meant writers give the rest of us a voice. Good authors lasso experiences and shock us with their value.

Aldo Leopold was such a writer. He wrote beautifully, taking the simplicity of a walk in the woods and turning it into a valuable lesson in conservation. His writings, particularly *A Sand County Almanac*, became classics. Further, Leopold helped define wildlife management, ecological restoration, environmental ethics, ecosystem management and the wilderness movement.

In 1999, *A Sand County Almanac*, celebrated its 50th anniversary, although it was conceived long before that.

Leopold was born in Burlington, Iowa, in 1887, the eldest of four children. From his parents, he gained a love for hunting and the outdoors, which shaped his thoughts on natural resources. His "official" entry into wildlife studies began after he completed his master's degree in forestry at Yale University. Leopold then moved to New Mexico as supervisor of the Carson National Park. While there, he organized local sportsmen interested in protecting land. That move defined his idea of conservation as more than a biological science.

Leopold's work took him to Arizona where he helped establish the Gila Wilderness Area, and then to Wisconsin as assistant director of the U.S. Forest Products Laboratory in Madison. His interest in lab work waned, pushing him into field studies of Midwestern game. He eventually chaired the American Game Conference and the game management division of the Department of Agriculture. He also started the Wilderness Society.

The most publicly known portion of Leopold's life began soon after this, with his purchase of a piece of land along the Wisconsin River, deemed "The Shack." It was there that Leopold's narratives of outdoor life were inspired and penned. His writings followed the simplicity of daily interaction with wildlife at a time when white-tailed deer and other animals were making a comeback from low population levels. His observations warned us how important natural resources would be to future generations.

AT A GLANCE

NAME: Aldo Leopold

HISTORICAL IMPORTANCE:
Considered by many as the father of modern wildlife management.

QUOTE:
"Government, no matter how good, can only do certain things. Government can't raise crops, maintain small scattered structures, administer small scattered areas, or bring to bear on small local matters that combination of solitude, foresight and skill which we call husbandry. Husbandry watches no clock, knows no season of cessation, and for the most part is paid in love, not dollars. ... Husbandry is the heart of conservation."

— *Photo courtesy of Aldo Leopold Foundation archives.*

Charles J. Alsheimer
Deer Hunting Author, Photographer, Lecturer

In 1979, Charles J. Alsheimer made a hasty retreat from the corporate world, bought $20,000 of camera equipment, and began a journey that would make him one of the most widely recognized members of today's outdoors media. Since then, Alsheimer's photography has appeared in *D&DH*, *Outdoor Life*, *Field & Stream*, *Whitetail Institute* and many other outdoor publications. His articles have been published in numerous magazines, and he has written four books. He also holds the title of Northern field editor for *D&DH*.

His insights into deer behavior originate from his family's 220-acre farm in rural western New York where Alsheimer has ample opportunity to hunt, view and photograph whitetails. His observations spawned articles on every realm of the whitetail's world, including his ever-increasing work with researcher Wayne Laroche into the moon's effect on the rut.

Although his knowledge of the whitetail is vast, Alsheimer's personal perspectives on hunting is probably what has made him so well-respected and frequently requested as a speaker and writer. Alsheimer takes readers past scent techniques and tree-stand placement into a lifestyle saturated by white-tailed deer. While writing for *D&DH*, Alsheimer has penned "One Man's Battle with Lyme Disease," a chronicle of the illness's effects on his own life; "The Journey," an article based on Alsheimer's relationship with his son, Aaron; and "More Than a Whitetail to Me," a narrative of the personal side of deer hunting. These features generated some of the most intense, heart-felt reader feedback *D&DH* has ever received.

In his article, "More Than a Whitetail to Me," Alsheimer discusses the importance of whitetails in his life. "As a teen-ager, the thrill of hunting whitetails was a big part of my life. But as I climbed the hill of life, the way I looked at life and the things around me changed. My desire to know everything about whitetails became far more important than hunting tactics."

This curiosity makes Alsheimer insightful and inspirational. He has succeeded in chasing a dream. "I can't think of anything I'd rather do," he said.

AT A GLANCE

NAME: Charles J. Alsheimer

HISTORICAL IMPORTANCE: One of the most recognized and respected white-tailed deer photographers in North America. Long-time field editor of *Deer & Deer Hunting* magazine and leading authority on how lunar influences affect white-tailed deer behavior.

QUOTE:
"For me, hunting is more than big antlers or shallow words. It's amber sunrises and the smell of leaves in an October forest. It's fluffy snowflakes landing on a cold gun barrel, and the smell of wet wool at the end of a day's hunt. It's experiencing all that nature offers."

Bill Jordan
Founder of Realtree Camouflage and Realtree Outdoors Productions

In evolutionary terms, the archery world has experienced a volcanic explosion of growth the past 20 years. The spirit and passion that drove archery pioneers like Fred Bear quickly permeated the hunting world, creating a fertile market for hunt-savvy entrepreneurs.

Recurves and military camouflage metamorphosized overnight into compounds and high-tech camo patterns. Anything that would bring a deer into bow range intrigued the new archers. And so it was that Bill Jordan found himself in the middle of a shifting sport, one that quickly accepted his patterns, ideas and expertise. At the onset of the archery revolution, Jordan had just graduated from the University of Mississippi with a degree in business administration. From there, he returned to Columbus, Ga., to join his family's boat dealership. He became vice president of Leon Jordan Marine in 1973, and remained until 1982.

But how could a businessman who loved hunting and the outdoors sit still when the sport was evolving around him? There was plenty of room for development in traditional outdoor clothing and accessories, so in 1982, Jordan began producing a line of camouflage headnets and bow-hunting accessories.

In 1986, Realtree camouflage was introduced. Jordan designed the pattern on environment rather than a generic coloring like previous military patterns. By 1994, Advantage camouflage joined the picture. Today, the two brands make up Jordan Outdoor Enterprises Ltd. The methods might have changed some, but Jordan still develops patterns with the same principle: Camo should resemble the environment in which it's used.

Readers said Jordan is inspirational because he put quality products in the hands of bow- and gun-hunters. Today, Jordan Outdoor Enterprises also produces the *Realtree Outdoor* television series along with *Monster Buck* videos and the *Realtree Outdoors* and *Bill Jordon's Advantage* magazines. These communication media have expanded Jordon's reach, and made him a leader in the hunting industry.

AT A GLANCE

NAME: Bill Jordan

HISTORICAL IMPORTANCE:
Founded Realtree Camouflage and Realtree Outdoors. His products helped bring deer hunting to mainstream America, making the sport highly visible.

QUOTE:
"Whenever I go to outdoor shows or give seminars, people often tell me how lucky I am to be doing what I'm doing. I couldn't agree more. Not only am I extremely lucky to be able to hunt big whitetails across North America, but I work with the greatest people in the world."

Daniel E. Schmidt

CHAPTER 2
BOW-HUNTER'S GUIDE

Technical Tips for Bow-Hunters

Ask any seasoned bow-hunter and they will probably tell you they were attracted to the sport by its beautiful simplicity. True, the challenge of taking a white-tailed deer with a mere bow, arrow and broadhead is perhaps the most difficult challenge in hunting.

While today's bow-hunters still enjoy the challenge, the sport is a bit more complicated, especially when it comes to equipment. Hunters must still possess skill and strength to shoot a bow accurately, but they also must know how to use high-tech equipment to achieve the same goal.

Each year, dozens of bow-hunters ask me "what's the best" equipment on the market. They oftentimes express disappointment when I tell them there are no easy answers. From bows to broadheads, the best product is usually the one that works best for the shooter. To that end, bow-hunting hasn't changed much over the years. The bow-hunter must first learn how to master his equipment — no matter how advanced it is — before he can expect to use it to tag a whitetail.

What follows are 12 of the most-asked questions by today's bow-hunters. Although I learned the answers to some of these questions by unfortunate self-taught lessons,

I learned the answers to others by consulting bow-hunters with decades of experience. The key point to remember is this: Don't go bow-hunting if you are unsure about the capabilities of your equipment. Instead, visit a pro shop and have a bow technician help you become properly equipped.

Taking shortcuts is not acceptable in the sport of bow-hunting.

Q: My buddy is an avid 3-D shooter, and he uses 2¾-inch vanes on his arrows. The vanes on my arrows measure 4 inches. He said his arrows are faster. Should I switch to shorter vanes for bow-hunting?

A: No. Although short vanes improve arrow speed on the 3-D course, they are ill-advised for bow-hunting. Longer vanes help stabilize an arrow while it is in flight, thereby improving accuracy. Accuracy, not speed, is the key to becoming a better bow-hunter.

Q: I shoot a compound bow with a draw weight of 55 pounds. I have always used fixed-blade broadheads for bow-hunting whitetails, but this year I want to try mechanicals because I'm told they shoot like field points. What types of heads should I try?

DANIEL E. SCHMIDT

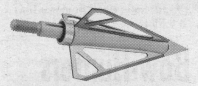

The Satellite Straight Razor, above, is a replaceable blade broadhead that offers continuous cutting surface. All broadheads should be sharpened regularly, regardless of how sharp they are out of the box.

A. Do not use mechanicals. Mechanical heads should be used for bow-hunting only if the hunter shoots a bow with a draw weight that exceeds 60 pounds. Using mechanicals with lower-poundage bows can cause the broadheads to not function properly.

Q. I shoot replaceable-blade broadheads. These broadheads are razor-sharp out of the box, so I don't ever need to resharpen them, right?

A. Wrong. Broadhead blades become dull in a hurry, even if they aren't pulled in and out of a quiver. Blades become dull through oxidation, a process in which metal loses its sharp characteristics through exposure to oxygen. Regardless of conditions, new broadheads should be touched up with a broadhead sharpener or sharpening stone before each hunt.

Q. I just purchased an expensive one-cam bow. I want to make this bow last for a long time. What can I do to protect the cam from wear and tear?

A. Besides taking your bow to a bow shop for regular tuning, buy several tubes of bow string wax and keep them handy — place one in your accessories box, one in your fanny pack and perhaps one in your vehicle's glove compartment. By waxing the bow string and the cam regularly, you can prevent costly repairs. Wax bow strings when they appear dry and matted. Wax cams, especially where they break, every few weeks.

Q. It seems as though one-cam bows are the rage among today's bow-hunters. Do one-cam bows have any disadvantages?

A. For many years, two-cam bows had the edge over one-cams when it came arrow speed. However, recent introductions have changed that trend. In fact, many of today's one-cams can be set up to produce comparable arrow speeds. Other than speed, one-cam bows have no inherent flaws. Many bow-hunters prefer one-cams because they aren't as fussy when it comes to tuning and timing.

The Fred Bear Epic Xtreme One-Cam

Q. I have hunted with aluminum arrows for years and have used them to kill several bucks.

However, I have heard that carbon arrows fly faster. Should I switch to carbon arrows?

A. Speed isn't everything. In fact, just because an arrow is made of carbon or graphite doesn't mean it will fly faster. Speed is directly related to weight. The lighter an arrow, the faster it will fly. However, a light arrow has drawbacks: The lighter the arrow, the less kinetic energy it provides. Most so-called professional hunters recommend that bow-hunters use arrows they feel comfortable with, and ones that fly the straightest for them.

Q. I'm thinking of replacing my old bow. It is quite long, measuring more than 40 inches from axle to axle, and heavy, weighing more

Today's one-cam bows are typically light, short and fast. To select a bow that's right for you, visit a pro shop and test-fire several models.

The Ultimate Deer Hunter's Quiz
Part 2, Bow-Hunting

17. You are bow-hunting and shoot a 150-pound buck. Because this deer carries about 8 pints of blood in its circulatory system, what is the minimum amount of blood the deer must lose before it falls and dies?

A. 15 percent, or 1⅕ pints.
B. 35 percent, or 2¾ pints.
C. 40 percent, or 3⅕ pints.
D. 75 percent, or 6 pints.

18. Which of the following statements is true in regard to a white-tailed deer's chest cavity?

A. A deer's chest cavity has a large "dead space" between the lungs and the spine, and, depending on the angle of the shot, an arrow can easily pass through this area without disrupting the deer's vital functions.
B. A deer's heart, lungs and network of blood vessels and supportive tissue continually overlap and cover nearly every square inch inside the chest cavity, whether the deer is inhaling or exhaling.
C. A deer's chest cavity is relatively small and should be avoided when aiming a bow or gun.

19. According to a study of bow-hunters in Camp Ripley, Minn., which of the following statements are true?

A. Bow-hunters wound and do not recover as many deer as they kill.
B. Bow-hunters wound and don't recover about 50 percent of the deer they shoot at.
C. Bow-hunters wound and don't recover slightly more than 11 percent of the deer they shoot at.

Continued on Page 31

Most shoot-through rests, such as this Chuck Adams Super Slam, are designed with bow-hunters in mind.

A: Most bow-hunters who shoot with their fingers prefer plunger-style arrow rests because arrows tend to stay on the rest better when the hunter draws. Hunters who shoot with release aids usually find the best success with prong- or launcher-style rests.

Q: I took up bow-hunting last season and used an older bow that my buddy gave me. I am going to buy a new bow this season. Should I also spend some extra money and get an overdraw?

A: Probably not. Overdraws are designed to increase arrow speed to compensate for misjudged yardage. Typically, overdraws are best for experienced shooters. In fact, an overdraw isn't necessary unless a bow-hunter can consistently shoot accurately at distances beyond 25 yards. Beginning bow-hunters should concentrate on improving their shooting form before moving on to advanced equipment.

than 6 pounds. This made for grueling practice sessions. I've read about new bows that are short, light and lightning fast. Should I buy a short model?

A: That depends. Some bow-hunters have problems when converting to the latest equipment. Short and light bows, especially the new one-cams, can be a pleasure to shoot, but they can be less forgiving than longer and heavier models. In fact, some bow-hunters learn that they must add stabilizers and other accessories to these new bows to get them to shoot consistent groups. It's wise to visit a pro shop and test-shoot several different brands and styles of bows before making a buying decision.

Q: My new archery catalog includes at least a dozen different kinds of arrow rests. Which style of arrow rest is the best?

Q: While shooting at an indoor range recently, I noticed that one archer had a small piece of string attached to his bow string. The string was tied near the nocking area, and he clipped his release to it to draw the bow. What was the string for?

A: What you saw was a string loop. They are becoming increasingly popular with today's bow-hunters. String loops consist of a super-strong cord that is tied above and below a nock. Loops help some release shooters shoot better, and they also reduce the odds of "arrow pinch" at full draw. Loops also virtually eliminate wear and tear on the bow string's serving. The only disadvantage is that loops slightly decrease arrow speed.

Q. My bow is very noisy. To make it quieter, I've tried everything, including tightening all bolts. I've even replaced the bow string, but the bow is still noisy. What is causing this excess noise?

A. Some bows are inherently noisy. Typically, noise comes from energy from the shot that is not absorbed by the bow. This energy causes the bow to vibrate and, therefore, create noise. It's wise to take your bow to a pro shop to have it inspected before deciding to replace it. Noise can also be created by accessories, bow strings and cables. A bow technician can pinpoint those problems and fix them at minimal cost. One possible solution is to attach Limb Savers to your bow. These small rubber buttons absorb shock and vibration and significantly reduce bow noise.

Q. I just finished reading the bow article

Limb Savers are small rubber discs that absorb bow recoil, reducing noise caused by vibration of the bow's limbs.

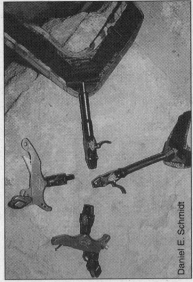

Daniel E. Schmidt

Hunters who want to use a string loop should consider switching to a caliper release that features no-gap jaws, such as the releases offered by Tomorrow's Resources, above.

in *Deer & Deer Hunting's Deer Hunters Equipment* annual. The description of each new bow lists a measurement called "brace height." What is a bow's brace height and why is it important?

A. The brace height is the shortest measurement from the back of the bow's grip to the string. Most of today's high-tech bows have short brace heights. For the most part, the shorter a bow's brace height is, the faster the bow will shoot. Beginning bow-hunters or bow-hunters with poor shooting form should shy away from bows with short brace heights because they are less forgiving — less accurate — than bows with longer brace heights.

How to Select Fletchings for Your Hunting Arrows

For hunting arrows tipped with broadheads, three 5-inch feathers or four 4-inch feathers work best. Individual differences in equipment and shooting style sometimes require the use of larger feathers. It is also possible that good flight can be achieved with smaller feathers. Test shooting is the best way to decide which setup is right for you.

It's important to remember that broadheads need more guidance than field points. Without proper guidance, a broadhead will cause the arrow to yawn or fishtail during flight. Yawning arrows cause inconsistent flight patterns, and lose velocity and penetration.

Use the following question-and-answer segment to determine which setups are right for your arrows:

➤ **Should I use right- or left-wing feathers?**

You can shoot either wing successfully. An arrow does not rotate noticeably until it is well clear of the bow. Left-wing feathers should be used to rotate the arrow counterclockwise, while right-wing feathers rotate the arrow clockwise.

➤ **How can I determine the alignment of the feather on my arrows?**

Two methods can be used to determine right- or left-wing alignment. First, look at the nock end of the arrow (aligned as though the arrow is ready to be shot), and rotate it so one fletching is on top of the shaft. If the "catch lip" is to the left of the web, it

FEATHER SPLICING

Cut quill only here

Cut quill only here

Butt quills together in clamp and fletch

(Smooth webs together after glue has set and the clamp has been removed.)

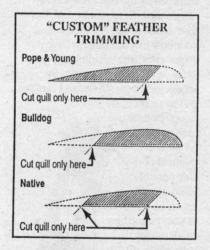

"CUSTOM" FEATHER TRIMMING

Pope & Young

Cut quill only here

Bulldog

Cut quill only here

Native

Cut quill only here

is a right-wing feather. If the "catch lip" is to the right of the web, it is a left-wing feather. (See diagram)

The second method involves holding the forward end of the die-cut (pointed end) or full-length feather (larger end) toward yourself. Look down from the top, and rotate the feather so its web is horizontal and its natural curve droops the end pointed away from you downward ("shedding rain" as opposed to "catching rain"). If the web is to the right of the quill base, it is a right-wing feather. If the web is to the left of the quill base, it is a left-wing feather.

> ## ➤ Should I use straight, offset or helical fletchings?

For compound bows, it is recommended that shooters use offset or helical fletchings on all arrows. Offset and helical fletchings cause arrows to rotate in flight just like the rifling in a gun barrel causes a bullet to rotate. This is important for arrows because the rotation acts like a gyroscope to stabilize the arrow during flight.

Helical fletchings offer more stability than a simple offset, and therefore should be the first choice for all broadhead-tipped arrows.

> ## ➤ How much fletching offset should I use?

If the forward end of a 5-inch feather is offset ¹⁄₁₆-inch from its rear, this equals about three-quarters of one degree. This works well for most offset or helical-fletched arrows.

> ## ➤ How should I prepare my arrow shafts for the fletching process?

Bow-hunters should begin by wiping the fletching area of their arrows with alcohol, then lightly scuffing the area with 600-grit sandpaper or fine steel wool. It's wise to perform a final alcohol wipe before starting the fletching process.

For more information on feathers and fletching, contact Trueflight Mfg., Box 1000, Manitowish Waters, WI 54545

The Ultimate Deer Hunter's Quiz
Part 2, Bow-Hunting

20. A 1986 study showed about 19 percent of all licensed hunters had tried bow-hunting. That percentage has steadily increased. By 1996, what percentage of licensed hunters had tried bow-hunting?

A. 25 percent
B. 35 percent
C. 45 percent
D. More than 75 percent

21. Which statement is true?

A. The Pope and Young Club is a recognized leader in bow-hunting.
B. The Pope and young Club is fiscally strong and has financial goals.
C. The Pope and Young Club promotes trophy hunting.
D. All of the above
E. None of the above

22. Where on a deer should a bow-hunter aim when the deer is broadside?
A. The lungs
B. The heart
C. The liver
D. The spine

23. In early fall, deer blood carries high levels of which vitamin?
A. Vitamin A
B. Vitamin E
C. Vitamin B
D. Vitamin K

24. A deer standing in what position offers the greatest margin of error for the bow-hunter?
A. Broadside
B. Quartering Away
C. Head-On
D. Quartering Toward

Continued on Page 33

Ol'Man's Tara AirElite II

Points to Consider When Shopping for Tree Stands

Most bow-hunters prefer tree stands that are roomy, yet easy to carry and set up.

The problem with most fixed-position stands is they're too heavy to carry in and out of the woods each day. Thanks to carbon technology, some of today's stands maintain the size and strength to make them safe and comfortable while keeping weight to a minimum.

For added weight reduction in a stand, consider a model that features a webbed seat and a cam-buckle attachment system. Webbed seats are more comfortable than bench-style seats, while cam-buckle straps are much lighter than chains.

— *Courtesy of **Ol'Man** Treestands, 32 Raspberry Lane, Hattiesburg, MS 39402.*

Select a Broadhead That's Right for You

Quality broadheads aren't cheap, and it's easy to spend a lot of money trying to determine which ones are right for you. With that in mind, follow this simple, four-step game plan to reduce your costs and select the perfect broadhead for your setup:

1. Conduct your own field test.

Most broadheads are sold in three- and four-packs, so get two or three of your hunting partners to split the cost of several packs of broadheads.

2. Research what types of broadheads are out there. You will want to try mechanicals and fixed-position heads, so do some homework and select three or four different brands of each category that you want to try.

Don't let cost scare you from trying what you want. For example, if three shooters spend $40 apiece on a field test, they could shoot at least six brands of broadheads. Furthermore, they will know exactly what heads they want to shoot, rather than spending $40 on two packs of one brand that "looks good."

3. Set up a test course. Present huge soft targets — foam blocks work best — and start by shooting the broadheads from short distances (10-15 yards).

First, however, organize the shoot. Give each shooter one broadhead from each pack. Shoot one arrow at a time, plot its performance on a sheet of paper, and retrieve the arrow before shooting again. You can ruin a lot of arrows, and perhaps a few broadheads, if you allow shooters to shoot several broadheads at the same 6-inch circle on the target.

4. Select the broadhead that shoots best for you, and purchase six or more that will be used strictly for hunting. Also, purchase replacement blades for heads that use. You will save a lot of money.

Finally, use the original field-test broadheads as your practice heads. And, unless your broadheads fly exactly like your field points, always practice with your broadheads.

— *Daniel E. Schmidt*

Tuning Tips for Broadheads

Broadheads should be checked for flight after shafts have been paper tuned. It's not uncommon for the impact point of a broadhead to be different than a field point.

1. Set up a broadhead target 20 to 30 yards away. Using the same arrow (with field point) that you used for paper tuning, shoot at the target. This will give you a reference point. If the shot is off, make the necessary adjustments to your sights.

2. Remove the field point and install a broadhead onto the shaft. Use the same aiming point, and shoot again. If the broadhead hits close to where the field point did, shoot the same arrow several times to be sure you are within a respectable group size.

3. The shot group is the key. If you are shooting good groups but the impact is off from your aiming point, simply make your sight adjustments.

— *Courtesy of **New Archery Products**, 7500 Industrial Drive, Dept. DDH, Forest Park, IL 60130.*

The Ultimate Deer Hunter's Quiz
Part 2, Bow-Hunting

25. With an estimated 340,000 bow-hunters, this state could claim the title as "bow-hunting capital of the world."
A. Wisconsin
B. Texas
C. Michigan
D. Pennsylvania

26. Who invented the compound bow?
A. Roy Case
B. Fred Bear
C. Howard Cam
D. H.W. Allen

27. In 1970, the compound bow was legal in all but one state. Which state was the last one to legalize the compound?
A. Wyoming
B. West Virginia
C. Iowa
D. Georgia

28. Which state held the nation's first modern-day bow-hunting season?
A. Michigan
B. Wisconsin
C. Minnesota
D. Iowa

29. According to broadhead manufacturers, bow-hunters should not use mechanical broadheads unless they shoot how much draw weight?
A. 50 pounds
B. 60 pounds
C. At least 70 pounds

30. Ishi, the California Indian who taught Saxton Pope and Art Young how to bow-hunt, came from what tribe?
A. Chippewa
B. Iroquois
C. Yana
D. Sioux

This is the end of the quiz for Chapter 2. The quiz continues on Page 47. Answers begin on Page 194.

A Predator's Prison

Although Kenneth wasn't raised in the vast, rich farmland of central Wisconsin, he quickly learned about its abundant deer herd after moving there in 1994. In fact, he discovered one hot spot while driving home from his first day of work at a manufacturing plant.

Kenneth knew little about the rural area surrounding the farmhouse he rented. It was a clear August evening, so he decided to tour the area and glass the fields for deer. He traveled only a few miles on a back road before spotting several deer feeding in a rye field.

He drove his pickup to the edge of the road's wide gravel shoulder, parked and cut the engine. He reached across the seat and grabbed his binoculars.

The deer, about a dozen does and fawns, grazed peacefully, apparently unbothered by the presence of the pickup truck. Kenneth watched in amazement as another five deer appeared at the field edge and trotted to join the others.

"This is incredible. I have got to find out who owns this ... ," he said, stopping in midsentence.

"Holy cow!" he gasped. With uncanny timing, a large buck stepped out from the nearby pine grove.

He watched the buck, which sported a tall, wide velvet-covered rack, as it alertly walked the edge of the field and nibbled at grass. It soon disappeared back into the woodlot.

Return Visits

During the next several weeks, Kenneth returned to the field to watch deer. Their pattern was predictable: Each night, about two dozen antlerless deer showed up at 7 p.m. Although the image of big buck was still vivid, Kenneth was more interested in the number of deer that showed up. He never saw that many deer in an entire season while hunting the Northern Forest that surrounded his father's cabin.

What's more, Kenneth was proud to be a meat hunter. He dreamed of taking big bucks, but that didn't fuel his hunting fire. His theory was simple: Take what he needed, give some venison to charity, and always portray hunting in a positive light.

It was that attitude that scored Kenneth what others declared "impossible" — permission to hunt Jack Butler's property.

The Investigation

Bow season was fast approaching when Kenneth stopped by the bank to purchase a plat book. He hadn't even got back to his pickup when he learned how Butler's 120 acres wrapped around the western boundary of a state park.

He was studying the map further when a voice interrupted his thought.

"What's up, man? Scoping out a place to hunt?"

Kenneth looked up to see Joe Peil, a friend from work who was also a bow-hunter.

DANIEL E. SCHMIDT

Tracy Schubert

"Hey, what's up?," Kenneth replied. "Yeah, I'm looking. Do you know Jack Butler?"

"Don't even think about it," Joe said. "Butler doesn't let anybody hunt his land. Believe me, I've tried. He's one of those old crusty types, ya know?"

"Yeah, I figured as much," Kenneth said, closing the book and changing the subject.

Making a Case

That evening, Kenneth decided to drive by the old man's farmhouse in hopes of getting a chance to meet him.

Luckily, the old man was working in a field when Kenneth pulled up.

"Good evening, sir," Kenneth said with an outstretched hand as he approached the man. "My name is Kenneth Chappell."

"Yeah, whadya want?" the man said gruffly.

Kenneth swallowed hard and continued.

"Well, sir, I recently learned you own the fields and woods adjacent to the park," he said. "I'm a bow-hunter, and I was wondering if we could work something out where I could hunt on your property."

"I don't allow hunting," the old man said. "I used to, but they were a bunch of slobs. They shot at everything that moved, and they threw garbage all over my property."

Kenneth knew this would be a tough sell.

"Well, not to badmouth anyone, but I'm not like other guys, sir. I respect all wildlife, and I respect landowner rights. I will play by your rules 100 percent.

"In addition, I will pay you for the privilege to hunt, and I will give you some venison if I get a deer."

The old man's expression went from irritation to intrigue.

"Pay to hunt deer? Why?" he said. "Why would you do that?"

"Because I love to hunt, sir," Kenneth said.

"Well, I'll think about it. Call me in a week," Butler said.

"I sure will," Kenneth said. "Thanks!"

Following Up

While heading to work the next morning, Kenneth stopped by the grocery store and bought a thank-you card. He wrote a quick note, thanking Butler for considering his offer, and then stopped by the post office to mail it.

Two days later, Kenneth was watching the evening news when the phone rang.

"Hello?"

"Yeah, this is Jack Butler. (Pause) You can hunt if want to. And I don't want anything."

Kenneth was ecstatic.

"Thank you, Mr. Butler. Thanks a lot. But I have to give you something."

"No you don't," Butler said. "What you can do is stop calling me mister. My name is Jack. And give me a steak or two if you get a deer.

"Come over after work tomorrow and I'll show you the property lines."

The Rules

Kenneth had a difficult time concentrating at work the next day. For the first time in his life, he knew he would see deer — lots of deer — opening day.

He left work at 6 p.m. and headed straight for Butler's farm. However, as he approached the rye field, he stopped to look at a group of deer that had entered the field early. There, among the herd, stood the buck.

Kenneth grabbed his binoculars and spied the buck. Its rack, now polished, had 10 perfect points.

"I'll be back for you next week," Kenneth whispered.

As he approached Butler's driveway, Kenneth saw the old man walking back to the house after getting his mail. Butler saw him coming and turned to meet him at the end of the driveway.

"Hi, Jack," Kenneth said as he rolled down the window. "Nice night."

"Sure is. You see all the deer out there?"

"Sure did," Kenneth replied.

"Yep, and there's one heckuva buck out there, too," Butler said. "You ain't one of those trophy hunters, are you?"

Kenneth didn't hesitate to respond. "Nope. That's not to say I wouldn't like to get him, but I would be just as happy to fill one or two doe tags."

"I know I'm going to like you," Butler said. "We have too many deer around here anyway. And I always said you can't eat the horns."

Butler walked around Kenneth's truck and got in. "C'mon, I'll show you the land."

A Game Plan

Kenneth spent the weekend hanging two portable tree stands in a nearby oak woodlot and constructing a ground blind in the small pine grove on the eastern edge of the rye field. Because deer were still showing up in the field regularly and opening day was just a week away, he decided to hunt from the blind on the opener if the wind was right.

The pine grove was a perfect location. Several well-worn deer trails wove through the pines, entering the field in a hub-like area a mere 35 yards from the blind.

Kenneth was tempted to trim shooting lanes, but decided not to out of respect for Butler's request not to "cut anything down." Instead, he used monofilament fishing line to tie back a few branches. The line wouldn't damage the trees, and he could replace it each time he hunted from the blind.

Opening Day

The first hunt from the ground blind came on the afternoon of opening day. The September day was glorious: 60 degrees, no wind and a clear, blue sky.

Kenneth parked in his designated spot — behind the barn — and removed an orange flag from a nearby gate post. Butler could see the post from his house. No flag signaled to him that Kenneth was out hunting.

Kenneth reached the blind at 4 p.m. and settled in for some field-watching.

First Arrivals

Within an hour, a doe and two fawns crossed the road bordering the state park. The deer were 300 yards away, but Kenneth's heart raced. His predatory instinct was on full alert.

He eventually calmed down and spent the next 25 minutes watching the deer move slowly across the field. They were soon joined by more deer; first a yearling doe, then a doe and two more fawns, and then two yearlings, an adult doe and three fawns.

The parade of whitetails was everything he had dreamed of. What's more, the deer were headed toward his blind. He would get a shot.

Within 10 minutes, several antler-less deer stood feeding on the grass just 30 yards from Kenneth's blind. He was preparing to draw when something caught his eye from across the field.

More deer.

Four whitetails crossed the road and bounded straight for the ground blind.

Visions of Antlers

The four deer were about 150 yards out when Kenneth realized two were bucks, including the massive 10-pointer.

"Oh yeah!" he thought to himself while nervously gripping his bow. "Don't look at the antlers."

The deer slowed their pace to a trot when Kenneth noticed something was wrong with the other buck. The buck, a mere forkhorn, walked with a noticeable limp.

The buck's left foreleg was broken at the upper joint, and it dangled life-lessly as the buck hobbled through the field.

Kenneth couldn't help but feel compassion for the deer, a probable victim of an auto accident. He also couldn't help think about what another predator might do in this situation. And, he couldn't help but recall the old man's words: "You ain't one of those trophy hunters, are you?"

"No one will ever know," Kenneth said to himself. "Besides, someone would probably shoot that forkhorn during gun season anyway."

Kenneth turned his attention back to the 10-pointer as it walked closer. Its rack was impressive: a 16-inch inside spread, 5-inch brow tines and 8-inch G-2s.

Decision Time

Kenneth paused momentarily and then drew. He had practiced this shot hundreds of times in his backyard. He placed his forefinger knuckle on the familiar spot of his cheekbone and pressed the bowstring to the tip of his nose.

By now, the bucks were just two of 17 deer feeding within bow range of the ground blind. A lone shaft of sunlight shone onto the spot, glitter-ing off the long tines of the 10-pointer. Meanwhile, the shorter forkhorn stood in the afternoon shad-ows.

Kenneth admired the 10-pointer's rack one last time before closing his left eye and peering through his bow's peep sight with his right eye. He settled the green fiber-optic pin on the crease behind the buck's right leg, paused and touched the release trig-ger.

Thwack!

The arrow hit its mark, and all the deer bolted. Kenneth watched as the buck sprinted 40 yards in a semicircle and then collapsed. The double-lung hit killed the deer within seconds.

"Woof!"

Turning to the alarm snort of one of the unscathed deer, Kenneth looked south. There, among the group of scattered deer, stood the 10-pointer. It blew once more before raising its flag and bounding gracefully across the field and back to the park's forest.

Kenneth smiled while stepping out of the blind to retrieve his buck, relieved with his decision to deny greed and listen to his predatory instinct.

Today's Hot New Bows

The **Fred Bear** Borsalino T/D is the first take-down compound bow. Hunters can fold the bow in half for compact carrying by simply releasing tension on the limbs.

The bow is built for speed, versatility and smooth handling. It can produce arrow speeds of 307 feet per second (IBO). Its draw weight can be adjusted from 60 to 70 pounds, and it has a 75 percent let-off module.

The Borsalino T/D also features the Perimeter Weighted Cam II, which puts more energy into the arrow while reducing hand shock and noise by 54 percent.

Mathews continues its trend of innovative technology with the introduction of the Q2, equipped with Mathews' Harmonic Damping System. When fired, recoil vibration encounters Harmonic Dampers that float in elastic bushings at key riser locations.

Each Q2 includes two sets of interchangeable dampers so hunters can create a custom feel. The Q2 also features the StraightLine MaxCam2, a perimeter-weighted cam, and a long riser/short limb design for maximum accuracy. Realtree X-tra camouflage is standard.

Golden Eagle's Litespeed Stealth is a compound bow designed to work with your natural body tendencies. The bow features a smooth draw with its StealthCam, a single cam with energy wheel characteristics.

The bow's Natural Grip enables the shooter's arm to reach the proper shooting position more naturally at full draw. Other features include an 8-inch brace height, 75 percent let-off module (65 percent is also available), and Golden Eagle's Solid Gold Assurance Policy.

High Country Archery introduces the Carbon 4-Runner Pro, a compound bow built for speed and durability. The bow features the Reflexed Carbon Riser, Vibra Damp Pocket and Center Line Sealed Bearing Idler Wheels.

The bow's carbon materials are 500 times stronger than traditional materials, and they reduce shock and vibration. A 6½-inch brace height provides forgiving shotting characteristics and smooth, quiet shooting.

Today's Slugs Turn Shotguns into Tack-Drivers

I've been around this business long enough to know the danger of referring to anything in extreme terms. For instance, "the best ever" of anything is usually quickly replaced by something obviously better in this high-tech world.

Over the past couple of years, the introduction of the expanding deer slug — beginning with Federal's Barnes EXpander in 1997 and Remington's revamped Copper Solid last year — represented landmarks in slug technology. And as you might know, these slugs flew off the shelves — provided buyers could find them.

Major manufacturers produced saboted slugs for most of the 1990s, but before the Federal and Remington breakthrough, only tiny Lightfield Inc. ever made a saboted slug that expanded well on deer-sized game. The move into mushrooming copper slugs that retained 100 percent of their weight was a huge advance. It was billed as the ultimate move in slug performance, and I would have echoed that sentiment if I hadn't known of other projects in the works.

Those projects have now reached fruition, and suddenly we're looking at another quantum leap in slug design and performance for 2000. The new millennium opens with new "ultimate" performers in the Winchester Supreme Partition Gold sabot and the Hornady H2K Heavy Mag sabot.

The new slugs again raise performance thresholds to unheard of levels. Both, suffice to say, are impressive.

The Winchester-Olin boys have been working on the Partition Gold project for 2½ years, causing one to suspect the scarcity of Hornady's XTP slug was the result of the Nebraska-based engineers' concentration in developing the new H2K.

Winchester is driving a specially designed .50-caliber, 385-grain version (ballistic coefficient of .220 compared to .101 in the Hi-Impact load) of the Partition Gold bullet loaded for pistols, rifles and muzzleloaders in excess of 1,900 feet per second. Hornady is using a 300-grain Hornady XTP Mag bullet with a BC of .200. It is getting 2,000-plus fps in a 30-inch test barrel, which projects to 1,930 fps in a 24-inch slug barrel or about 1,900 in a 22-inch version.

What does that mean in trajectory? Well, the rule of thumb for a 100-yard zero with past saboted

Federal loads a line of slugs with the Barnes EXpander bullet. This combination makes for one of the most accurate and reliable slugs on the market.

loads was to center them 2 to 2½ inches high at 50 yards. The new Winchester and Hornady loads need only be .7 inches high at 50 to zero at 100. In fact, print them 2 inches high at 50 now and you'll have a 150-yard zero. That translates to a maximum point-blank range (plus or minus 3 inches from zero, meaning no hold-over) of 178 yards. These are shotgun slugs we're talking about, with performance that rivals the .45-70 centerfire rifle.

The improved ballistic coefficients, an extra 400 fps to 500 fps over standard saboted loads, and the bullet's expansion characteristics simply flatten deer. The new slugs boast a previously unheard-of muzzle velocity of around 3,300 foot pounds (a half-ton advantage over the rest of the market) and retain a full ton of energy at 125 yards. That's 600 foot pounds more than the expanding copper slugs, and the new ones still have 1,500 foot pounds available at 200 yards.

I had an opportunity to do some range testing and field testing with the new Winchester load in a Browning Gold Deer Hunter at a cull deer hunt at the Wingmead Farms waterfowl plantation near Little Rock, Ark., last November. I killed five deer (including the first buck ever taken with the Partition Gold) at Wingmead and added three more at home in New York before I ran out of tags.

All the kills were devastating one-shot wonders. Seven of the eight deer fell in their tracks and the last deer — hit in the lungs while running — managed another stride purely on momentum before plowing a furrow in

Daniel E. Schmidt

Some hunters still rely on smooth-bore shotguns and iron beads for slug-hunting. However, with today's rifled slug guns and high-tech slugs, hunters can greatly improve their accuracy and effective range.

Daniel E. Schmidt

The Ithaca Deer Slayer is a deadly accurate slug gun, especially when it's topped with a quality scope. Shown here is the Bushnell Holosight, a sight featuring a luminous red dot and circle. The sight's brightness can be adjusted for low-light conditions.

the leaves with its nose. In 35 years of serious slug-shooting, I've never experienced such performance.

Yes, shotgun deer hunters never had it so good.

Remington's new Copper Solid was limited in availability last year but that will improve. Big Green is also campaigning for its 20-gauge version this year to run neck-and-neck with the similar Federal Barnes EXpander line.

Brenneke, which is finally in full production with its K.O. slug, made some guarded moves toward a new slug at the '99 SHOT Show, but isn't introducing anything publicly for 2000.

Don't look for anything new in slug guns, except some refinements (sight systems, camo coverings, etc.) on existing models. In fact, for 2000, expect to see slug guns geared toward renewal rather than innovation. Some models that were available

sparingly last year are in full production for 2000.

Meanwhile, Remington sold out production of its new heavier cantilevered rifled barrel for the 870 pump in 1999, and dealers can expect increased availability on that front in 2000. After all, there are more than 6 million 870s sitting out there with the potential of being converted to an effective rifled-barrel deer gun.

Beretta's ES100 slug gun, formerly the Pintail Slug, was introduced two years ago, but wasn't produced until last year. The recoil-operated autoloader, a virtual twin to the more expensive Benelli Super Black Eagle, was plagued by delivery problems, which helped make for disappointing sales last year, but dealers and customers can look for a renewed push this year.

All in all, slug hunting for deer will take another big step forward to start the new millennium.

Which Rifle Bullets Drop Whitetails in Their Tracks?

To quickly answer the question asked in the headline above, the best rifle bullets for quick kills on whitetails are those that open quickly upon impact without falling apart. Avoid heavy or solid bullets that are designed for North America's larger big-game animals, such as elk, bears and moose.

That statement shouldn't surprise anyone who spends much time hunting whitetails or reading about the best loads for deer hunting. Still, such questions will probably be asked as long as whitetails are hunted with a rifle. It seems that even when we know the best answer, we go prospecting for an argument with someone who might not agree with our choice.

Charles Ruth, a wildlife biologist with the South Carolina Department of Natural Resources, has been asked such questions so many times over the years that he sought a scientific way to back up his time-tested answers. As he told the 22nd meeting of the Southeast Deer Study Group in February 1999, professional wildlife managers are often expected to answer hunting-related questions with authority, even if their expertise is biology-based deer management.

Therefore, Ruth recently conducted a study at the Cedar Knoll Club — which is located in South Carolina's coastal plain — to examine several hunting-based questions he hears. He strived to conduct his study as scientifically as possible. He wanted to obtain some objective numbers to back up whatever answers he gave inquiring hunters.

The Study

The Cedar Knoll Club is no stranger to deer research. The club's members and guests have taken part in several university studies since the late 1980s. The club's land has been intensively managed for whitetails since 1984. The work includes various habitat techniques like logging, burning, mowing, fertilizing and plantings. As a result, deer habitat is excellent, and features dense woods and long clearings planted as food plots for deer.

It's impossible to exaggerate the thickness of the region's underbrush. Hunters who spend any time hunting South Carolina's coastal region know the value of a well-placed shot that drops deer in their tracks. Typically, this means aiming for the scapula, or shoulder blade. If the shot narrowly misses the scapula, it will likely hit the spine, heart or lungs. Shots directed at the spine, neck or head are usually considered too risky.

PATRICK DURKIN

Most of Cedar Knoll's hunting takes place from elevated platforms with a shooting rail. During the study, if a deer ran off after the shot, the researchers returned to the site with a trained tracking dog, even if the hunter thought the shot missed.

Researchers recorded all shots taken, shot placement, the estimated range of each shot, the distance deer traveled after being shot, and the type and amount of sign left by the fleeing deer. Researchers also recorded the rifle's make and caliber, as well as the type of ammunition. In addition, they recorded information on tracking results and how much the trained dogs aided the recovery of each deer.

What Did Researchers Find?

The club's hunters fired 603 shots and killed 493 deer during the one-year study, for an 82 percent shooting success. The mean distance for all shots was 132 yards, and the average distance of killing shots was 127 yards. The average distance of missed shots was 150 yards.

Of the 493 deer shot and recovered, 253 (51 percent) dropped when shot and 240 (49 percent) ran. Those that ran were put into three categories:

Class A: 155 fell within 46 yards.

Class B: 61 fell within 83 yards.

Class C: 24 fell within 152 yards.

Researchers believe deer in the final group wouldn't have been found in the dense brush and wetlands without the help of track-

ing dogs. With these deer, no evidence of a hit was found where the deer was standing. In most cases, dogs were needed to discover the sign.

Overall, researchers believe the trained dogs accounted for 15 percent to 20 percent of the recovered deer. Besides finding the 24 deer in the Class C hits, dogs also found many of the Class B hits, as well as 19 deer that weren't killed by the hunter's shot. These 19 poorly hit deer were usually wounded in the jaw, legs or lower abdomen. They were trailed by the dogs until they could be dispatched.

Shot Placement

Researchers in this study used the following categories for bullet placement: neck, spine, shoulder, heart, lungs and abdomen. The study revealed the following results from such hits:

Location	Number	Distance Traveled
Neck	25	< 1 yard
Spine	27	< 1 yard
Shoulder	170	3 yards
Heart	14	39 yards
Lungs	152	50 yards
Abdomen	58	69 yards

Based on those findings, and assuming most spine hits resulted from shoulder-aimed shots going high, Ruth recommends the shoulder shot. Deer hit in the scapula traveled an average of three yards, and generally didn't leave the hunter's sight.

As Ruth wrote in his report: "The broadside shoulder shot essentially gave results similar to what most hunters expect from a neck shot. Presumably, it works well because it strikes part of the heart and/or lungs, which itself is a mortal blow. However, a shot through the scapula damages the *brachial plexus*, which is part of the central nervous system, thereby rendering the animal immobile. It knocks the animal out and it never regains consciousness. Also, the shoulder is a large target that offers room for error. A high shot hits the spine; a low shot, the heart; and a rearward shot, the lungs."

Caliber and Firearms

Like most of us, Ruth often hears many strong opinions on which calibers and rifles work best for whitetails. As he bluntly states in his report: "The old saying 'I use this magnum because you can hit them in the butt and blow their head off' is still common. Also apparent are skeptical remarks implying smaller-caliber centerfire firearms are less effective, increasing crippling rates and resulting in deer running farther."

Hunters in Ruth's study used more than 20 types of centerfire cartridges to kill deer. To simplify and reduce variability in the results, researchers defined five caliber groups: .243 caliber, .25 caliber, .270 caliber, .284 caliber and .30 caliber. To objectively measure how the calibers performed, the researchers studied the distance deer traveled after being hit — whether they ran or fell on the spot.

Perhaps not surprisingly, the study found no significant perfor-

The Ultimate Deer Hunter's Quiz
Part 3, Gun-Hunting

31. This company's lever-action rifle, introduced in 1894, is the most popular deer rifle of all time.
   A. Winchester
   B. Remington
   C. Savage

32. This firearms manufacturer introduced a bolt-action deer rifle in 1964. That model is the second most popular deer rifle of all time. Who made it?
   A. Winchester
   B. Remington
   C. Marlin
   D. Ruger

33. Of the following four magnum cartridges, which one was introduced first?
   A. 7mm Remington Magnum
   B. .300 Winchester Magnum
   C. .338 Winchester Magnum
   D. .300 Weatherby Magnum

34. Which cartridge is considered the most versatile for deer hunting?
   A. .308 Winchester
   B. .270 Winchester
   C. .30-06 Springfield
   D. .30-30 Winchester

35. Which state has the most muzzleloading-hunters?
   A. Michigan
   B. Ohio
   C. Wisconsin

36. Which state attracted the most firearms hunters (not including muzzleloading hunters) in 1998?
   A. Michigan
   B. Pennsylvania
   C. Texas
   D. Wisconsin

This is the end of the quiz for Chapter 3. Quiz continues on Page 67. Answers begin on Page 194.

mance differences between calibers. The mean distances deer traveled ranged from 14 to 40 yards, but "there was no apparent relationship with increasing or decreasing caliber size or the inherent differences in velocity or energy related to the different caliber groups."

Caliber	Number	Distance Traveled
.243 (6 mm)	48	40 yards
.25	36	14 yards
.270	84	31 yards
.284	160	26 yards
.30	116	33 yards

Custom vs. Factory Equipment

Ruth said he also hears many questions and assumptions from hunters who buy custom firearms and ammo in their quest for pinpoint accuracy. Most of these hunters are highly experienced. Even so, Ruth found no statistical differences in the results produced by factory and custom rifles and ammo. Regardless of the make of the rifle and ammo, deer traveled about 30 yards after being hit.

"The guys with the custom equipment could drive tacks on paper, but you generally don't need that for deer hunting," he said. "From what we could see, they would have had virtually the same results if they had been using factory rifles and ammo."

Which Bullets Work Best?

Anyone who spends any time studying today's great offerings of big-game bullets knows the choices seem infinite. Therefore, it's difficult to make simple judgments and all-inclusive conclusions. For the purpose of his study, researchers grouped bullets into two basic categories:

Group 1: Soft, or rapidly expanding bullets. This includes ballistic tips, bronze points or any soft-point bullet that is an appropriate caliber-specific weight for whitetails. In .30-caliber rifles, for example, appropriate weights are 150 and 180 grains, but not 200.

Group 2: Hard, solid or other slowly expanding premium bullets designed more for North America's larger big-game species. Also included were bullets generally considered heavy for whitetails, such as 200-grain bullets in .30-caliber cartridges.

To judge a bullet's effectiveness, Ruth again examined the distances deer traveled after being hit. Here's what he found in his analysis:

Bullet Type	Number	Yards Traveled	% Dropped	% Poor Sign
Soft	360	27	58	12
Hard	84	43	40	21

Deer struck by Group 1 bullets, which are rapidly expanding "soft" or light bullets, traveled a mean distance of 27 yards, while deer struck by Group 2 bullets, "hard" or heavy bullets, traveled an average of 43 yards.

As you can also see, deer struck with the soft bullets were more likely to drop in their tracks or leave more tracking sign when fleeing.

Hunter Experience

Ruth said there was no conclusive way to document the impact of hunting experience. In general, though, he found that hunters who

Daniel E. Schmidt

Which bullets work best on deer? This question appears to have no clear-cut answer, according to a South Carolina study.

used Group 2 bullets were often nonresidents from Northern states who might think they need such bullets for whitetails.

"A big part of bullet choice and shot placement was very likely local hunting experience," Ruth said. "Anyone who has shot deer and tracked them through this region's underbrush understands the importance of dropping a deer in its tracks. Even though heart and lung shots are quickly fatal, the deer usually still makes it back into the cover before dying. Ideally, hunters at Cedar Knoll want the deer to drop where it's standing. When they're hit in the shoulder blade, they often resemble a cow lowering itself into its bed. It's like they just pass out and collapse."

Conclusion

What can deer hunters take from Ruth's research, both for fireside debates and in-the-field application? The most obvious conclusion is that if you want facts and figures to back up your preferences, you'll be better served if you limit your choices and discussion to bullet types and shot placement. You simply won't find much scientific evidence to back up any beliefs you might have about your favorite caliber or rifle type.

Of course, as with many things, if you have confidence in your rifle or caliber that was achieved through years of good results, faith might be more important than cold, hard facts.

How to Mount a Riflescope

Mounting a riflescope properly can mean the difference between success and failure in the deer woods.

Tools required
- ✓ Hex wrench set (English)
- ✓ Gunsmith screwdrivers
- ✓ Scope-mounting adhesive
- ✓ Gun oil
- ✓ Long cotton swabs
- ✓ Soft cotton cloth
- ✓ Acetone, ether, or other cleaning/degreasing agent
- ✓ Riflescope bore-sighting device and arbors
- ✓ Scope alignment rods
- ✓ Shims
- ✓ Rubber hammer
- ✓ Rifle vise
- ✓ Short steel ruler
- ✓ Lapping kit
- ✓ Reticle leveler

Instructions

1. Place the gun's safety in the "on" position. Unload firearm and remove bolt, cylinder, clip, etc. Make sure the chamber is empty.

2. Remove old bases or rings. If the gun is new, you might have to remove the factory screws from the receiver. These screws protect the scope's mounting holes until needed.

3. Degrease the base screws and the receiver's mounting holes.

4. Temporarily install the bases. Shimming might be required under part of the base if the top of the receiver is not parallel to the axis of the bore. Mismatches might require a different set of bases.

5. Install the scope alignment rods into the rings and place them on the firearm. If there is a misalignment,

When the scope is mounted on the gun, make sure there is at least ⅙-inch clearance between the bell of the scope and the gun.

some shimming might be required. Very small adjustments can be made later by tapping the base with a rubber hammer.

6. Remove the rings when the rods indicate the system is aligned. Apply a light coating of gun oil to the underside of the base and the top of the receiver.

Also install the base and screws, using adhesive. Be sure the adhesive does not drip into the action. Use cotton swabs to check clean spillage.

7. Re-install the rings with the alignment rods. Again, if there is a small alignment problem, tapping with the rubber hammer might correct it. If there's gross misalignment, shimming might be required.

8. Once you are satisfied the rings and the base are aligned, install the riflescope in the rings. Degrease the inner surface of the rings and the area of contact on the scope.

Inspect the fit of the rings to the riflescope. Some inexpensive rings are not perfectly round, making for a poor fit between the ring and the scope's body tube.

If you're using Weaver-style rings, install them loosely, then attach them to the base. For Redfield-style rings, attach the twist-lock front ring by using a 1-inch metal or wooden dowel.

When the scope is mounted on the

gun, make sure there is at least ⅛ inch clearance between the bell of the scope and the gun. Also, make sure the action isn't touching the scope during cycling.

9. Set up the bore-sighting system on the firearm. Adjust the ring screws so the scope can rotate, but not wobble. Adjust the distance the scope is from the eye to prevent injury during recoil — about 3 inches.

10. Turn the scope to high power and adjust the windage and elevation controls so the image of the bore-sighting grid and the scope reticle don't move with each other as the scope is rotated.

11. Gently rotate the scope in the rings so the horizontal portion of the reticle is level when the gun is held in the shooting position. To aid this adjustment, use a bubble level or reticle leveler. Next, tighten all rings and base screws. Use adhesive on the screws, and let set over night.

12. Adjust the windage and elevation controls to place the center of the reticle on the center of the bore-sighting grid.

Shimming might be required to bring it in alignment with the bore. If so, consider using a system with windage control.

13. With everything secure, the riflescope is now ready for the range. The shooter should pick a common distance — 25, 50 or 100 yards — and adjust accordingly. Remember, ammunition, outside temperature, temperature of the barrel and cleanliness of the barrel all affect a gun's accuracy.

14. Make sure the scope's rings and bases are tight.

— For more information on scope mounting, contact BUSHNELL SPORT OPTICS, 9200 Cody St., Dept. DDH, Shawnee Mission, KS 66214.

Tips for Sighting Deer Rifles

Sighting-in a deer rifle is best accomplished by shooting from a bench and steady rest at a paper target from a range of 50 to 100 yards.

If your scope is equipped with an adjustable objective, be sure it is adjusted to the range at which you are sighting.

The traditional method of sighting a rifle is, from a solid rest, to aim at the bull's-eye and carefully fire one or more shots. Make note of the vertical and horizontal distances between the resulting bullet holes and the desired point of impact. Adjust the scope the required number of clicks to move from the initial point of impact to the desired point of impact. Fire additional shots and make adjustments as required to achieve the desired result.

The "two-shot" sighting method is much easier, but it requires the help of another person.

With the rifle on sandbags, take careful aim at the bull's-eye and fire one shot. Arrange the rifle back on the bags and aim carefully at the bull's-eye again. Without moving the rifle, have a friend adjust the scope reticle while you watch through the scope. Direct the person to move the reticle until it's centered on the first bullet hole. Now the rifle should shoot where the scope is looking.

Fire a second shot to confirm the rifle is sighted. You might need to perform some fine tuning, but this method is quick, easy and accurate.

— Courtesy of PENTAX, 35 Inverness Drive East, Englewood, CO 80112.

A Spike for Scott

I was really getting sick of the hype. It started sometime in August and continued building slowly as the weeks rolled by. It seemed like every time I picked up a newspaper, the outdoors columnist was reaching off the page and hitting me on the head with a large rubber mallet.

"DNR Predicts Best Season Ever."

"Hunters Brace for Record Harvest."

"State to Sell Extra Bonus Tags."

It wasn't that I didn't want to go hunting. I certainly wouldn't miss it. My pessimism had more to do with the fact that I had but one weekend to scout my favorite Bayfield County woods, and I didn't want to be one of the unlucky few who didn't kill a buck during this "season to end all seasons."

My job prevented me from hunting up North much the past few years. I had already used three of my seven vacation days on nonhunting trips, and I always saved three vacation days for gun season. It was late October when I decided to use that final day to hunt grouse and scout for deer.

Well-Laid Plans

I smiled widely when I stepped out on a dew-soaked logging trail that quiet Friday morning. I was surrounded by what must be one of God's greatest creations: a North Woods autumn.

The road was lined with red, yellow and burnt-orange leaves. Red-oak acorns tumbled intermittently onto a nearby deer trail. A slight breeze carried a scent of musky earth and evergreens.

This was supposed to be a pleasure walk. I uncased my shotgun and loaded five shells, but I really didn't expect to do much grouse hunting. My thoughts were on deer, and I knew I would have to find a couple of good stand sites that day if I expected to have any luck during the gun season.

Thirty minutes into my walk, I found a fork in the logging trail. To the left, it wound past a creek and into a cedar swamp. To the right, it turned uphill through a 2-year-old aspen clear-cut. My instincts told me to go left, but my curiosity made me go right.

Fifty yards later, I was thankful I had gone right. Along the trail, there were rubs on three wrist-size trees, including one that featured a scrape and licking branch. I followed the trail for another 400 yards until it ended at a small 1-acre grass field.

"This is too perfect," I thought as I observed numerous deer trails leaving the aspen regrowth and crisscrossing into the field. Only one mature tree, about 20 inches in diameter, bordered the

TEXT AND PHOTO BY DANIEL E. SCHMIDT

> **By noon, everyone was well-prepared. Inside, the gun rack sported freshly oiled rifles. Outside, blaze-orange overalls hung swaying from a clothesline, and portable tree stands and climbing sticks were lined up along the woodshed.**

field. Best of all, it grew in the field's northeastern corner — a perfect spot to hunt with a portable tree stand.

The trail leading to the spot was overgrown enough that I knew no other hunters had walked it in quite a while. I discreetly slipped out of the area and returned to my truck.

Planning for the Big Day

I located two more new stand sites before the day was finished, and they all held promise for opening day. They were secluded, near food and water, and off the beaten trails other hunters would surely use. I saw numerous deer while scouting those areas, but none of the other sites compared to what I called "The Clearing."

After driving home that night, I couldn't wait to get on the phone with my father and brother to tell them about the promising signs. I'm sure the news made their evenings.

"Can I hunt one of the spots?" my dad asked.

"No problem," I replied.

"Can I hunt one of the spots?" my brother asked.

"No problem, I've found three," I replied.

Of course, I planned to let them hunt the two spots I'd found later in the day. The Clearing was mine, I assured myself.

Another Phone Call

The next few weeks passed quickly. It wasn't easy getting good sleep when thinking about what might walk into that grass field opening day. It seemed like I spent all my free time running to the sports shop to pick up last-minute items and making sure my hunting clothes were scent-free. Work had become, well, just that — something I did when I wasn't getting ready for the hunt.

I can't remember exactly when I received the phone call — a week, maybe 10 days before the opener.

"Hi Danny," my dad said. "Scott just called and said he can get off of work for the opener. Do you know of a spot where we can put him?"

He was greeted with several seconds of silence.

"Uh, well, yeah," I stuttered. "Yeah, we can find something for him, I guess."

"Oh, that's great," my dad replied. "He's really excited because I told him about all the deer you've been seeing. He's even going to work overtime next week just so he can get off for two days."

My dad went on to tell me that Scott, my new brother-in-law, hadn't hunted much the past few years. It seems his job as a chef demanded that he work grueling schedules — sometimes 70 hours per week.

What's more, he had been busy at home helping my sister take care of their new baby boy. She insisted he take some time for himself, but he had always declined, saying his family and job came first.

Numerous images flashed through my mind while I held the receiver to my ear. I thought of my little sister on her wedding day, looking at her husband with eyes filled with joy, hope and happiness. I also thought of Scott, physically and emotionally drained, driving home after a 14-hour shift.

I couldn't disappoint them.

"Tell him not to worry," I said. "Tell Scott he's going to hunt the clearing."

Gathering at the Cabin

The morning before gun season opened, our six-man hunting party rolled into camp. We quickly unloaded our trucks, filled the refrigerator with groceries and split enough dry maple to warm the cabin for several days.

By noon, everyone was well-prepared. Inside, the gun rack sported freshly oiled rifles. Outside, blaze-orange overalls hung swaying from a clothesline, and portable tree stands and climbing sticks were lined up along the woodshed.

> **Numerous images flashed through my mind while I held the receiver to my ear. I thought of my little sister on her wedding day, looking at her husband with eyes filled with joy. I also thought of Scott, physically and emotionally drained, driving home after a 14-hour shift.**

With everything in order, a couple of the guys left for a last-minute run to the general store 20 minutes away. My dad was cleaning the garage so it could serve as a temporary meat cooler, and one of my brothers was in the kitchen with Scott, peeling potatoes for dinner.

"Hey Scott!" I hollered. "You want to check out the clearing?"

He didn't answer. Within two minutes, he met me outside, carrying his hiking boots and heavy wool shirt.

"Let's go!" he said.

Here's Your Spot

While driving to the stand area, I took Scott on a short detour, showing him spots we might hunt later in the week. I could tell he was listening, but I knew he was more interested in seeing the spot I had described in detail.

By 1 p.m., I drove to an area

about a half-mile from The Clearing, parked and whispered to Scott the route we would take.

As we walked down the logging trail, I admit I felt a rush of selfishness in my veins. I told myself I should have kept my big mouth shut and kept the stand a secret. After all, I had done the work to find it.

Then I looked at Scott.

His eyes twinkled with excitement, and the corners of his lips were curved upward. My jealous feelings instantly subsided and were replaced by humility and pride.

I was proud to have found such a spot, and convinced myself that a deer — any deer — killed from it would be cause for celebration — even if someone else shot it.

Within minutes, we were slugging up the now-familiar aspen thicket. I showed Scott where the creek crossed the trail, and I tied an orange ribbon on a sapling at the fork in the trail where he would have to turn north.

Then, he spied one of the signs I had talked about all week.

"Whoa, check it out!" Scott gasped, pointing toward the three wrist-sized rubs. "There's at least one good buck in here!"

"You ain't seen nothing yet," I whispered.

During the next 400 yards, Scott did something I hadn't during my scouting trip. He counted the rubs.

"Eighteen, 19, 20," he said while keeping pace with me. "This is insane!"

Meeting at the Meat Pole
It was just before noon

Saturday when I drove back to camp for lunch. My morning had been unproductive: Three gray squirrels, two raccoons and a fisher were the only animals that had walked into view of my stand, the ledge of a rock formation in the middle of nowhere.

Rounding a bend in the road near the driveway, I caught a glimpse of a brown form swaying from the meat pole.

I couldn't help but hoot loudly and press my hand firmly on the truck's horn.

Scott was out of the cabin and at the driver's-side door before I could turn off the ignition.

His eyes showed no hints of the redness visible when he drove all night to get there. And his face showed none of the anxiety I knew came with working so hard.

"I got a buck," Scott said. "A nice spike. He came out right where you said he would.

"I thought about holding out for a bigger one, but then I thought, heck, a buck's a buck, right?"

"You got that right," I said, stepping out of the truck. I smiled and slapped him on the shoulder. "Way to go, Scott. Let me get a closer look at this deer."

I slapped him on the back once more as we walked to the meat pole, but this time I paused for a moment to hang onto his shoulder.

Was I hoping his luck would rub off on me? Maybe a little. But above that, I was hoping to grasp a handful of his wide-eyed euphoria.

And hang onto it forever.

Today's Hot New Deer Guns

■ Marlin intro-duces the Model 336M, a .30-30 lever-action rifle. The first stainless-steel lever-action to carry the Marlin name, the 336M is ideal for hunting deer in rain and snow. Almost all of the major parts are stainless steel — the rest are nickel-plated. The 20-inch barrel has Micro-Groove rifling, a hammer-block safety and offset hammer spur for scope use. Sights include an adjustable folding semi-buckhorn rear and front ramp sight that includes a brass bead and removable Wide-Scan hood.

The Model 336M weighs 7 pounds and measures 38½ inches.

■ U.S. Repeating Arms expands its Winchester line of shotguns with the Model 1300 deer and turkey shotgun. The deer shotgun is light and easy to handle. The 20-gauge version features a fully rifled barrel, while a rifled sabot tube is optional for the 12-gauge version.

■ Left-handers have another option for deer rifles with Weatherby's Mark V Ultra Lightweight Magnum. At less than 7 pounds, the rifle is a good choice for southpaws who hunt in rugged country or for extended periods. The Ultralightweight Magnum features a bolt, bolt sleeve and chrome/moly receiver.

The barrel is 26 inches and features weight-reducing flutes to increase portability while main-taining velocity. The gun also sports a hybrid composite stock of Kevlar and fiberglass.

The rifle is available in the following Weatherby Magnum calibers: .257, .270, 7mm and .300. It is also available with a 24-inch barrel in 7mm Rem. Mag. and .300 Win. Mag.

■ Shotgun-hunters looking for a versa-tile gun should check out the new 20-gauge Encore from Thompson/Center. The Encore features a 26-inch slug barrel with blued finish.

It has a steel click-adjustable fiber-optic rear sight with ramp-style fiber-optic front sight. With the 20-gauge barrel, the Encore weighs about 7 pounds and is 40½ inches long.

Switching barrels on the Encore is easy. Simply detach the forend, tap out a hinge pin and change barrels. T/C offers a variety of barrels in popular deer hunting calibers for the Encore.

The Long and Short of Muzzleloader Performance

"Two good bucks are coming off that willow island every afternoon, and they feed along the edge of my hay field by those big cottonwoods."

I couldn't suppress a large grin as I thought those words over. My rancher friend didn't hunt, but he knew I wanted to try out my new long-barrelled muzzleloader. This was good information, and I knew the bucks would continue their feeding pattern because there weren't any other hunters around. I hiked down to the area and scouted the riverbank carefully. A well-used trail led from the little overgrown island, and I decided to sit in a jumbled pile of driftwood just downwind from it. I moved a few logs to make a hiding spot, cleared some vegetation and quietly left.

That afternoon I made myself comfortable in the driftwood pile. I was only yards from the dried-up riverbed and the island. A 5-foot-tall screen of willows and tall weeds grew right along the bank, so I couldn't see the river or the island. I was startled when a doe, and later a forkhorn, leaped from the hidden riverbed, bursting through the willow wall just yards from my hiding spot. Both deer fed less than 15 yards away, the closest I had ever been to shootable deer. I was excited. This was a great spot and the deer were moving.

Barbed wire squeaked softly behind me. I slowly turned and was amazed to see two big bucks standing by a fence line that ran down to the riverbank. I hadn't seen or heard them until one touched the wire as he jumped the fence. They had left the island on a different trail than I had expected. Both bucks were trophies with nice width, heavy beams and long tines. They walked through some willows and weeds, slowly making their way toward the hay field. Just yards from heavy cover, the two stopped broadside and looked over their shoulders. I cocked the hammer, set the trigger and put the front blade on the biggest buck. With the heavy rifle resting on a log, my aim was steady, the sight picture was perfect. Seconds ticked by. The bucks walked into cover. I couldn't shoot. Although the bucks were about 75 yards away, I wasn't confident I could make a killing shot. I never saw another deer all evening.

IAN MCMURCHY

How to Prepare for Long Shots

Long-range accuracy with scoped in-line muzzleloaders (or scoped caplocks) entails two things — knowledge and ability. You must know the bullet drop or trajectory, distance to the target, and the effect of any wind that might be present. You must also refine some of the former, and obtain the shooting skills to ensure that your shot will strike the vitals of a deer. Here are some key tools that hunters should use for long shots.

1. Drop chart — Memorize or write a drop chart on the side of your rifle.

2. Laser rangefinder — These items are crucial for determining exact distances.

3. Shooting rest — Underwood shooting sticks, Harris bipods, Snipe Pods or any handy rest can be helpful.

4. Back-up — If possible, have your buddy ready to help put down a wounded animal.

5. Practice — Take shots at a variety of distances and learn what effect wind has on your bullet.

6. Be prepared to pass on shots — Only take ideal shots within your ability. Wishing to undo a shot is no way to end a hunt.

The In-Line Craze

Although that hunt was almost 20 years ago, I still don't regret my decision not to shoot. I was not confident in the ability of that side-hammer beyond 50 yards. This was very frustrating, and cost me a chance at a great buck. I had shot the rifle a lot in preparation for the early muzzleloader season. Although I varied the black-powder charge and loading technique, I could not keep three shots on the paper at 100 yards. Even at 50 yards, the average group was just good enough to stay in the vital area of a whitetail.

I gave up on that rifle about the time Tony Knight started the in-line craze that has taken over muzzleloading. My first MK-85, scoped and shooting easy-loading sabots, shot five shots into two- to three-inch groups at 100 yards. The rifle handled like the center-fires in my gun rack. I killed deer cleanly at 95 yards and was confident I could extend that if necessary.

As in-line muzzleloaders took over the muzzleloading industry, I was fortunate to test and hunt with virtually all of the new rifles. Many people involved in muzzleloading wondered just how far these changes would go and if the new technology was really good for the sport. Some manufacturers raced to bring out centerfire-like options, and advertisers touted significant performance increases.

The in-line evolution occurred when deer populations were reaching record numbers, so game agencies used the popularity of muzzleloader-hunting to control deer numbers as well as provide an extra means of recreation.

Other Improvements

Along with fast-twist barrels attached to in-line actions, manufacturers concentrated on improving the performance of the projectile, propellant and ignition devices. Manufacturers developed saboted bullets that offered simplified loading and flatter trajectories. Initially .44- and .45-caliber pistol bullets were pressed into service, seated in various

Distance (yards)	100	150	200	250	300
Bullet Drop (inches)					
Knight	0	-3.5	-13	-27	-48
T/C	0	-2.7	-10.4	-24.5	-45
Velocity (feet per second)					
Knight	1,625	1,502	1,320	1,095	—
T/C	1,686	1,555	1,366	1,130	—
Five-shot Group Size (inches)					
Knight	1.3	1.6	7.0	4.6	
12.4*					
T/C	1.2	1.5	6.0	9.9	
14.0*					

*three-shot group

The test used 250-grain Barnes bullets in orange MML sabots with three 50-grain Pyrodex Pellets and CCI No. 209 primers. An Oehler 35P chronograph was used to measure velocity.

	Muzzle Velocity	100-Yard Velocity	Difference
Black Belt Conicals			
295-grain	1,467	1,149	318
348-grain	1,395	1,157	238
405-grain	1,334	1,136	198
444-grain	1,286	1,130	156
520-grain	1,226	1,096	130
Barnes Redhot Bullets			
180-grain	2,127	1,688	439
200-grain	2,128	1,689	439
220-grain	2,083	1,669	414
250-grain	2,045	1,626	419
300-grain	1,923	1,545	378

This test used a Knight Wolverine LK93 with a 24-inch barrel to test bullet velocities. A 100-grain charge of RS Pyrodex powder was used with the Black Belt Conicals and a 150-grain charge of Pyrodex Pellets was used for the Barnes Redhot Bullets.

sized and shaped plastic sleeves or sabots. Unfortunately, some of the early handgun bullets were not intended to perform at muzzleloader velocities, resulting in shed cores and poor penetration. Hotter, 150-grain loads pushed velocities of lightweight bullets over 2,000 feet per second, so belted/bonded and thick-jacketed bullets were developed. Enter onto the scene Pyrodex Pellets, "souped-up" musket caps and 209 shotshell primer ignition systems, further changing the traditional front-stuffer. With such significant changes occurring so quickly, some sportsmen and game agency officials wondered if things had gone too far. Rumblings of "Might as well shoot Ruger single-shots..." and "They (in-lines) aren't muzzleloaders any more," floated about.

Field Tests

I wondered that myself, so I set out to learn just how well current in-lines perform, particularly if they offer greater killing distances. I asked a number of muzzleloader shooters to participate in a simple field test to see how far they could accurately shoot a scoped in-line. I also did extensive range tests myself and attempted to obtain chronograph information to find out velocities at distances over 100 yards. My field tests are not large enough to be statistically valid, but they did provide me with information I can use to make decisions and form opinions.

In my tests and through several seasons worth of experience shooting muzzleloaders, I have found that in-lines don't offer any ballistic performance advantage — period. (Notice that I said ballistic performance advantage, there are other significant differences to consider when comparing the two types of muzzleloaders.) Igniting the current maximum of 150 grains, either in a charge of black powder, Pyrodex powder or Pyrodex Pellets behind a fairly light, saboted-bullet will result in identical velocities whether the action is sidehammer or in-line. Although I am not a proponent of unnecessarily heavy loads, and the factories clearly stipulate maximum suggested powder

Today's souped-up muzzleloaders, like this Thompson/Center Encore, push bullets to never-before-seen speeds. What's more, magnum muzzleloaders allow hunters to shoot 150-grain charges.

charges, virtually any modern sidehammer replica can handle the 150-grain saboted bullet load.

As mentioned, I performed long range field accuracy and chronograph tests. I decided long range extended to 300 yards. Anything past that is futile or a fluke. While shooting a pair of scoped in-lines, I concentrated on the highest performance loads to find out what they would actually do in the field. I shot my Knight Disc rifle and T/C 209x50 .50-caliber rifles, each mounted with Nikon scopes in Warne mounts. Each rifle had a history of excellent accuracy, which I consider to be three shot groups under two inches.

Each of these rifles consistently shot groups under 1½ inches. The chart on the previous page shows the results of my shooting tests.

This table shows the performance of the hottest loads available. More popular charges of 90 to 100 grains of powder and 250- to 300-grain sabots will have much more looping trajectories. I've seen almost eight inches of drop between 100 and 150 yards with some loads. We commonly measure over 55 inches of drop at 300 yards with hunting loads, which is more than four and a half feet! The above graph uses 100-yard zeroes to show downrange bullet drop. Most hunters adjust their scopes to 2½ or 3 inches high at 100 yards.

Because of rainbow trajectories, I couldn't get 300-yard velocities. My shots at that range destroyed too much of my Oehler Skyscreen before I could properly adjust it for long-range trajectories. I did chron-

Advanced sabots and shotgun primers push the envelope for muzzleloading technology. However, while modern in-lines can shoot accurately enough to kill deer at long range, not every shooter can do so. Consistency requires lots of practice.

ograph some conical bullets to compare velocity loss, and was amazed at how well the long, heavy bullets retained speed (and therefore energy). Unfortunately, heavy bullets drop like stones after 100 yards, so I did not get velocities past that. To compare big bullets with current lightweights, I shot the latest Knight/Barnes saboted bullets through the same chronograph screens. I chronographed the lighter bullets to 200 yards with good results.

The data show that the trend to lighter, faster bullets is not providing extra distance. Lightweight bullets are inefficient and shed velocity quickly. The big 520-grain conical lost 130 fps while traveling 100 yards, and the 180-grain hot-rod lost 439 fps! At 200 yards, the 180-grain bullet had lost 40 percent of its initial velocity. The important

thing here is retained energy — there is no comparing the two. I fired each type of bullet into clay at 100 yards, and the heavy 520-grain bullet penetrated at least four times as deeply, plus retained virtually all of its original weight. The lighter bullet tended to split and shed pieces, which greatly reduced the penetration ability. I am aware of several deer taken at 250 to 275 yards by 300-grain Barnes, Speer and Hornady bullets that completely passed through. I am confident that most loads would be lethal at 300 yards if they hit a vital area.

Field Accuracy

In my test to establish field accuracy, I set up full size white-tailed deer targets at distances varying from 50 to 400 yards. I then asked each participant to shoot one shot

.50 Cal. Ballistics - Lead Conicals with Black Powder or Pyrodex

Bullet	Black Powder or Pyrodex®	Range in Yards	Impact from line of Sight	Velocity f.p.s	Energy ft./lbs.
350 Grain Maxi-Hunter® or 370 Grain Maxi-Ball®	100 Grains	50	+1.9	1383	1572
	100 Grains	100	0.0	1176	1137
	100 Grains	150	-8.1	1041	891
	100 Grains	200	-21.8	951	743
350 Grain Maxi-Hunter® or 370 Grain Maxi-Ball®	150 Grains	50	+1.5	1574	2036
	150 Grains	100	0.0	1326	1445
	150 Grains	150	-4.6	1142	1072
	150 Grains	200	-15.2	1016	848

.50 Cal. Ballistics - Mag Express Sabots with Black Powder or Pyrodex

Bullet	Black Powder or Pyrodex®	Range in Yards	Impact from line of Sight	Velocity f.p.s	Energy ft./lbs.
240 Grain XTP™	100 Grains	50	+1.1	1696	1532
	100 Grains	100	0.0	1539	1261
	100 Grains	150	-4.8	1399	1043
	100 Grains	200	-14.1	1276	867
240 Grain XTP™	150 Grains	50	+.7	2006	2143
	150 Grains	100	0.0	1830	1783
	150 Grains	150	-3.2	1660	1468
	150 Grains	200	-9.6	1507	1210
275 Grain XTP™	100 Grains	50	+1.4	1571	1506
	100 Grains	100	0.0	1420	1232
	100 Grains	150	-5.7	1289	1014
	100 Grains	200	-16.6	1177	846
275 Grain XTP™	150 Grains	50	+.8	1887	2175
	150 Grains	100	0.0	1705	1775
	150 Grains	150	-3.8	1540	1447
	150 Grains	200	-11.4	1393	1185
300 Grain XTP™	100 Grains	50	+1.4	1573	1649
	100 Grains	100	0.0	1452	1404
	100 Grains	150	-5.6	1343	1200
	100 Grains	200	-15.9	1244	1030
300 Grain XTP™	150 Grains	50	+.8	1862	2310
	150 Grains	100	0.0	1718	1965
	150 Grains	150	-3.8	1583	1669
	150 Grains	200	-11.1	1461	1421

The information provided here is based on testing done by Thompson/Center Arms with components as specified in the chart. 26" barrels were used to produce the data. Magnum charges of 150 grains of FFG Black Powder or Pyrodex equivalent should be used only in those guns approved by the manufacturer for use with magnum charges.

Muzzleloading Supplies

Barnes Bullets
Box 215
318 S. 860 E., Dept. DDH
American Fork, UT 84003

Connecticut Valley Arms
Box 7225, Dept. DDH
Norcross, GA 30091

Goex Black Powder
Belin Plant, Dept. DDH
1002 Springbrook Ave.
Moosic, PA 18507

Gonic Arms Inc.
134 Flagg Road, Dept. DDH
Gonic, NH 03839

Hodgdon Powder Co.
6231 Robinson, Dept. DDH
Shawnee Mission, KS 66202

Hornady
Box 1848, Dept. DDH
Grand Island, NE 68802

Knight Rifles
234 Airport Road, Dept. DDH
Centerville, IA 52544

Markesbery Muzzle Loaders Inc.
7785 Foundation Drive, Suite 6
Florence, KY 41042

Muzzleloading Technologies
25 E. Hwy. 40, Suite 330-12
Roosevelt, UT 84066

Prairie River Arms
1220 N, 6th St., Dept. DDH
Princeton, IL 61356

Remington Arms Co. Inc.
870 Remington Drive, Dept. DDH
Madison, NC 27025-0700

Thompson/Center Arms
Box 5002, Farmington Road
Rochester, NH 03867

Traditions
1375 Boston Post Road, Dept. DDH
Old Saybrook, CT 06475-0776

White Shooting Systems
25 E. Hwy. 40 (330-12), Dept. DDH
Roosevelt, UT 84066

at each of the following distances (unknown to them): 50, 90, 125, 165, 200, 245, 275, 305, 330 and 370 yards. Each shooter could refrain from attempting a shot when he got beyond his personal perceived capability. Shots were taken from any position with any hunting rest the shooter might normally use. Each muzzleloader was loaded with the individual's preferred hunting charge. Everyone used saboted bullets in the range of 250 to 310 grains. No one shot round balls or conicals. Powder charges were consistently in the 90- to 100-grain weights of Pyrodex RS or Select. No black powder was brought out. Pyrodex pellets were shot by five shooters, each one preferring the heavy 150-grain charge.

The shooters ranged from very experienced black-powder hunters to new owners of in-lines. I placed a full body buck decoy beside the target so that participants could estimate distance realistically. How did they do? Range estimation accuracy dropped significantly after 90 yards, and most individuals failed to come within 10 percent to 15 percent from 90 to 275 yards and within 15 percent to 20 percent past 275 yards. What does that mean in practical terms? Given that some muzzleloader bullets drop almost eight inches between 100 and 150 yards, miss-judging the distance will probably result in a wounded animal.

One shooter was very accurate out to and including 125 yards, with virtually all shots striking the vital zone of the target (95 percent). Accuracy at 165 yards dropped to

82 percent and down to 63 percent at 200 yards. No shooter chose to shoot at 245 or 275 yards, so 200 was the unanimous maximum range for participants. I got most of the shooters to try shots at 245 and 275 yards and results indicated that they were correct in not trying the shot — no vital hits.

Can long shots (200-250 yards) be part of muzzleloading today? Yes. Should they be? That depends completely on the knowledge and skill of the individual. Any muzzleloader hunter can improve his distance shooting so that his kill zone is extended as far as his equipment can allow. This requires a lot of practice, with an emphasis placed on trajectory and wind drift. The shot should be doable, not just an attempt. Many modern in-lines will shoot accurately enough to kill at "long range" but not every shooter can do so. I am aware of a growing interest to use the potential of modern loads to enhance hunting opportunities. Obtaining the skill and knowledge to shoot your muzzleloader out to 200 yards will definitely expand your chances of taking a trophy.

During the Hunt

My friend Gregg Ritz, national sales manager for Thompson Center, was hunting Texas whitetails on the Nail Ranch, northwest of Abilene. Gregg and his guide, Calvin, were hunting in early November, and the bucks were starting to show good rutting activity. Setting up on a large hill, Calvin clashed his rattling horns, hoping the sound would carry into a mesquite thicket below. Soon, the

The Ultimate Deer Hunter's Quiz
Part 4, Muzzleloading

37. Including nonresident hunters, which state attracts the most muzzleloading hunters each year?
A. Pennsylvania
B. Michigan
C. Tennessee
D. Arkansas

38. Which state leads the nation in deer harvest by muzzleloaders?
A. Pennsylvania
B. Michigan
C. Tennessee
D. Arkansas

39. Which state has the longest muzzleloading season in the nation?
A. Michigan
B. California
C. South Dakota
D. Oregon

40. Why do some hunters prefer Pyrodex Pellets over traditional black powder?
A. A 100-grain pellet is easier to load.
B. Pellets do not cause barrel fouling.
C. Pellets burn erratically, causing increased muzzle energy.
D. Pellets can increase a bullet's velocity by up to 200 feet per second.

41. Which four items are parts on a traditional, Hawken-style muzzleloader?
A. Tang, hammer, lock plate, breech plug
B. Tang, nipple, safety, hammer
C. Tang, hammer, nipple, patch box
D. Nipple, hammer, tang, receiver

42. Which of the following is not a muzzleloading bullet?
A. Round ball
B. Steel conical
C. Sabot with a jacketed bullet
D. Lead conical

This is the end of the quiz for Chapter 4.
Quiz continues on Page 79.
Answers begin on Page 194.

hunters saw movement in the mesquite. A buck started thrashing a tree. Calvin rattled again, and Gregg got a good look at the buck. The buck was a wide 9-pointer; just what Gregg had come to Texas for. The fellows watched as the buck buzzed around in the thicket, herding does together and chasing off a couple of lesser bucks. Every time Calvin rattled, the big buck moved over to look uphill, but he was not going to leave the does. After it became apparent that the buck wouldn't come any closer, Calvin started to sneak back to the truck.

"I asked Calvin where he was going," Gregg recalls. "He replied that 'We're burnin' daylight, the buck's not comin' up this hill and you're not shooting a 7 Mag.' I asked how far he thought the shot was and Calvin gave me a look like I had three heads and said it was easily 200 yards. Then he asked me if I was planning to take the shot."

With a confident grin, Gregg set up his Underwood shooting sticks and began preparing for the shot. Calvin sat on a rock, with that "customer is always right attitude," and resumed glassing the buck. The big buck continued his activities, frequently offering broadside shots. Gregg checked the wind with his lighter and was relieved to see that it was head-on and very light. Knowing his rifle was sighted two inches high at 100 yards and five inches low at 200 yards he put the cross hairs right across the buck's back with the vertical cross hair down the right foreleg. Taking a deep breath, he let the shot go and white smoke filled the air.

Gregg quickly turned to Calvin to see the veteran guide shaking his head in disbelief. Calvin exclaimed, "That buck is dead in his tracks. He died without so much as a kick. That would have been an impressive shot with a 7mm Magnum. I can't wait to tell the guys a muzzleloader killed a buck stone dead at 200 yards!" Later, Gregg lasered the shot at 187 yards, so their estimate was close. Gregg had practiced with his rifle, and he knew the trajectory — resulting in a clean kill.

I was involved in another big buck kill last year. My son, Glen, set up in a location where we had seen a buck the previous afternoon. He sat quietly in a light rain, hoping the buck would return to feed. He used his Bushnell Yardage Pro-800 to determine distances of possible shots, including readings of 175 and 200 yards to the far side of the field. The hunting gods smiled, and a huge buck walked out in front of Glen. Settling his Knight MK-85 in his Underwood shooting sticks, my boy calmed himself and slowly squeezed off a shot at the buck of his dreams. One shot equalled one buck that grossed well over 175 points. Distance: 28 yards.

Conclusion

Why do I mention my son's close-range hunt in an article on long range? To make my key point — get as close as you can but be prepared to shoot accurately at longer distances if you must. Even 28 yards might look pretty long when a monster buck is looking back over his shoulders.

Editor's Note: *This article originally appeared in the* 1999 Deer Hunters Equipment *annual.*

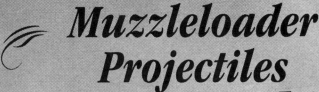

Muzzleloader Projectiles

Round Balls

The Round Ball

The earliest and most traditional projectile; an all-lead sphere. Used with a lubed patch; either pre-cut or trimmed during loading (with a patch knife). A .50-caliber round ball weighs approximately 175 grains. Using 100 grains of FFG Black Powder, muzzle velocity is about 2,000 feet per second. At 100 yards, terminal energy will be only half of what a conical delivers.

Maxi-Balls

Lead Conicals

An all-lead, conical-shaped projectile, with grooves to hold a lubricant. Although weights might vary, the most popular weight used (.50 cal.) for deer is approximately 350 grains. Using 100 grains of FFG black powder, muzzle velocity is about 1,400 fps. At 100 yards, terminal energy will be about twice that of a round ball.

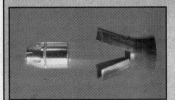

Mag Express

Sabots

A jacketed bullet (usually .44 or .45 cal.) housed in a plastic or polymer sleeve. The weight of a .50-caliber bullet is usually between 240 and 250 grains. Using 100 grains of FFG black powder, muzzle velocity is approximately 1,600 fps. At 100 yards, terminal down range energy is between 1100 and 1250 ft lbs; on a par with a 350-grain all-lead conical. At longer ranges, 150 yards or greater, down-range energy starts to surpass that of a conical because of the higher retained velocity.

Up in Flames

T he painful hours of sitting silently in below-zero temperatures suddenly seemed worth it when I heard a twig snap and leaves rustle to the north.

It was the waning half-hour of the last day of muzzleloader season. I had hunted hard for four days for this moment. Another twig snapped, and I finally saw movement.

It was a deer, and it was sneaking through the tangle of briars and new-growth aspen that wove through the edge of the woods about 100 yards from my stand. The deer stopped occasionally to browse, but a combination of brush and the setting sun obscured my vision enough that I couldn't tell if it was a buck or doe.

Regardless, I would tag it given the opportunity. My views on muzzleloading mimic those I have of bow-hunting: Any deer is a trophy, especially on the last day of the season.

Preparing for the Moment

The muzzleloading season holds special charm in my home state of Wisconsin. The season lasts but a week, usually the first one of December, and it isn't greeted with even a fraction of the media attention given to the bow- and gun-hunting seasons.

In fact, my favorite woodlots are their own versions of the Dead Sea when muzzleloading season rolls around. Gone are the grouse hunters and granola crunchers who stomp past my early-season bow stands. Absent are the blaze-orange-clad mobs who conduct drive after drive during the rifle season. And, even when the snow falls, snowmobilers are still a few weeks away from getting serious about blazing up and down the logging roads.

In other words, I pretty much have the woods to myself.

So, a few days before muzzleloader season opens, I head to the basement to find my possibles bag and fill it with all the necessities. While watching the deer move through the thicket, I was extra thankful I opted to pack the new percussion caps and flask of Pyrodex I bought a week earlier.

With a deer finally in front of me, I was extremely confident my gun's load was ready to deliver a killing shot.

Back to the Hunt

I had watched the deer for 10 minutes before finally getting a look at its head. Then, just as the last rays of sunlight dipped below the tree line, I saw a spectacular flicker.

Antlers.

I'm often amazed at how many times I see bucks in the woods and fail to immediately pick out their racks. I often blame that on the fact that most of the bucks I see are small. However, this time I had no excuse. This buck was big.

When a nearby pine squirrel

DANIEL E. SCHMIDT

ripped loose with ear-piercing chatter, the buck threw his head up and surveyed his back trail. He stood motionless for a minute and then went back to browsing.

In that brief moment, I studied and memorized his rack. It featured eight perfect points on massive, chocolate-brown beams that stretched about two inches beyond his ears.

By now the buck was standing about 75 yards from my stand, but I fought the urge to shoulder my muzzleloader. He was still in thick cover, and I knew the muzzleloader's iron sights were most accurate for shots less than 50 yards.

Drastic Measure

While the buck stood in the thicket, I looked down at my watch. Only 10 minutes of shooting time remained. Something had to happen pretty soon if this dream encounter was going to turn into a success story.

Gently and quietly raising the gun to shooting position, I pressed the gun's butt into my shoulder and held onto it with one arm while using the other to slowly reach for my grunt tube. I pressed the reeds to my lips, pointed the sound chamber to the back end of the tree and let out one soft grunt.

Big mistake, especially on a windless afternoon like this one.

As if he were hit by a stray electrical charge, the buck made two short bounds away from me. However, that's all he did.

His bounds placed him on the edge of the thicket about 80 yards from my gun barrel. He stood statue-like, facing directly away

from me, apparently unsure where the sound came from. Everything but his head and neck were obscured by brush.

I immediately tucked the call back in my coat pocket and placed the iron sight pin on the base of the buck's neck.

"This is a no-brainer," I thought to myself. "If I hit him, he's dead."

The Moment of Truth

Despite convincing myself I had nothing to lose, I held off on taking the neck shot. I knew I could wait a few minutes to see if the buck would step into a nearby opening.

He didn't. He merely stood still, swiveling his ears every few moments in an attempt to pick out further clues of my presence.

The suspense was killing me. I glanced at my wristwatch only to notice shooting time had just expired. I briefly listened to the little devil on my shoulder that told me to shoot now and make excuses later, but, I dismissed the temptation.

The buck was still scanning his surroundings when I took the iron pin off his neck and placed it on a white birch stump about 20 yards in front of my stand.

Pow!

I don't know which was more blinding — the fire that shot across the darkening woodland light, or the white tail that skyrocketed out of the thicket and danced into the deepest recesses of the forest.

After outsmarting this hunter, that wise, old buck deserved the reprieve.

Today's Hot New Muzzleloaders

■ Thompson/Center's Encore rifle has been chosen as an official Team Realtree designated product. The Team Realtree Encore rifle system is available in three models: two centerfire rifles in .308 Winchester and .300 Win. Magnum, and the 209x50 Magnum muzzleloader. All models are blued with walnut stocks and forends. Each rifle features T/C's Gold Medal barrel.

■ Modern Muzzleloading's Knight Master Hunter DISC Rifle is an in-line muzzleloader built for serious deer hunters. The Master Hunter is built around Knight's patented No. 209 primer DISC technology. It features a 26-inch Green Mountain stainless-steel barrel.

Before the barrel is laid into a custom stock, its 1-in-28-inch rifling is air-gauged to ensure exact tolerances. The .50-caliber muzzleloader features a jeweled bolt and gold-plated adjustable trigger. It also features an engraved trigger guard, TruGlo fiber-optic sights, satin ramrod and premier laminated thumb-hole stock with Monte Carlo cheekpiece.

■ Connecticut Valley Arms offers the Hunterbolt, Firebolt and Eclipse rifles with the Musket Mag 3-Way ignition system. This system hunters the added versatility of using 209 shotgun primers or No. 11 musket caps.

CVA's Hunterbolt, Firebolt and Eclipse rifles feature Illuminator II fiber-optic sights, and come in Realtree Hardwoods and Advantage camouflage. Barrel options include blued and nickel finishes.

Shown here is the FireBolt MusketMag, a .50-caliber muzzleloader. It is available in Advantage and Realtree Hardwoods synthetic stocks.

■ Traditions offers the Lightning Lightweight muzzleloader that has the capability of firing magnum saboted pistol bullets and up to three Pyrodex pellets.

The Lightweight comes with TruGlo adjustable fiber-optic sights, the Lightning Fire System, a stainless steel removable breech plug, and a lifetime warranty.

A quick-release bolt allows for easy removal with no tools required and each model includes a built-in weather shroud for protection from the weather. A 22-inch blued, nickel or stainless barrel is available.

Lohman's Brad Harris killed this 170-class whitetail on Day 1 of the 1999 **Deer & Deer Hunting** *sweepstakes hunt. Harris killed the buck while bow-hunting in eastern Kansas.*

CHAPTER 5
BIG BUCKS OF NORTH AMERICA

Rackin' Up Bucks

I used to have a knack for being in the wrong place at the wrong time. Especially when it came to deer hunting.

Well, my luck changed in 1999 when, as a co-host of the two *Deer & Deer Hunting* sweepstakes hunts, I watched some of the best whitetail action unfold in front of my own eyes. Best of all, I shared these camps with two top-notch deer hunters: sweepstakes winners Peter Whittaker of Spencer, Mass., and Howard Adams of Castleton, N.Y. Their names were drawn randomly from tens of thousands of entries.

Both hunts not only produced what we were after — sightings of big bucks — they emphasized the fact that readers of this magazine are dedicated whitetail hunters.

Heading West

For the 1999 gun-hunt, Whittaker and I traveled to Joplin, Mo. There, we met Brad Harris, a famous wildlife caller and expert deer hunter. We soon learned that Harris knows western Missouri's draws and woodlands about as well as anyone.

Harris is the director of public relations for Outland Sports, makers of Lohman and M.A.D. game calls, Blueridge targets, API

tree stands and Feather Flex decoys. He was accompanied by videographers Andy Swift, Mike Haviland and Chadd Duncan.

Success on the Prairie

Harris was the first to strike it rich. He had drawn a bow-hunting permit for Kansas, which was minutes from the western Missouri ground we were hunting. After selecting two prime stand locations for Whittaker and me, Harris grabbed his bow and headed for the border on the afternoon of Day 1.

His hunt didn't last long. Harris was in his stand just a short time when a massive 16-point nontypical strolled into range. He killed it cleanly with a double-lung shot.

Whittaker and I met Harris that evening at a gas station that processed venison. Our jaws hit the ground when we stepped into the walk-in cooler and saw what we both agreed was the buck of a lifetime. The buck's tines were long and many, and the main beams were studded with massive burrs. The rack gross-scored 170 inches.

We admired the buck for several minutes before Harris turned to us and said, "Well, guys, now it's your turn!"

TEXT AND PHOTOS BY DANIEL E. SCHMIDT

The author killed this 160-class whitetail in Missouri on Day 2 of the 1999 sweepstakes hunt.

He wasn't kidding.

My Turn

Harris knows whitetails. Despite daytime temperatures of nearly 80 degrees, big bucks, like any animal, can be outsmarted if you know where to find them.

Harris knew deer would move sparingly but seek water several times a day in that kind of weather. Thankfully, he had just the spot where I could sit and wait for a big buck.

In the predawn darkness of Day 2, Harris walked me and videographer Andy Swift to the edge of a grass field and then pointed to a small hill. "That's where you want to set up," he said. "The deer will funnel out of the woods and enter this field at daybreak. There's a pond on the other side

of the hill where they've been going to drink. The wind will be in your face, and the deer will never smell you."

That was the key to the set up. The area we hunted was dotted with small ponds, but most were surrounded by thick brush and offered poor visibility. What's more, the predominant winds made the other spots less than ideal.

Swift and I quickly climbed the hill and found a perfect spot to set up. I found two small trees on the edge of the hill that grew next to each other. One made for the perfect back rest, while the other had a small limb that made an ideal gun rest. Meanwhile, Swift backed himself into some brush and set up his video camera's tripod about five feet behind me.

Within minutes, the sun was pushing its way toward the horizon. However, cloud cover made for a gray morning, and, when legal shooting time arrived, Swift whispered that we needed another 20 minutes until he had "good light" for filming. I nodded and took my rifle from its rest and laid it across my lap.

The Vision

While watching the morning unfold, I began daydreaming about past hunts. Suddenly, I heard something rustling in the leaves behind me at the base of the hill. The sound was so close that I didn't think it could possibly be a deer. However, I didn't move a muscle and tried alerting Swift.

"Here comes something," I

whispered.

He didn't hear me.

"Here comes some...," I began whispering louder when I noticed movement at the base of the hill.

Without moving my head or body, I glanced over my shoulder. The vision almost made me lose control.

Antlers. Lots of antlers.

Standing at the base of the hill — a mere six yards from my boot laces — was the biggest buck I had ever seen in the wild. The buck looked directly at me, but it wasn't alarmed. I could have turned quickly and shot, but I knew Swift wanted to get video footage. I figured if I stayed still, the buck would eventually put his head down and walk to the pond. If he stayed on course, he would pass within four yards of my rifle barrel.

That didn't happen.

Our setup left us unprepared for this situation. We figured deer would come from the other end of the field, so Swift was in no position to see the deer. I wanted to whisper to him, but I knew it would probably spook the buck.

Swift knew I was watching a deer, but he had no idea how close it was. Assuming he had time to move his camera into position for filming, he shifted slightly, rustling some leaves under his feet.

Woosh! The buck snorted loudly and bounded into the field. The deer, however, hadn't seen us. It merely knew something was out of place. It stopped after leaping twice and looked back at me. At this point, the buck was still

Sweepstakes winner Peter Whittaker took this three-beam buck on Day 4 of the hunt in Missouri.

only 13 yards away. It lifted its tail high in the air as it prepared to take one last look before fleeing.

I knew Swift was far enough behind me that he couldn't see the buck. As much as I wanted him to videotape the scene, I knew my chance at the buck of a lifetime was going to quickly vanish.

In one motion, I shouldered my rifle and swung my body toward the buck. I quickly looked at his rack to confirm it was absolutely huge before settling the scope's cross-hairs on his lung area. The buck was flexing his hind quarters in preparation to leap when I squeezed the trigger on my Browning .30-06.

Pow!

The buck did a mule kick and

The sweepstakes hunters met Randy Berwald of Missouri while registering their deer with a venison processor. Berwald took this 180-class buck on opening day.

ran straight across the field. It crossed a tree-line, jumped a logging road and plowed into a thick stand of scrub oaks.

"Man, he was huge!" Swift exclaimed. "Did you hit him?"

"I sure hope so," I said with trembling lips. "But at that range he should be lying in his tracks."

Thankfully, my shot was true. The buck ran only 94 yards before collapsing. The buck's rack roughscored 168 inches, not including two 1-inch sticker points near his brow tines.

Another Buck of a Lifetime

After dragging the buck to the middle of the field, Swift and I waited for the rest of the Outland Sports crew. When they pulled up, Whittaker was one of the first ones out of the truck. His eyes sparkled with excitement as he jogged to the buck to admire it.

In fact, he was almost as excited as I was. Despite the fact he hadn't seen but a few antlerless deer in two days, he was upbeat and positive. I couldn't help but say a silent prayer that he would experience the same success.

Whittaker is a newcomer to deer hunting. And although he took up bow-hunting only four years ago, he has tagged bucks three years in a row. Going into the sweepstakes hunt, his largest buck was a yearling 5-pointer, and he had yet to tag a deer with a gun.

That all changed when my prayer was answered on Day 3.

Perched in a tree stand overlooking a grassy field, Whittaker and cameraman Mike Haviland readied themselves for a productive morning. The temperature had dropped into the 30s, and they had a feeling the deer would be active.

They were right.

The sun had barely crested the horizon when Whittaker heard crunching in the leaves behind him. He waited patiently, then watched as several antlerless deer stepped out of the woods and entered the field.

Within a few minutes, Whittaker spotted a large deer moving through the timber. He readied himself when the deer turned and headed toward his stand.

"It didn't take long to realize it was a buck," he said. "His antlers were just awesome."

The buck passed within bow range of Whittaker's stand, but he didn't shoot because he was waiting until Haviland could turn around with his video camera. The close encounter didn't shake Whittaker. He took a couple of deep breaths and watched as the buck entered the field and began angling away from him. At that point, Haviland gave him the green light.

When the buck was about 75 yards away, Whittaker calmly raised his Remington bolt-action, peered through the scope and touched off a shot. The deer buckled and ran a short distance. Whittaker thought his shot was true, but he didn't take any chances. He immediately chambered another round and dropped the deer in its tracks.

Whittaker couldn't contain his excitement. He and Haviland exchanged a high-five and quickly descended to claim the buck. And what a buck it was. Although it had lost a brow tine in a fight, the buck's 115-inch rack featured two main beams on the right side.

"That's a scene I'll never forget," he told me when we met back at the motel that afternoon. "He trotted across that field with his head up (and looked) all proud."

The euphoric feeling stayed with Whittaker for the rest of the trip.

The Ultimate Deer Hunter's Quiz
Part 5, Big Bucks

43. According to the Boone and Crockett Club, this man is credited with killing the biggest typical-antlered buck of all time.
A. Milo Hanson
B. James Jordan
C. Mitch Rompola
D. Chuck Adams

44. A person can enter a buck into the Boone and Crockett Club's record book after killing it with which of the following methods?
A. Bow and arrow
B. Shotgun
C. Rifle
D. Road kill
F. All of the above

45. In which instance would a bowhunter not be allowed to enter a bow-kill into the Pope and Young Club?
A. If the hunter killed the buck over a bait pile.
B. If the hunter killed the buck in an enclosure.
C. If the hunter killed the buck near a water source.
D. If the hunter used more than 60 percent let-off on a compound bow.

46. Of the top 10 typical-antlered bucks in the Pope and Young Club's record book, five came from this state.
A. Minnesota
B. Iowa
C. Colorado

47. True or false: It is unlikely for a rack to score 125 inches unless it has a width of at least 16 inches.

48. True or false: To enter a buck into Boone and Crockett, it must score 170 inches as a typical or 195 inches as a nontypical.

This concludes the quiz for Chapter 5. Quiz continues on Page 101. Answers begin on Page 194.

Ed McDonald of Ontario, Canada, killed this massive nontypical in 1998. The 22-pointer's rack had 28-inch main beams and an inside spread of more than 21 inches. The longest tine measured 12¾ inches.

Gun-Hunters Rewrite Record Books in Ontario and Wisconsin

In 1998, gun-hunters in Ontario and Wisconsin bagged two of the largest nontypical bucks in the history of white-tailed deer hunting. Combined, the bucks have more than 491 inches of antlers.

The tremendous eastern Ontario buck was killed Nov. 6 in Lanark County by Ed McDonald.

McDonald was part of a 12-man drive-hunting party that day. After a solid morning of hunting, five of the hunters had to leave the woods to return to work. The remaining seven hunters decided to keep hunting, and they moved to an area one of the hunters knew well.

McDonald said his friend Earl Ennis, who is an expert deer driver, told him to take a stand near a familiar deer runway.

"I was standing along a fence line separating two hayfields, with a bush about 100 yards in front of me," McDonald said. "I had been using this particular stand for the past nine years. Ironically, I had been thinking that morning of the fact that I had never shot a deer from this spot. I had numerous does and fawns pass in front of me, all of which I had let go in hopes that a monster buck would come out behind them.

"He never did."

McDonald's luck changed that day.

Ennis placed one hunter between McDonald and a section of woods that ended at the banks of a river. He then walked another hunter to the shoreline. Ennis walked about a mile downstream with his dogs, which is legal in Ontario.

"This (type of) hunt usually took from an hour and a half to two hours, which on a cold day could seem like a very long time," McDonald said.

McDonald said he sat on a large rock under a huge oak tree along the cedar-rail fence that separated the two fields. After 90 minutes, he began daydreaming about past hunts. Suddenly, he heard two of the dogs baying in the distance.

"They definitely picked up a deer and had him on the run — straight up the shore of the river," McDonald recalled.

"I heard the chase for a good 15 minutes, and, as it got closer, I thought for sure that one of the other lads would get shooting. Then, as quickly as I heard the chase start, I heard the dogs turn from the river and start coming in my direction. It didn't take long before I could see a massive set of horns just above the long wild hay. He was heading straight for me."

By then, McDonald's heart was pounding, and his mind was racing.

"I decided to take him the second he broke out of the long hay —

Arnold Stalsberg killed this massive nontypical whitetail in Wisconsin. The rack, which sports 25 points, weighs more than 16 pounds.

before he had a chance to see me."

McDonald didn't have to think much longer. The 22-point buck continued its path, and McDonald quickly found it in his riflescope when it ran within 80 yards of his setup. One shot dropped the buck in its tracks.

"I could hardly believe my eyes," he said. "I had seen a lot of huge deer over the years, but never anything that came close to this."

The buck's age was estimated at 6½ years.

The rack was scored at 246⅞ inches by the Foundation for the Recognition of Ontario Wildlife. Its score after deductions was 236⅝.

The buck's 22-point rack has an inside spread of 21⅞ inches with 28-inch main beams. The longest tine is 12⅝ inches.

Another Monster Buck

The massive Wisconsin buck was killed by Arnold Stalsberg on opening day of the state's November gun-hunting season.

The 66-year-old veteran hunter shot the buck in the same Vernon County deer woods where he has killed about a dozen other white-tails over the years.

Stalsberg said he hunted all morning from a blind, but decided to leave at 11:40 a.m. to go home for lunch. He spied the buck while slowly still-hunting back to his vehicle.

"In 20 minutes, I moved 150 yards after leaving the blind," Stalsberg said. "I took a few steps and stopped; took a few steps and stopped. If you're going to shoot a deer, you have to see him first. When I got across a ditch, I took a break."

Stalsberg was hunting near a big ravine that was at least 300 yards across. He said there was plenty of cover for whitetails in the ravine and adjoining hardwood ridges.

While taking his break, Stalsberg saw the big buck moving through some cover about 150 yards away.

"I could only see his antlers at first," he said. "The rack was something bigger than I ordinarily saw, but not as high. 'Arny, wake up now,' I said to myself. I thought I better get a shot at this deer.

"I had both eyes open as I got my rifle up," he continued. "He was moving at a fast gait. I looked ahead along the route he was taking and saw two (aspen) trees where it was more open. That's where I planned to shoot. When he went through the opening between those two trees, I shot, and he went right down."

Stalsberg said he didn't know exactly where the bullet hit, so he put another shell in his .308 and shot the deer in the neck.

The buck wasn't going anywhere. The first 150-grain bullet hit the buck at the base of the neck near its shoulder, killing it instantly.

Stalsberg said he knew the buck was big, but he was shocked to see how big.

The right side of the rack sports 12 scorable points, while the left has 13. What's more, the rack weighs 16 pounds!

The 4½-year-old buck had a field-dressed weight of 179 pounds.

Wisconsin's previous state record nontypical was recorded in 1973 by Elmer Gotz in Buffalo County. The Gotz Buck sported 30 points and scored 245 points on the Boone and Crockett scale.

Steve Ashley of the Wisconsin Buck & Bear Club said Gotz shot one of the brow tines off the buck in the process of killing it. Gotz found the broken tine, but it couldn't be used in the official score. If the brow tine had remained intact, the rack would have scored 253 and remained the state's No. 1 nontypical.

— Daniel E. Schmidt and Richard P. Smith

Massive Alabama Buck Tipped Scales at More than 300 Pounds

More than 200 yards away, a heavy buck stepped into a shooting lane across a bean field. Glen Roberts of Sulphur, La., waited with his rifle ready in his tree stand.

The morning had been foggy, and Roberts had passed up shots at two yearling bucks. He wanted a big buck, and now he saw one. Although the 9-pointer carried a respectable rack, it certainly didn't look like a record-book buck. However, the buck's massive size told another story. As the buck moved closer, Roberts couldn't believe his eyes.

"It looked like a yearling calf," Roberts joked. "The deer made the rack look little."

Roberts placed his scope on the deer and tracked it as it walked across the field. When it crossed through another shooting lane about 175 yards away, he fired. The buck dropped after a short run.

That's when Roberts' story became interesting. He quickly found the buck, but he was unable to move it. Hunting at a lodge near Aliceville, Ala., Roberts returned to camp to enlist the help of his guides.

"When the guides loaded it onto the the back of the three-wheeler, (the three-wheeler) flipped," he said. "When I sat on the front, it was still bouncing, and I weigh 270 pounds."

The guides returned to the lodge and lifted the buck onto a scale. However, the buck's weight buried the needle at the scale's 300-pound limit. The hunters then took the deer to a feed mill where they weighed it on a commercial scale.

Glen Roberts of Sulphur, La., killed this buck in Alabama in 1997. The buck, weighing 315 pounds on the hoof, is believed to be the heaviest whitetail ever killed in Alabama.

It weighed 315 pounds on the hoof. The buck shattered The Roost's record by 11 pounds. The previous record of 289 pounds was set in 1963.

Roberts did not weigh the buck when it was field dressed, but it could have easily weighed 240 pounds. The buck's neck measured 28 inches.

Although such records aren't kept, Roberts' buck is believed by many to be the heaviest deer ever taken in Alabama.

"The people I've talked to have never heard of one going over 300 pounds," said David Hayden, assistant chief of the Alabama Department of Game and Fish. "It's definitely an impressive deer."

The buck's jawbone indicated the buck was 3½ years old.

— *John N. Felsher*

Bow-Hunter Says He's Happy He Held Out in 1999

Tony O'Kon never considered himself a trophy hunter before last season, and that's probably a good thing. After arrowing a massive nontypical 18-pointer, O'Kon will be hard-pressed to hold out for a bigger buck.

O'Kon lives and hunts in northeast Wisconsin. When Nov. 11 rolled around, he had already passed up eight bucks with his bow, including a couple of wide-racked 2½-year-olds. He knew his odds of tagging a buck with his bow were dwindling. The state's firearms season would begin in less than two weeks, making bow-hunting for a mature buck a tough, if not impossible task afterward.

O'Kon was only in his stand for about 30 minutes when a one-antlered buck appeared. He decided he would shoot the buck if he could call it in, so he placed his grunt tube to his mouth and made a few soft grunts. The buck didn't respond, so O'Kon grunted again. This time, the buck threw its head up and bounded away.

Dejected, O'Kon put his call away. Then, after waiting just 15 minutes, he noticed movement from the same area. "I put my binoculars up, and my jaw just dropped," he said.

There, just 75 yards away in the woods, stood the biggest buck O'Kon had ever seen.

"He was moving along at a fast walk, probably looking for does. I figured grunting might scare him away, but I grunted anyway, hoping to turn him around."

The tactic worked. The buck

Tony O'Kon and his 18-pointer.

stopped and looked in O'Kon's direction. O'Kon grunted again, and the buck did an about-face.

"He kept coming, but it seemed like he wanted to wander, so I kept giving him short tending grunts. When he was about 20 yards away, he stopped behind a big oak tree, so I drew. I shot when he stepped out and quartered-away."

O'Kon didn't let the sight of the big rack rattle his nerves. The arrow hit its mark and pierced the buck's heart. The buck ran about 40 yards before falling.

The rack features 18 scorable points and an 18-inch inside spread. The bases measure 5⅛ and 5⅜ inches. The rack netted 189 nontypical points on the Boone and Crockett scale.

The kicker of the story? O'Kon's hunting land consists of a mere 20 acres that abuts farmland and public hunting ground.

— *Daniel E. Schmidt*

Saskatchewan Gun-Hunter Bags 7-Point 'Unicorn' Buck

When John O'Higgins pulled the trigger on a big-bodied Saskatchewan buck, he was so excited he couldn't wait to call his wife, Nita, and tell her about it.

John no sooner reached his downed buck when he dialed Nita's number on his cellular phone. Nita, a schoolteacher, was on break between classes when the phone rang.

"You got one?" she exclaimed! "How big? ... A 7-pointer with a 9-inch spread," she inquired skeptically. "John, what did you do?!"

"You just have to see it to believe it," he replied.

O'Higgins, who intended to hold out for a record-class buck, shot the buck because it sported just one massive beam, which sprouted from a single pedicle located in the middle of its head. The "unicorn" buck was so odd that he passed it up the first time he saw it because he wasn't sure what was going on with the buck's headgear.

O'Higgins was hunting near Regina, Saskatchewan, on a huge tract of Indian land with outfitter Ron Nemechek.

The hunt took place in December 1999. Mornings temperatures dipped below zero, and a foot of snow blanketed the ground. Hunters had been taking stands in mornings and evenings, but some conducted small deer drives at midday.

It was noon on a Tuesday when O'Higgins left his stand to seek a more remote area to set up another stand. Nemechek told O'Higgins to

John O'Higgins killed this odd-antlered white-tailed buck in Saskatchewan in 1999.

investigate a remote valley, an area that could only be reached by a long drive with an all-terrain vehicle and a lengthy walk.

O'Higgins was quickly satisfied with his choice. "Walking into the (valley), I found a number of huge, high rubs — the work of big deer," he said. "The location overlooked a clearing about 125 yards long and 75 yards wide. A frozen river ran to my left and thick brush was to my back. It seemed 'bucky,' a great place to kill a deer."

O'Higgins watched several deer pass through the clearing that afternoon, including two bucks. One of the bucks was a 130-class 9-pointer with a 22-inch spread. Seeing that buck excited O'Higgins, but he didn't shoot, hoping something bigger would come along.

He hunted the same spot the next afternoon, but the weather changed dramatically. "The constant wind stopped dead still," he said. "You could hear a pin drop.

"I waited about 15 minutes, then gave a series of grunt calls, casting sounds in several directions."

In less than two minutes, a big-bodied deer appeared at the far end of the clearing. "The buck's hair was standing on end," O'Higgins recalled. "He moved in a stiff-legged walk, and his neck was swollen from the rut."

O'Higgins slowly raised his binoculars and examined the deer. Its antlers looked heavy, but something about the rack seemed strange. He studied the animal further.

"I noticed that it had no spread whatsoever, and it had a 9- or 10-inch spike over its nose."

He kept his rifle on his lap and reached for his video camera. O'Higgins filmed the buck for five minutes as it walked about the field searching for the rival it thought it previously heard. The buck surveyed the area and then exited the field.

O'Higgins immediately questioned himself for not shooting the buck. Through the camera, he got a good glimpse at what might have been the buck of a lifetime.

As minutes passed, he wondered why he didn't shoot the buck when he had the opportunity. Suddenly, a stick snapped behind his tree stand.

It was the same buck, but this time, it was only 15 yards away.

"Looking down on the deer, I noticed it had just one base — one solid pedicle," he said.

O'Higgins immediately decided to shoot the buck, but it soon saw him and bolted. O'Higgins shouldered his rifle and followed the buck as it bounded toward thick cover. Fortunately for O'Higgins, the buck stopped in a small clearing about 50 yards away. He placed the buck in his cross-hairs and pulled the trigger. The buck dropped dead in its tracks.

"We see bucks in the 180- to 200-inch range all the time," said Nemechek, "but nothing like this."

The buck soon became the talk of the town. It not only sported just one massive pedicle, it had a 9-inch spike growing up and out from the middle of it. What's more the pedicle split the buck's skull.

"You could feel the horns move when you applied pressure," O'Higgins said. "After caping the head, the crack was visible from the eye socket to the rear of the skull, down to the cortex."

O'Higgins wondered if the buck would have survived the winter. He believes it would have been difficult for the buck not to contract a disease and die because the top of its head would have been completely exposed after it shed the odd antler.

Since the antlers had one pedicle, they technically couldn't be scored for base mass. However, using the split as a separation point, an antler scorer came up with two base measurements of 6⅛ inches each. Using this method, the rack grossed 115⅛ points! That's incredible, considering the inside spread was just 7 inches.

The buck's teeth indicated it was 4½ years old. Further research indicated the buck was probably a breeder, therefore, it could have passed its genes on to other bucks.

You can bet O'Higgins is anxious to find out.

— *Joe Byers*

Hunter Bags Buck After Finding its Shed Antlers

For 23 hunting seasons, I had daydreamed about seeing a monster buck while on stand. My dream came true in 1999 when I not only saw a big buck while hunting, I got to hunt him all year long.

It started in February when I went shed hunting on my hunting land in northeast Wisconsin. You can imagine my excitement when I found the matching set of a huge 10-pointer. The sheds were enough to keep me pumped for the upcoming bow and gun seasons.

The excitement increased when I saw the buck six times in a bean-field behind the farmhouse on our hunting land. He was in velvet and looked huge! Then, my dad and I saw him the evening before September's opening day of bow season.

I saw the buck on opening day, but he was more than 250 yards away from stand. The buck disappeared for a few weeks, and I began wondering if we would ever see him again.

One afternoon in early October, I placed a stand on a well-used deer trail — a trail I knew he used previously. An hour before closing time, I saw the buck emerge from a stand of pines and head for my stand. At one point, he stood broadside just 27 yards away. However, I decided not to shoot. All summer long and into the season, I promised not to shoot beyond 20 yards. I would never forgive myself if I wounded him.

Tim Eierman and his 10-pointer.

That was the last time I saw the buck during the early bow season.

When gun season opened in late November, I was excited to get another chance at the big 10-pointer. I bought a new shotgun equipped with a cantilever scope. I practiced a lot, and could shoot confidently out to 100 yards.

Opening day arrived in a flash. I carried the big buck's sheds for rattling antlers, but I never got a chance to use them. Deer were everywhere. I saw five bucks and numerous antlerless deer throughout the day, but not the big buck.

On Sunday, I set up in a ground blind I had prepared earlier in the fall. I expected to see deer early, but none showed. By 9 a.m., I was bored. Two of my hunting partners were nearby, so I decided to do some one-man drives for them because they were looking to fill some doe tags. I did three drives within an hour and flushed several deer, including a big 10-pointer. I would have tagged that buck, but he ran through some brush and I couldn't get a clear shot at him.

It was now 10 a.m. Everyone was supposed to meet in an hour to discuss hunting strategies for the rest of the day. Seeing that I had some time, I decided to go back to my blind and retrieve some of my gear. When I got there, I decided I might as well sit down and hunt for the last hour.

I had just sat down, put my feet up and started reading a magazine, when I heard a noise. Looking up, I spied a doe walking into a shooting lane 90 yards away. Seconds later, I saw a huge buck standing behind her. I grabbed my gun, put the cross-hairs on the buck's chest and squeezed the trigger. The buck dropped in his tracks.

It wasn't until I walked up to the buck that I knew it was the same 10-pointer I had watched all year. His rack was almost identical to the sheds I found earlier in the year. Even more incredible, I killed the buck less than 100 yards from where I found his sheds.

I admit this was an incredible dream hunt for a once-in-a-lifetime buck. It is definitely one year I will never forget!

— *Tim Eierman*

Editor's note — *Tim Eierman's buck gross-scored 164 points on the Boone and Crockett scale.*

At 94, Wisconsin's Chauncey Weitz is one of the nation's oldest — and most dedicated — deer hunters.

Hunter Hasn't Missed a Deer Season Since 1928

Chauncey Weitz last shot a buck in 1996, but that doesn't stop him from preparing for next season.

That desire might not set Weitz apart from the more than 600,000 other Wisconsin gun-hunters who head to the woods each November, except that he's probably one of the oldest participants.

Weitz turned 97 in 2000, and hunting runs thick through his veins.

He began deer hunting in the 1920s, and, from 1932 to 1965, worked as a conservation warden for the then-Wisconsin Conservation Department.

"I killed my first buck in 1928 and have hunted every year since," Weitz said. His hunting skills have not deteriorated with time. Although he saw few deer during his 1999 gun-hunt, he still managed to tag a doe.

Weitz has seen a lot of changes in

the woods and in hunting practices in nine decades of hunting. In fact, he said he isn't pleased with modern-day deer seasons. He said he thinks deer hunting has turned into "deer shooting," and that hunting doesn't involve as much sportsmanship as it used to.

Weitz opposes baiting and the use of tree stands. He said he could have tagged a deer in 1998, but he refused to shoot because it was on its way to a bait pile.

"There is only way to really hunt deer and that is to be on your feet and still-hunt for deer," he said.

Weitz has seen an amazing change in deer populations.

"In 1928, eight of us spent 14 days in the woods, and we only saw two bucks during all of that time, one of which I killed," Weitz recalled.

Back then, the season was only 10 days long, but the group went up three days early to set up their camp and scout the woods. They stayed a day after the season ended to pack their camping gear.

Back then, deer season was open every other year. Weitz's group returned to the same location in 1930 and shot three bucks in two days.

"The deer season opened on Dec. 1, regardless of whether it was a weekend or a week day, and it extended for 10 days," Weitz said. "The limit was one buck, and the bucks were hard to see. Nowadays we've got an unlimited number of deer."

Weitz said there is no state in the nation that has done as good a job of managing its deer population as has Wisconsin.

That success can be linked to Weitz and his former coworkers. In the 1950s, Weitz, along with Stan DeBoer and the late Burt Dahlberg, travelled to Colorado to learn more about big-game registration systems. They used that knowledge to implement a mandatory registration system in Wisconsin, which is now regarded as one of the best in the nation.

Initially, wardens were the only ones who could register deer. Those duties were eventually shifted to wildlife management employees.

"Deer really started to increase in great numbers around 1950," Weitz said. Weitz said deer became so abundant that he and his eight coworkers routinely filled all their buck tags by 9 a.m. on opening day.

Weitz's son Dave, who now works for the Wisconsin DNR, said he remembers his father was often on the road attempting to infiltrate poaching activities.

"One of the lessons I learned was watching Dad and another warden, Ben Little, investigate a father and young son who attempted to register a bow-killed deer that the father said the son had shot," Dave Weitz said.

Bow-hunting was just in its infancy then and it became obvious the father shot the deer. It took some work, but the wardens convinced the father it was not only illegal but also unethical to have his son tag a deer he didn't shoot. The man confessed and was allowed to do the right thing — place his tag on the deer.

At this writing, Weitz was planning to hit the woods for a November 2000 gun-hunt. He also planned to try a new hunting location, but he vowed to stay true to the code that kept him in the woods for nine decades — ethical hunting behavior.

— *Tim Eisele*

Double Drop-Tine Buck Surfaces on Lakeshore

This double-drop tine buck was found dead on the northern Wisconsin shore of Lake Superior. It ranks among Wisconsin's highest nontypical entries in the Boone and Crockett Club.

Hunting is a team effort for the Jean Schultz family. Every detail is organized to ensure a successful hunting season. Every member of the hunting party gets an important assignment, including cutting firewood months in advance of the annual fall hunt.

The family hunts the woods of northern Wisconsin, just off the Lake Superior shoreline. In 1998, Schultz was taking a break from firewood detail when she found the buck of a lifetime.

Schultz's late husband, Wallace, had hunted the area for years. She knew her discovery, which she calls "Destiny," was the type of buck he had always dreamed of tagging.

Schultz was searching for driftwood with one of her sons and two grandsons when an unusual piece caught her eye. As she walked towards it, she realized it wasn't a piece of driftwood but an enormous 22-point rack attached to a badly decomposed white-tailed buck.

The group could barely contain their excitement, and quickly decided to summon Schultz's two other sons, both avid deer hunters, to assess the situation.

Brad Schultz was skeptical when he heard about the "monster buck," but he agreed to make the 1-mile trip back to the shoreline on an ATV to investigate. The moment he saw the deer, he said, "This was the type of buck Dad was looking for all his life!"

After examining the pungent animal, they felt it was best to separate the head from the rest of the carcass. Scavengers had already stripped the meat from the body and the hide was in tough shape.

After registering their find with a game warden, the group elected Brad Schultz as guardian of the head. He initially placed the head in a shed behind his home, but curious rodents, and even a black bear, took turns at breaking into the building and dragging the skull and antlers into a nearby woodlot. Both times Schultz had to use his tracking ability to re-discover the head. He then decided to cut the antlers away from the head.

Jean Schultz later registered the rack with the Boone and Crockett Club. Its nontypical score of 236⅝ points ranks as the fifth all-time highest score for a non-hunting entry in Wisconsin.

— *Linda Hess*

Father Denies Greed, Lets Son Shoot Buck of a Lifetime

The 1998 gun-deer season proved more than memorable for one father-and-son hunting team.

Florida residents Keith Emit and his 14-year-old son Cole were eager to get to their ranch in northwestern Nebraska, but their plane was delayed in Minneapolis, Minn. They finally made it to their ranch in the afternoon of opening day, and they were in their hunting blind by 4 p.m.

Amazingly, it wasn't long before a 130-class buck entered the field they were hunting. Because they had only been in the blind for a short while, they decided not to shoot, hoping an even bigger buck might show up.

"All of a sudden it (the 130-class buck) turned around and ran as hard as he could," Keith Emit said. "I knew then that a big deer was coming."

Within moments, a giant buck emerged from a draw about 300 yards away. The Emits knew the buck was huge, but they had a problem deciding who would shoot it.

The two hunters made a lot of commotion in their blind, shuffling around trying to get into shooting position, but the buck continued in their direction. "If it hadn't been for the wind, he would have heard us," Emit said.

Finally, Keith decided that his son would get the chance at the buck of a lifetime. Keith had already bagged a deer that season, so he handed Cole his .300 Magnum.

While Cole was bracing for a

Cole Emit, 14, shot this massive 14-point buck on opening day of Nebraska's deer season in 1998.

Keith Emit

shot, Keith leaned out the side of the blind and grunted in an effort to lure the buck within shooting range.

"The funny thing is I was trying to grunt with my mouth and Cole thought I was trying to scare the deer off," Emit said.

The tactic worked. The deer walked within 140 yards of the blind before stopping to scratch its head with its hoof. Cole didn't miss the opportunity. He carefully aimed and shot. The deer dropped instantly.

After reaching the deer, the Emits discovered the bullet hit the buck in the jaw as the buck turned its head. However, the bullet continued into the buck's body, hitting its spine.

They also realized the buck was bigger than they had thought. The 14-point nontypical rack grossed 217⅞ points on the Boone and Crockett scale. It netted 201⅝ points.

"It's the deer of a lifetime," Keith Emit said. "The score doesn't even do it justice."

— *Joe Shead*

Nontypicals Shared Similar Deformities, Home Ranges

Whe John Bazile found an odd-antlered buck dead on his central Wisconsin hunting property in Winter 1996, it closed the book on what turned out to be two similar nontypical bucks.

The story began in Fall 1995 when Bazile saw a mature buck with a bizarre rack. The buck's right antler featured five massive points. The left antler, however, was a stunted beam that curved up and out. At the time, Bazile thought it was a massive beam with possibly one short point.

Bazile noticed something else: The buck's right hind leg was badly injured.

"The leg joint appeared to be smashed," Bazile said. "The buck limped badly and actually traveled with that leg up in the air."

Bazile instructed visiting hunters to kill the buck if given the chance. The story seemed to have a successful, although odd, ending when Bazile received a phone call during the gun season. A friend, Jack Kasson, whose deer camp is five miles from Bazile, said he

John B. Bazile photos

These bucks were killed within five miles of each other. Both bucks had grown nontypical racks after sustaining injuries to their right hind legs. The 6-pointer, top, was killed by a gun-hunter in November 1995, and the 7-pointer was found frozen in a snowdrift three months later. The buck was probably killed by a coyote.

killed the buck. He told Bazile the buck's right hind leg was badly injured, probably from an automobile accident. When Bazile drove to the property to see the dead buck, he was convinced it was the one he had seen earlier that fall. It sported five points on its right beam, while its left beam was a long, twisting spike — longer than he remembered and with no sticker points.

Although he was amazed the buck was killed five miles from where he saw it, Bazile thought the case was closed. That is, until he went shed-hunting in February 1996.

Bazile was walking through his woodlot — not far from where he saw the odd-antlered buck — when he noticed something sticking out of the snow. Upon closer examination, he discovered it was an antler. And under it was a buck's body.

Bazile kicked the snow away and made a surprising discovery. The frozen buck had five points on its right antler, and its left antler was a short, massive beam with an underdeveloped brow tine. He soon realized this was the buck he had seen several months earlier. Its right hind leg had also been crushed from a previous injury.

Bazile realized how odd it was for two bucks to suffer nearly identical injuries and, subsequently, grow similar racks. He later obtained the rack from the hunter-killed buck and displayed it in his home.

— *Daniel E. Schmidt*

Above are the skulls and antlers of two bucks Aaron Phelan found floating in an Ontario lake. The bucks' massive antlers were locked together.

Fishing Trip Nets 2 Big Bucks

Day 1 of a fishing vacation in Canada turned up more than fish for the Al Phelan family of Madison, Wis.

Phelan and his son Aaron were fishing on Lake of the Woods in Ontario when Aaron noticed what looked like a dead moose floating about 60 yards away. Closer inspection revealed the partially decomposed bodies of two massive white-tailed bucks with their antlers locked together.

The bucks were found more than 100 yards from shore. Phelan said he believes the fight occurred during the previous fall's rut. The lake was frozen earlier than normal that year, and Phelan said it appeared as though the locked bucks, desperate to free themselves, pushed each other onto the thin ice. He believes the ice collapsed from the weight of the two massive animals.

It took the Phelans 45 minutes to get the deer unlocked. Aaron rough-scored the larger head, which also had a broken jaw, at 134 inches.

Phelan aged the jawbones at 3½ and 4½ years old.

— *Amber Paluch*

How to Age a White-tailed Deer

Biologists and deer researchers agree that analysis of tooth replacement and wear — though not perfect — is the most handy and reliable field method for aging whitetails. That's because, regardless of where they live, whitetails lose their baby "milk" teeth and wear out their permanent teeth on a fairly predictable schedule.

At birth, white-tailed fawns have four teeth. Adult deer have 32 teeth — 12 premolars, 12 molars, six incisors and two canines.

Aging analysis often is based on the wear of the molars, which lose about 1 millimeter of height per year. It takes a deer about 10½ years to wear its teeth down to the gum line. Therefore, it's difficult to determine the age of a deer that's older than 10½ years.

Most importantly, the ability to estimate a deer's age based on the wear of its teeth is something most hunters can learn with a little study and practice.

To order a full-color poster of our complete guide to tooth aging, call 888/457-2873.

Instructions: Cut one side of the deer's jaw all the way to its socket. Prop open the jaws and compare the lower jaw to these photos to estimate the deer's age.

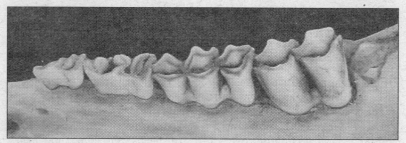

Fawn

Few hunters have difficulty aging a white-tailed fawn, whose short snout and small body are usually obvious when viewed up close. If there is doubt, simply count the teeth in the deer's lower jaw. If the jaw has less than six teeth, the deer is a fawn.

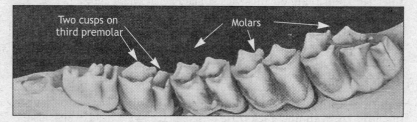

Two cusps on third premolar

Molars

Yearling: At Least 19 Months

About 1 year, 7 months, most deer have all three permanent premolars. the new teeth are white in contrast to pigmentation on older teeth. They have a smooth, chalk-white appearance and show no wear. The third molar is partially erupted.

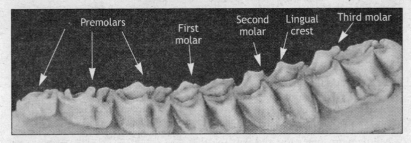

2½ Years

The lingual crests of the first molar are sharp, with the enamel rising well above the narrow dentine (the dark layer below the enamel) of the crest. Crests on the first molar are as sharp as those on the second and third molar. Wear on the posterior cusp of the third molar is slight, and the gum line is often not retracted enough to expose the full height of this cusp.

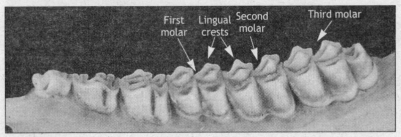

3½ Years

The lingual crests (inside, next to tongue) of the first molar are blunted, and the dentine of the crests on this tooth is as wide or wider than the enamel. Compare it to the second molar. The dentine on the second molar is not wider than the enamel, which means this deer is probably 3½ years old. Also, the posterior cusp of the third molar is flattened by wear, forming a definite concavity on the biting surface of the teeth.

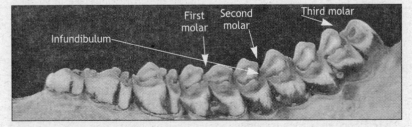

4½ to 5½ Years

At this point, it's often hard to distinguish between the two age classes. The lingual crests of the first molar are almost worn away. The posterior cusp of the third molar is worn at the cusp's edge so the biting surface slopes downward. Wear has spread to the second molar, making the dentine wider than the enamel on first and second molars. By age 5½ wear has usually spread to all six teeth, making the dentine wider than the enamel on all teeth. Because the first molar is the oldest, it wears out first. Also, by 5½, there might be no lingual crests on the first and second molars, although rounded edges might appear like crests. A line drawn from lingual to outside edges of first and second molars generally touches the enamel on both sides of the infundibulum.

Pope and Young Club Propelled Bow-Hunting

The formation of the Pope and Young Club arose from a need to show the world the bow was an effective, viable hunting tool. Most hunters and state game agencies of the 1940s and 1950s believed the bow was little more than a toy, and few recognized it as a hunting weapon.

It was Glenn St. Charles and a group of dedicated bow-hunters who conceived the idea of pulling together all the nationwide bow-hunting successes they could document. Their idea was to bring all of the information together and show it to those who believed bow-hunting was ineffective.

Today, the bow is accepted nationwide.

Although few people in the non-hunting world think of the hunter as a conservationist, the hunter has always been one. Aldo Leopold, the father of the modern conservation ethic, was a bow-hunter and advocate of land stewardship. It was Theodore Roosevelt — an avid hunter — who conceived the idea of the Boone and Crockett Club, of which *P&Y* is modeled after.

— Reprinted courtesy of the Pope and Young Club

Scoring System Helps Quantify Antler Size

The Boone and Crockett scoring system, with few changes, is essentially the same one developed by a committee of Boone and Crockett Club members and staff in 1950. The system was developed in the 1940s with valuable additions by Grancel Fitz. It was Fitz, who had his own

scoring system, that emphasized antler symmetry in the rack's final score.

A B&C score chart for typical-antlered bucks is included on the facing page.

For B&C record-keeping purposes, official scores can be disputed, even years after the original measurement. Repeat measurements are allowed because of the enduring nature of white-tailed deer antlers.

Scoring a rack begins with careful reading of the official score charts reproduced in this book. Be sure to follow the instructions carefully. After taking a rough measurement, the owner must contact a volunteer B&C measurer to get an official measurement for the records program.

An official measurement cannot be made until the rack has dried 60 days after the date of kill. A drying period is necessary to allow for normal shrinkage. The drying period also ensures shrinkage will be relatively the same for all trophies, an impossible condition if "green" scores were allowed.

Boone and Crockett Score Sheet

OFFICIAL SCORING SYSTEM FOR NORTH AMERICAN BIG GAME TROPHIES

Records of North American
Big Game

BOONE AND CROCKETT CLUB®

250 Station Drive
Missoula, MT 59801
(406) 542-1888

Minimum Score:	Awards	All-time
whitetail	160	170
Coues'	100	110

TYPICAL
WHITETAIL AND COUES' DEER

Kind of Deer: _____

	Abnormal Points	
	Right Antler	Left Antler
Subtotals		
Total to E		

Detail of Point
Measurement

SEE OTHER SIDE FOR INSTRUCTIONS				Column 1	Column 2	Column 3	Column 4
A. No. Points on Right Antler		No. Points on Left Antler		Spread Credit	Right Antler	Left Antler	Difference
B. Tip to Tip Spread		C. Greatest Spread					
D. Inside Spread of Main Beams		(Credit May Equal But Not Exceed Longer Antler)					
E. Total of Lengths of Abnormal Points							
F. Length of Main Beam							
G-1. Length of First Point							
G-2. Length of Second Point							
G-3. Length of Third Point							
G-4. Length of Fourth Point, If Present							
G-5. Length of Fifth Point, If Present							
G-6. Length of Sixth Point, If Present							
G-7. Length of Seventh Point, If Present							
H-1. Circumference at Smallest Place Between Burr and First Point							
H-2. Circumference at Smallest Place Between First and Second Points							
H-3. Circumference at Smallest Place Between Second and Third Points							
H-4. Circumference at Smallest Place Between Third and Fourth Points							
			TOTALS				

ADD	Column 1		Exact Locality Where Killed:	
	Column 2		Date Killed: Hunter:	
	Column 3		Owner:	Telephone #:
	Subtotal		Owner's Address:	
SUBTRACT Column 4			Guide's Name and Address:	
	FINAL SCORE		Remarks: (Mention Any Abnormalities or Unique Qualities)	

Copyright © 1997 by Boone and Crockett Club®

(Sample — Not for Official Use)

CHAPTER 6
MANAGING YOUR LAND FOR QUALITY DEER

How to Rejuvenate Native Vegetation

For many years, hunters and outdoor enthusiasts have planted food plots to improve the nutrition available to their deer herds. Of course, most hunters put in the time and effort to increase their chances of seeing bigger bucks.

While this is a good practice, food plots typically represent only 1 percent to 5 percent of the available habitat on most hunting properties. What about the other 95 percent to 99 percent? Clearly, food plots are only one piece of a total management program. The purpose of this article is to introduce you to a relatively new management concept: total vegetation management. This program involves managing native vegetation and supplementing these forages with planted food plots during critical periods of the year.

The white-tailed deer is a herbivore and is characterized as a browser. It is also a ruminant — an animal with four stomachs. The extra stomachs help with the digestion of various foods. This gives a deer versatility in its feeding habits. Deer consume a variety of leaves, twigs, bark and buds, plus hard and soft fruits, vines, forbs, lichens, mushrooms, cultivated crops and grasses. The majority of these food items are native plants available throughout much of the year. However, most hunters and managers pay little attention to native vegetation or ignore them completely when formulating land-use plans. On the contrary, a successful QDM plan lists native vegetation as its primary concern.

Why Native Plants are Important

A deer's food preferences change considerably throughout the year in response to its changing nutritional requirements. Three key periods of the year should be considered when attempting to maximize the availability of native forage. These include spring, when deer are trying to recover from the stress of winter and the rut; summer, when antler growth occurs, does are lactating, and newborn fawns are growing; and fall when deer are preparing for winter and the rut.

The whitetail's diet is significantly different during each of these periods. Therefore, by managing the native vegetation on your property during these periods and implementing good herd management practices, like those suggested by the Quality Deer Management Association, you can significantly increase your chances of producing healthier deer and bigger bucks.

JOHN JOHNSON

Daniel E. Schmidt

Fall is the time to prepare winter food plots — wheat, oats, rye and clover — because winter is the other stressful period of the year when native plants are least available.

Spring

During early spring, white-tailed bucks are usually recovering from the stress of winter and the weight they lost due to the rut. During this time, bucks need a high-protein diet. Luckily, this is also the time of the year when Mother Nature provides "first green-up," the time of the year when plants start putting on new growth. This new growth is readily available in most areas and it's highly preferred by whitetails. If managed properly, new growth can be highly nutritious by providing crude protein levels exceeding 16 percent.

Spring Management Techniques

Fertilizing woodlands and patches of native vegetation is an effective but underused method of attracting deer, according to Dr. Lee Stribling of Auburn University. In fact, some fertilizers can increase nutritional content and production of native plants like Japanese Honeysuckle. This is possible because the nitrogen contained in some fertilizers is coated with a proprietary timed-release agent that enables the nitrogen to be gradually released to the plant over several months. The recommended application schedule is one application in the early

Southern Native Plants and Preference Levels

Crop	Preference Level
Japanese Honeysuckle	High
Blackberry, Raspberry	High
Greenbrier	High
Strawberry Bush	High
Wild Grapes	Moderate
Common Persimmon	High
Ashes	High
Southern Crab apple	High
Oaks	High
Hollies	Moderate

spring followed by another in late summer.

For those who like a more hands-on approach, they can make light, periodic applications of a complete fertilizer every 45 to 60 days from spring through late summer. Be sure to perform an annual soil test and apply lime and fertilizer accordingly.

Stribling said these natural food plots become excellent areas to hunt during the early fall. "Deer are attracted to these natural food plots by the improved nutrition and taste of fertilized plants," he said.

Fertilizing mast trees and shrubs in spring is often overlooked by hunters because these plants are not utilized by wildlife until late summer or early fall. However, spring is the best time to start a tree fertilization program. To make fertilizer application easier and more effective, hunters can use "Tree Tablets" or compressed fertilizer discs that are inserted into the soil around the perimeter of a tree's root zone at a rate of four tablets per one inch of tree trunk diameter. Like other fertilizers, these tablets are also timed-release so they provide gradual fertilization for up to two years with a single application.

Summer

Summer is one of the most critical, but often overlooked times of the year for managing wildlife habitat. In summer, mature bucks are growing antlers, does are lactating, and newborn fawns are growing. Late summer is also one of the two times of the year when

The Ultimate Deer Hunter's Quiz
Part 6, Deer Management

49. In the North, a well-fed mature white-tailed buck (older than 4½ years) is how much larger than a well-fed mature doe?
A. 40 percent
B. 45 percent
C. 50 percent
D. 55 percent

50. At what age do bucks normally grow their largest set of antlers?
A. 4½ to 5½ years
B. 5½ to 6½ years
C. 6½ to 7½ years
D. 7½ to 8½ years

51. Which statement is true?
A. Bucks grow faster than does.
B. With adequate nutrition, bucks reach their maximum body weight when they're 3½ years old.
C. Antler growth takes precedence over body growth.
D. Bucks don't reach their mature weight size until they're 2½ years old.

52. What percent protein does a buck need for maximum antler growth?
A. 5 to 10 percent
B. 10 to 15 percent
C. 15 to 20 percent
D. More than 20 percent

53. Concerning malnourished bucks, which statement is true?
A. They begin antler growth sooner, shed velvet later and cast antlers later than well-fed bucks.
B. They begin antler growth later, shed velvet sooner and cast antlers sooner than well-fed bucks.
C. They begin antler growth later, shed velvet later and cast antlers earlier than well-fed bucks.

Continued on Page 103

Charles J. Alsheimer

During fall and early winter, the whitetail's diet switches to high carbohydrates as deer prepare for winter and stresses of the rut. In fall, deer feed heavily on mast crops such as acorns and soft fruits.

native food sources are least available and in poor condition. Consequently, supplementing native vegetation with food plots at this time of the year is critical for optimum nutrition.

Use the chart on the next page to determine nutritional needs for deer in summer. Remember, late summer is also the time to make an additional applications of fertilizers to native plants. This will ensure these plants grow well and provide good nutrition into early autumn.

Fall

During fall and early winter, the whitetail's diet switches to high carbohydrates as deer prepare for winter and stresses of the rut. In fall, deer feed heavily on mast crops such as acorns and soft fruits. Therefore, for maximum results, it's important that you properly prepare these trees and shrubs in early spring.

Fall is also the time to prepare winter food plots — wheat, oats, rye and clover — since winter is the other stressful period of the

Summer Food Plot Options

Crop	Planting Date*
Soybeans	April to June
Cowpeas	April to June
American Jointvetch	March to June
Biologic Summer	March to June
Rape	April to July
Lablab	April to June
Corn	March to May
Millet	April to July
Grain Sorghum	May to June

Forage species should be planted progressively later from Southern to Northern climates.

year when native plants are least available.

Fall Food Plot Suggestions

What should you plant for your fall food plots? Well, it's generally best to plant a mixture of cereal grains and legumes or forage plants such as those recently introduced by Biologic. This will provide nutritious forage during winter, spring and early summer.

I would also suggest using a single application of timed-release food plot fertilizer. This eliminates the need to make multiple fertilizer applications, saving time and money.

Conclusion

The most important thing to remember when instituting a total vegetation management program is to manage your native vegetation and food plots to meet the nutritional needs of your deer herd. Native vegetation provides the nutritional basis for deer, but during the critical stress periods of late summer and winter, planted food plots are generally required to maintain optimum nutrition.

A total vegetation management program coupled with good harvest management practices, like those supported by QDMA, will ensure a healthy deer herd. It will also greatly improve your chances of tagging the buck of a lifetime.

Editor's note: *John Johnson is an avid deer hunter and strong supporter of Quality Deer Management and the Quality Deer Management Association.*

The Ultimate Deer Hunter's Quiz
Part 6, Deer Management

54. Generally speaking, if a Northern white-tailed buck is stunted when he's 1½ years old, he will probably be undersized and grow smaller-than-normal antlers when mature.
A. True
B. False
C. Inconclusive

55. During most winters, what kinds of deer comprise 80 percent to 90 percent of the winter-killed deer in northern Michigan?
A. Mature bucks
B. Mature does
C. Fawns
D. Bucks older than 6½ years

56. Who is considered by many as the father of Quality Deer Management movement?
A. Charles Alsheimer
B. Al Brothers
C. Brian Murphy
D. Bill Gibbons

57. What is the No. 1 problem facing the Northern QDM movement?
A. Hunters shooting too many yearlings.
B. Hunters not shooting enough does.
C. Rising land prices.
D. Small land parcels.
E. Depending on region, all of the above.

58. A lush 35-acre clover field, which grows 20 percent protein food, could ideally provide enough food to sustain how many whitetails?
A. 50 to 75
B. 25 to 50
C. 10 to 25
D. No more than 10

59. Lime is the cornerstone of food plot preparation.
A. True. It's extremely important.
B. False. It's need only in small amounts.
C. Lime is not needed at all.

Continued on Page 105

Charles J. Alsheimer

The Deer Hunter's Guide to Food Plots

The concept of Total Vegetation Management has been supported by most wildlife specialists and universities for many years, but it is just now finding its way into the general public because of the interest in new management techniques.

The focal point of this management technique is to provide sound nutrition to wildlife through the management of native habitats and supplementing these native habitats with planted food plots during critical times of the year — late summer and winter.

The focus of this article is on planting fall food plots to maintain the carrying capacity of whitetails during the critical winter months. Over the years, this technique, when combined with TVM, should increase your chances of raising quality deer.

Building Blocks for Success

For any food plot program to be successful, landowners must take a few initial steps when planning to implement a food plot management program. Planting food plots with a specific plan is like trying to find your way into a new city without a road map.

Use this checklist when considering a food plot program:

✓ Determine your goals. What do you want to accomplish?
✓ Develop a budget.
✓ Determine the total acres to be planted.
✓ Conduct soil tests of the planting areas.
✓ Determine what to plant.
✓ Apply lime the soil according

JOHN JOHNSON

to the soil test's recommendations.

✓ Determine when to plant.

✓ Fertilize at planting to the soil test's recommendations.

Budgeting/Goals

Many hunters and landowners believe that planting a green field late in summer will give deer ample time to become familiar with it. They also believe that such a plot will give them the best chance at taking a big buck. While dreaming is good, this scenario seldom unravels to plan.

The deer herd will benefit more, and you will increase your chances of growing big bucks, from well-laid plans.

For starters, determine well before hunting season what your herd management goals are and how much time and money you can spend. For instance, if your goals are to implement QDM practices but are unwilling to shoot does and let young bucks walk, you will fail. Likewise, if you have a goal of producing quality whitetails, but lack the time, or the program costs more than what you can afford, you have conflicting goals.

The most precious resource is time. Make sure you are willing to spend the time to see it through!

Food Plot Site Selection and Size

When selecting food plot areas, remember the four key requirements for wildlife are cover, water, food and space.

To maximize these four requirements, food plots should be planted in areas that are far away from property boundaries but near water and bedding areas. My hunting group tries to plant areas that are accessible

The Ultimate Deer Hunter's Quiz
Part 6, Deer Management

60. An adult deer requires how much dry food matter each day?
A. 5 to 10 pounds
B. 10 to 15 pounds
C. 15 to 20 pounds
D. More than 20 pounds

61. To properly feed 40 deer per square mile in summer, the land must produce how much food per square mile?
A. 10 to 40 tons
B. 40 to 80 tons
C. 80 to 120 tons
D. More than 120 tons

62. Under QDM principles, some hunters won't have meat for the freezer.
A. True
B. False

63. What is the primary goal of Quality Deer Management?
A. To produce big bucks.
B. To shoot as many does as possible.
C. To balance deer populations with the habitat's carrying capacity.
D. To promote a natural balance of the herd's adult buck-to-doe ratio at about 3-to-1.

64. Which scenario describes the healthiest deer herd?
A. A herd that exceeds the land's carrying capacity.
B. A herd that is at about half the land's carrying capacity.
C. A herd that includes a doe-to-buck ratio of 1:1.
D. A herd that includes a doe-to-buck ratio of 2-to-1.

65. To reach maximum size, a buck must:
A. have access to high-protein food.
B. live on land that isn't overrun with deer.
C. have access to good nutrition.
D. live on land that produces food with a 20 percent protein content.

This concludes the quiz for Chapter 6. Quiz continues on Page 121. Answers begin on Page 194.

Daniel E. Schmidt

Fertilizing woodlands and patches of native vegetation is an effective but underused method of woodlands management. To supplement the deer's diet, plant food plots near areas of natural habitat.

to trucks and equipment, and we concentrate on the wildlife in the inner areas of the property. This reduces outside pressures and keeps poaching and hunting pressure to a minimum.

If possible, use old loading deck areas where timber has been cut. It's also wise to use fields that border bedding areas like stands of pines or hardwood feeding areas. If you lease land, be sure to get the land-owner's permission before planting food plots.

A sound food-plot program includes 1 percent to 2 percent of total acreage in food plots. Anything less is not going to be enough to support your herd through the critical late-summer and winter months when native plants are at their lowest

levels. For example, a 500-acre lease needs to have 5 to 10 acres in food plots.

Soil Testing

Would you attempt to drive from Virginia to California without a road map? Would you attempt to bake a cake without a recipe? Of course not. Then why would someone plant a food plot without first performing a soil test?

Soil testing food plots is the road map that gets you from Point A to Point B. It's your recipe for success. Soil tests are the least expensive part of the whole program, costing about $3 to $10 per sample, depending on what services are used.

My hunting group annually takes at least one soil test on each food plot. To perform soil testing correctly, you will need a small bucket, soil probe and test kits. These items can usually be obtained free from agriculture extension offices.

The next step is to take seven to 10 samples with the soil probe in different areas of the food plot. Combine the samples in one bucket.

After obtaining all of the samples, mix the soil with your hand and then pour it into the test kit. Label the kit with a name or number so you know which food plot it came from.

The soil-testing process is the time when you want to determine what types of crops you want to plant. If you prefer small grains like wheat, rye, ryegrass and oats, mark the samples accordingly. If you want to plant legumes like clover, alfalfa or the new varieties of Biologic, be sure to mark those samples accordingly. Keep in mind that no seed variety meets the needs of deer on a year-round basis, nor does one seed type thrive in all climatic or soil types. Therefore, it's wise to use combination plantings of cool- and warm-season crops and a mixture of small grains and legumes.

Whatever you plant, be sure to label your samples so that you receive the best information. Soil tests are conducted by land grant universities and agricultural offices.

Neal Mishler

The most important thing to remember when instituting a total vegetation management program is to manage your native vegetation and food plots to meet the nutritional needs of your deer herd.

Lime

Soil test results list, in tons, how much lime needs to be applied per acre to the soil to make it compatible with the crop listed on the test kit. Most farmer's cooperatives can be hired to apply lime to food plots. Keep these points in mind when scheduling an appointment with your farmer's co-op.

✓Co-ops are very busy in spring providing services to farmers. Plan accordingly.

✓The trucks they use for liming are big and heavy. Make sure your land is dry enough before asking them to deliver lime.

✓Request dolomitic or agricultural limestone. Dolomitic limestone is slow-acting. It must be applied 90 to 120 days before planting.

✓You can apply lime with your own equipment, but it is very time consuming.

✓After the lime is applied, prepare the food plot's seed bed for planting. This extra step is especially helpful when planting legumes.

Don't cut corners, especially if you live in an area with acidic soils. This is a determining factor in raising the soil's pH to the proper levels

This is the result of well-laid Quality Deer Management plans. Given the proper nutrients, mature bucks grow antlers to match their big bodies.

for maximum plant growth, yield, fertilizer efficacy, and plant palatability. Most wildlife biologists and universities agree that it's a waste of time and money to apply lime to a food plot without knowing exactly how much should be applied.

Fertilization

Soil tests provide guidance for applying fertilizer to food plots. Just like a recipe for baking a cake, the soil samples will tell you how much of each ingredient needs to be added to maximize production.

Fertilizers come in all shapes and sizes, but they all include the three major elements for plant nutrition: nitrogen, phosphorous and potassium. These elements are always listed in the same order on the bag, N-P-K, and the number associated with each is the percentage of that component contained in each bag.

For example, a 10-10-10 fertilizer is 10 percent nitrogen (10 pounds of nitrogen per 100 pounds of fertilizer), 10 percent phosphorous and 10 percent potassium. This is commonly referred to as a "1-1-1 formula" or "balanced formula."

What separates fertilizers are the ingredients used to make up the N-P-K contents. Another thing to remember about most soil tests is they often list requirements such as "100 pounds of nitrogen, 30 pounds of phosphorous and 30 pounds of potassium per acre." Don't be fooled, this is the actual pounds of N-P-K that are needed. To achieve that, you would have to apply 300 pounds per acre of a 30-

Daniel E. Schmidt

Landowners can improve the production of mast trees by fertilizing them regularly.

10-10 fertilizer to reach those soil test recommendations, or 1,000 pounds per acre of a 10-10-10 fertilizer to meet nitrogen requirements.

Your soil test, based on what type of crop you want to plant, will determine the formula or percentage of each ingredient to use. The only decision left is to determine what type of ingredients you want to use. Until recently this has been relatively easy because the most widely used ingredients for food plots were

---

For More Information

For more information on food plot management and products, contact these companies:

The Scotts Company, 1-800-811-2545

Mossy Oaks Biologic, 1-888-MossyOak or www.mossyoak.com

Mississippi State Web Page (Wildlife Food-Plot Planting Guide, SE) ext.msstate.edu/pubs/pub2111.htm

Alabama Cooperative Extension System (White-Tailed Deer Management) http://www.aces.edu/department/extcomm/publications/anr/ANR-521/anr521main.html

agricultural-grade fertilizers or fertilizers that are readily dissolved by moisture and then used by the plant or leached out of the soil profile. That's the reasoning behind recommendations of follow-up applications of ammonia nitrate (34-0-0) 90 to 120 days after planting small grains.

Nitrogen requirements are lower for legumes and combinations of legumes and small grains.

The Scotts Company offers a line of timed-release wildlife fertilizers that are specifically formulated for food plots, trees and native plants. Scotts Food Plot Fertilizer is a 28-10-10 formula that utilizes a proprietary timed-release coating on the nitrogen that provides months of continuous fertilization. A single application at planting time will provide nutrients throughout the growing season.

Determining When to Plant

Most hunters plant fall food plots based on when they have time. For some reason, most Southerners assume that Labor Day weekend is that time. Although this could be a good time to get the most out of some food plots, Mother Nature should determine the time to plant. If you want to get the most out of your fall/winter food plots, it's critical that the seed germinates. Moisture is the key for seed germination.

Keep in mind that as bad as you want to have beautiful green fields in October it's more important that you have nutritious green fields in January and February.

Do yourself and your deer a favor and wait until there is enough moisture in the ground to germinate the seed. This will save a great deal of time and money from having to replant the crop.

Remember that after the food plots are established to install utilization cages to monitor feeding. These can be constructed from a 4-foot by 10-foot piece of dog wire per plot. Roll the fencing into a circle and attach the ends. The cage will be 4 feet high and about 3 feet wide when complete. Place one or two cages in each food plot for monitoring throughout the year.

Conclusion

The most important thing to remember when instituting Total Vegetation Management is to manage your native vegetation and food plots to meet the nutritional needs of your deer herd.

Native vegetation provides the nutritional basis for your deer herd, but during the critical stress periods of late summer and winter, planted food plots are generally required to maintain optimum benefits.

How White-Tailed Deer Affect Your Woodlot

Deer eat a lot. And, as deer feed, they affect more than just the plants they consume. Browsing whitetails also affect other animals and even insects.

Deer feed on some plants more than others, often leading to fewer plant species in the woods. Studies in northern Wisconsin have shown that deer can keep hemlock and Canada

Len Rue Jr.

Daniel E. Schmidt

Forest plant diversity and deer populations can more easily coexist — if alternate food sources, such as farm crops, are available.

yew from reproducing, leading to their disappearance in some areas. The loss of some plant types can lead to the local elimination of insects that are dependent on them. Repeated browsing by deer can also alter the vegetation's structure, reducing the variety of songbirds found in an area.

A Pennsylvania study revealed that when deer densities were high versus moderate, areas lost a quarter of the songbirds that nest in the middle tree branches, and birds that were still present in the woods declined by 37 percent. Eastern wood pewees, indigo buntings, least flycatchers, yellow-billed cuckoos and cerulean warblers were not found on plots with more than 21 deer per square mile. The Eastern phoebe and American robin were no longer observed in areas with deer densities of 65 deer per square mile. In rare cases, even small mammal communities were affected.

Therefore, it's wise to share this information with landowners. It's safe to say most of these landowners would allow hunting if they realized it could create a more natural plant and animal community on their land.

Deer browse lines are easily distinguishable from the browsing of other animals. Deer do not have upper teeth in the front part of their jaw. Biting with its lower teeth, a deer rips vegetation when eating, leaving a ragged edge. Rabbits and hares have upper and lower front teeth, leaving smooth cuts on twigs.

Some plants commonly browsed by deer include:
- ✓ Gray dogwood
- ✓ Chokecherry
  - ✓ Nannyberry   ✓ Gooseberries
  - ✓ Blackberries   ✓ Raspberries
  - ✓ Sweet cicely   ✓ Wild geranium
  - ✓ Solomon's seal
- ✓ Lopseed
  - ✓ Bellwort   ✓ Viburnum
  - ✓ Enchanter's nightshade
  - ✓ Virginia creeper

Deer usually won't eat wildflowers until these plants send up their reproductive shoots. However, deer readily munch on the shoots when they become available. Once the plants have flowered and fruited, deer generally avoid them.
— *Bob Cooney*

Plants and Deer Can Coexist in Farm Country

Forest plant diversity and deer populations can coexist more easily— if alternate food sources are available. A University of Wisconsin-Madison study shows that while deer numbers in parts of south-central Wisconsin are above most damage-threshold estimates, foraging whitetails did little damage to woodland plants after filling up on farm crops.

However, the same can not be said of whitetails that live in the farm-poor areas of North America.

Wildlife ecologists studied eight areas in Wisconsin's Baraboo Hills. The Baraboo range contains the largest contiguous tract of southern upland forest and more than 50 percent of the native plant species in the state. Many of the plants are considered rare.

Graduate student Rebecca Christoffel studied both large (500 acres or more) and smaller (100 acres or less) sites, all with nearby crop land. Deer numbers at the sites were estimated at 29 to 47 per square mile. Biologists previously calculated over-winter goals for the management units at 26 to 36 deer per square mile. In general, deer densities were 30 percent to 40 percent above over-winter goals in 1996, and at or just above over-winter goals by 1997.

To measure the effects of deer browsing at each site, Christoffel built fenced exclosure plots that kept out deer but let in rabbits and other plant-eaters. Over two years, she monitored browsing rates, changes in plant density and reproductive rates in the exclosures and nearby unfenced plots.

"The over-winter deer density estimates in the management units in which our sites were located were equal to or higher than previously published damage-threshold estimates," Christoffel said. "However, despite these density estimates, no herbaceous plants that we sampled were browsed more than expected given their availability, and most plants had browse rates under 10 percent."

"Nothing that we observed or measured suggested that deer impacts on native communities warranted a management response," she said. "The threshold for deer damage to native plant communities in this agricultural landscape may be much higher than in heavily forested, nonagricultural landscapes."

According to the study, no plants were heavily browsed in oak woods — there are just too many crop fields surrounding these patches for deer to forage in oak forests. "Crop fields provide a concentrated, nutritious forage base, and I believe they are buffering the surrounding native plant communities," Chrisoffel said.

"Had we sampled exclusively along deer trails in oak forests, I might draw a different conclusion. Where I did find significant browse, it was along established deer trails or very near them," she continued. "It would be very interesting to compare browse preference ratings for the same 21 herbaceous plant species that were examined in this study with browse preference ratings in a nonhunted deer population, or in an extensively forested area without the buffering element of agricultural crops nearby."

— *Bob Cooney*

CHAPTER 7
HUNTING WHITETAILS BY THE MOON

How the Moon Affects Deer

"When the hunter's moon occurs, bucks are consumed by their breeding instincts, and the doe's reproductive process is set to go off about a week afterward. Therefore, the period just before, during, and immediately after that full moon offers potentially incredible rutting activity."

— *Charles J. Alsheimer*
"Lunar or Loony? The Best Moon Phases for Hunting"
Deer & Deer Hunting magazine, *September 1998*

Over the years, hunters have shown much interest in the moon and deer movement, but mystery still remains.

Many old-timers believe deer activity is poor on mornings during the new moon. However, many deer hunters have found the opposite to be true, especially for bucks.

According to 25 years of data gathered by Derrick Woodlen, a whitetail hunting fanatic from Ringgold, Ga., hunters will see more bucks from daylight until noon on days when the moon is full than any other day or time during the hunting season.

"Some hunters like to spend their days afield on days that might bring them the most success. If this describes you, and you prefer to hunt specific times, you will probably see the most buck activity from daylight to 9 a.m. on days of a full moon. In my 25 years of observation, 53.12 percent of the deer I saw during this time on full-moon days were bucks," Woodlen wrote in his arti-cle, "The Best Time to Hunt: One Man's Perspective," which appeared in the October 1998 issue of *Deer & Deer Hunting*.

Since rutting activity varies regionally, you will have to apply this information to your region. Longtime *D&DH* reader Greg Coumos used that advice while hunting northeastern Ohio in 1999.

"We had Indian Summer with temps in the 70s," he wrote. "However it did not affect the bucks.

"Compared to other years of 'non-lunar' hunting, this was amazing! The rut activity for the last week of October convinced me to hunt the week after the hunter's moon!"

Remember that factors such as the rut, food availability, weather conditions, hunting pressure and type of habitat have more impact on deer movement than moon phases do.

Many theories exist on this topic. Deer hunters should use these theories as guides and simply hunt whenever they can.

Tapping Age-Old Lore for Moon-Phase Insights

The lunar cycle begins with the new moon. During this phase, the moon is in the earth's shadow and the night-time sky appears almost completely black. For the next 14 days, the moon begins to reflect light and becomes brighter each evening and eventually peaks with the full moon.

For centuries, cultures have had various beliefs about the moon's phases. Among these is a belief that humans and animals exhibit more energy during the new-to-full moon phase period. Conversely, lore has it that humans and animals exhibit less energy during the full-to-new moon phase period.

The second full moon in a calendar month is called a "blue moon." The phrase, "once in a blue moon," as referring to a rare event, dates back to the 16th century. On average, a blue moon occurs once every 2.7 years, but the actual interval can vary considerably.

The last blue moon occurred June 30, 1999. The next blue moon will occur on Oct. 31, 2001.

The moon goes through a complete cycle of phases in 29½ days. A month was originally defined as the time it takes the moon to go through one cycle. Each month began with the sighting of the new moon, but for reasons of convenience, our calendar has been modified so months have fixed lengths of 30 or 31 (or even 28 or 29) days.

Since the calendar month is slightly longer than the actual time it takes the moon to go through one cycle, each phase occurs once a month. If, however, a certain phase occurs within the first day or two of the month, the same phase can reoccur, and there can be two full (or new) moons in the same month. Of course, this is not true for February, which occasionally has only three of the four lunar phases.

Hunters should note that there will be a total lunar eclipse on Jan. 9, 2001. A partial eclipse will occur July 5, 2001, and a penumbral eclipse will occur Dec. 30, 2001.

Editor's note: *The moon-phase data in this article and elsewhere in this chapter were calculated at the Griffith Observatory in Los Angeles. The observatory has been a Los Angeles landmark since 1935. It attracts nearly 2 million visitors annually, and it ranks seventh on the list of major tourist attractions of Southern California. The Griffith Observatory sits on the southern slope of Mount Hollywood where it commands a stunning view of the Los Angeles basin.*

The observatory is a non-profit educational institution whose purpose is to provide information on astronomy and related sciences to the public. It is not a research institution, although from time to time it carries out modest research projects.

For more information, write: Griffith Observatory, 2800 E. Observatory Road, Los Angeles, CA 90027-1255.

Moon Phases for 2001

Central Standard Time
(Corrected for Daylight Saving Time April 1 to Oct. 28)

New Moon	First Quarter	Full Moon	Last Quarter
	Jan. 2, 4:36 p.m.	Jan. 9, 2:26 p.m.	Jan. 16, 6:34 a.m.
Jan. 24, 7:09 a.m.	Feb. 1, 8:04 a.m.	Feb. 8, 1:13 a.m.	Feb. 14, 9:23 p.m.
Feb. 23, 2:23 a.m.	March 2, 11:02 p.m.	March 9, 11:24 a.m.	March 16, 2:46 p.m.
March 24, 7:24 p.m.	April 1, 5:46 a.m.	April 7, 10:23 p.m.	April 15, 10:33 a.m.
April 23, 10:28 a.m.	April 30, 12:04 p.m.	May 7, 8:54 a.m.	May 15, 5:14 a.m.
May 22, 9:48 p.m.	May 29, 5:07 p.m.	June 5, 8:41 p.m.	June 13, 10:33 p.m.
June 21, 7:59 a.m.	June 27, 10:20 p.m.	July 5, 12:05 p.m.	July 13, 1:50 p.m.
July 20, 2:46 p.m.	July 27, 5:11 a.m.	Aug. 5, 12:57 a.m.	Aug. 12, 2:57 a.m.
Aug. 18, 9:56 p.m.	Aug. 25, 4 p.m.	Sept. 2, 4:45 p.m.	Sept. 10, 2:02 p.m.
Sept. 17, 5:28 a.m.	Sept. 24, 4:37 a.m.	Oct. 2, 8:51 a.m.	Oct. 10, 11:21 p.m.
Oct. 16, 2:24 p.m.	Oct. 24, 10:03 p.m.	Nov. 1, 11:43 p.m.	Nov. 8, 6:22 a.m.
Nov. 15, 12:41 a.m.	Nov. 22, 5:23 p.m.	Nov. 30, 2:51 p.m.	Dec. 7, 1:52 p.m.
Dec. 14, 2:49 p.m.	Dec. 22, 2:57 p.m.	Dec. 30, 4:42 a.m.	

Seasons

Spring equinox	March 20, 7:31 a.m.
Summer solstice	June 20, 1:38 a.m.
Autumn equinox	Sept. 22, 10:56 p.m.
Winter solstice	Dec. 21, 7:15 p.m.

Source: Griffith Observatory, Los Angeles, Calif.

Conversion Chart

The above moon phases are in Central Standard Time. Use the following formula to convert the phases to your area.

Time Zone	Difference
Pacific	Subtract 2 hours
Eastern	Add 1 hour
Mountain	Subtract 1 hour

American Indians Relied on Moon Phases for Deer Hunting

Although modern man tries to take credit for many deer hunting tactics, the truth is American Indians mastered decoying, grunt tubes and yes, hunting by the moon, long before Europeans set foot on this continent.

Many historians credit the Iroquois as the first group to truly understand white-tailed deer behavior in relation to the moon.

Although the Iroquois relied mainly on agriculture for sustenance — corn, beans and squash were known as "keohako," or "life supporters" — hunting was also important.

While the women owned and tended the fields under the supervision of the clan mother, men usually left the village in the fall for the annual hunt. They hunted hard for white-tailed deer and small game, and returned to their clans in midwinter.

The Iroquois knew all about the best times to hunt rutting white-tails. According to historians, the terms "harvest moon" and "hunter's moon" came from American Indians, and, more likely, the Iroquois. Because their survival depended on knowing the best times to hunt, they became masters of how the moon affected deer movements, especially during the breeding time, which they called the hunter's moon.

For more information on Iroquois history, visit the web site www.dickshovel.com/iro.html.

Deer Hunting Guide to Full-Moon Dates* in 2001

Month	Date	Day
January	9	Tuesday
February	8	Thursday
August	5	Sunday
September	2	Sunday
October	2	Tuesday
November	1	Thursday
November	30	Friday
December	30	Sunday

*Based on Central Standard Time

Plan Your White-Tailed Deer Hunts by the 'Rutting Moon'

In most areas, the rut usually peaks in late October or early November.

Many deer biologists and hunting experts believe it's possible to accurately predict the peak times for deer activity during the rut. Three in-depth research articles on this topic were published in the August, September and October 1997 issues of *Deer & Deer Hunting*. These articles revealed a new theory on the moon's influence on deer activity.

The dates on this page are nearest to the full-moon phases for the rutting months. This guide will help you plan this year's hunts, enabling you to be in the woods when deer are most active.

For an in-depth look at how the moon influences deer behavior, check out Charles Alsheimer's book, *Whitetails by the Moon*.

To order, call 888/457-2873, or visit our Web site:
www.deeranddeerhunting.com.

Harvest Moon and Hunter's Moon are Not the Same

The "Harvest Moon" occurs during the full moon after the autumnal equinox. In 2000, it occurs Oct. 13.

This date ushers in a period of several successive days when the moon rises soon after the sun sets. For centuries, farmers have relied on the extra hours of light during this period to harvest their crops. The next full moon after the "Harvest Moon" is called the "Hunter's Moon," and is accompanied by a similar phenomenon.

In 2001, the "Hunter's Moon" occurs Nov. 1.

Some deer researchers say the days leading up to and following this date produce extraordinary movement by rutting white-tailed bucks.

You Can Track the Moon Throughout the Year

If you observe the moon at the same time each evening, you will notice that it changes position in relation to the stars. The moon's path carries it through the traditional 12 sections of the sky. During most deer hunting seasons, the moon begins in autumn's Virgo, and continues through winter's Capricorn.

The moon also passes through Scorpius and Sagittarius during this time. It takes about 56 hours for the moon to travel through a sign. During these periods, the moon makes angular relationships with other bodies in the solar system. For centuries, people have believed certain alignments have affected human and animal behavior.

For More Information

A great source for learning and understanding deer and the moon is Charles Alsheimer's three-part series, "Lunar or Loony? Studying the Moon's Impact on Rutting Whitetails," which appeared in the August, September and October 1997 issues of *Deer & Deer Hunting*.

After 10 years of intense deer photography and hunting across the North, Alsheimer came to believe November's full moon — the Indians' harvest moon, greatly influences when does enter estrus. Alsheimer's insights ran contrary to the commonly held belief that the best time to kill a huge buck is during the new moon when night skies are black.

While conducting research with wildlife biologist Wayne Laroche, Alsheimer found that more than 70 percent of does bred from Nov. 17 to Nov. 28, with the earliest research doe being bred Nov. 13, and the latest Dec. 6. The research was conducted on Northern range.

What are his predictions for 2001? "The hunter's moon will be Nov. 1," Alsheimer wrote. "From what we now know, it appears that Nov. 4 through Nov. 18 will see the best buck activity. After Nov. 18 — with most does in or nearing estrus, hunting will get tough."

Standard Time Differences Across North America

City, State	Time
Akron, Ohio	12:00 p.m.
Albuquerque, N.M.	10:00 a.m.
Atlanta, Ga.	12:00 p.m.
Austin, Texas	11:00 a.m.
Bismarck, N.D.	11:00 a.m.
Boise, Idaho	10:00 a.m.
Buffalo, N.Y.	12:00 p.m.
Butte, Mont.	10:00 a.m.
Charleston, S.C.	12:00 p.m.
Chattanooga, Tenn.	12:00 p.m.
Cheyenne, Wy.	10:00 a.m.
Chicago, Ill.	11:00 a.m.
Colorado Springs, Colo.	10:00 a.m.
Dallas, Texas	11:00 a.m.
Detroit, Mich.	12:00 p.m.
Duluth, Minn.	11:00 a.m.
Erie, Pa.	12:00 p.m.
Evansville, Ind.	11:00 a.m.
Fort Wayne, Ind.*	12:00 p.m.
Frankfort, Ky.	12:00 p.m.
Halifax, Nova Scotia	1:00 p.m.
Hartford, Conn.	12:00 p.m.
Jacksonville, Fla.	12:00 p.m.
Juneau, Alaska	8:00 a.m.
Kansas City, Mo.	11:00 a.m.
Lincoln, Neb.	11:00 a.m.
Little Rock, Ark.	11:00 a.m.
Los Angeles, Calif.	9:00 a.m.
Milwaukee, Wis.	11:00 a.m.
Mobile, Ala.	11:00 a.m.
Montreal, Quebec	12:00 p.m.
New Orleans, La.	11:00 a.m.
Norfolk, Va.	12:00 p.m.
Oklahoma City, Okla.	11:00 a.m.
Phoenix, Ariz.	10:00 a.m.
Pierre, S.D.	11:00 a.m.
Portland, Me.	12:00 p.m.
Portland, Ore.	9:00 a.m.
Reno, Nev.*	9:00 a.m.
St. John's, Newfoundland	1:30 p.m.
Salt Lake City, Utah	10:00 a.m.
Santa Fe, N.M.	10:00 a.m.
Savannah, Ga.	12:00 p.m.
Seattle, Wash.	9:00 a.m.
Sioux Falls, S.D.	11:00 a.m.
Toledo, Ohio	12:00 p.m.
Toronto, Ontario	12:00 p.m.
Vancouver, British Col.	9:00 a.m.
Wichita, Kan.	11:00 a.m.

Denotes cities that do not observe Daylight Saving Time.

The Ultimate Deer Hunter's Quiz
Part 7, The Lunar Influence

66. Which factor can drastically suppress rutting activity?

A. The day of the week.
B. Ground-point pollution.
C. Lack of hunting pressure.
D. A high doe-to-buck ratio.

67. The breeding season is most intense and concentrated at _____ latitudes where the difference between day length in summer and winter is greatest.

A. Northern
B. Southern
C. Eastern
D. Western

68. Place in sequential order the following five primary activities of mature white-tailed bucks during the rut.
   A. Resting, seeking, feeding, tending, chasing.
   B. Feeding, chasing, seeking, tending, resting.
   C. Resting, feeding, seeking, chasing, tending.
   D. Feeding, seeking, chasing, tending resting.

69. Intense seeking activity by white-tailed bucks makes for great hunting by what method?
   A. Ground blinds
   B. Tree stands
   C. Still-hunting

70. What is the No. 1 suppressant of rut activity?
   A. Rainy weather
   B. Skewed doe-to-buck ratios
   C. Hot temperatures
   D. Baiting
   E. High hunting pressure

This is the end of the quiz for Chapter 7.
The quiz continues on Page 127.
Answers begin on Page 194.

A Rut-Hunter's Guide to Hunter's Moon Dates

Throughout much of the whitetail's range, the rut usually peaks in late October or early November.

Charles J. Alsheimer, Northern field editor for *Deer & Deer Hunting*, and Vermont wildlife biologist Wayne Laroche believe it's possible to accurately predict the peak times for deer activity. The following chart, provided by Alsheimer, lists the Hunter's Moon dates for the next several years. Use this guide to help plan future rut-time hunts.

Peak deer activity usually starts about a week after the Hunter's Moon.

Alsheimer's lunar insights are included annually in *Deer & Deer Hunting's Whitetail Calendar.* Here's a sample of the responses the *D&DH* editors have received concerning Alsheimer's lunar predictions:

➤ "I try to take days off from work according to Charlie Alsheimer predictions. I hunt 77 acres in Alden, N.Y., that consists of thick brush, pines, a pond and hardwoods. I observed the chase phase increase the last five days of October. Most of the smaller bucks I saw were chasing does, but the bigger bucks were not far behind. I tagged a 120-class buck on Nov. 1 at 8:45 am.

"I took Alsheimer's advice and used deer scent and a grunt tube to lure the buck within 20 yards of my tree stand.

"I would like to thank Charlie Alsheimer for his work on the lunar predictions and *Deer & Deer Hunting* for a quality magazine."
— *Steve Pundt, Buffalo, N.Y.*

Year	Hunter's Moon
2000	Nov. 11
2001	Oct. 31
2002	Oct. 21
2003	Nov. 8
2004	Oct. 28
2005	Oct. 17
2006	Nov. 5

➤ "Mr. Asheimer was right on with his 1999 rut prediction! Only wish I had the info when I scheduled my vacation. I normally take a week off and try and time it with the rut. Last year, my attempt was too late, but I did get some hunting opportunities during the time frame he predicted would be hot. Each time I hunted in that period, bucks were chasing does all day.

"Next year I will definitely use this method to determine when to take off from work."
— *Greg Swan, Amissville, Va.*

➤ "My experience with Charles Alsheimer's lunar predictions in the Little Belt Mountains of Montana have been 'on the mark.' For the past three years, on the exact day he predicted the chasing phase the bucks chased, tended, then relaxed. In attempting to pattern bucks, this is extremely valuable and accurate information."
— *W.C. Bowser, chief of wildlife research, W.R. Strain Foundation, Monarch, Mont.*

Editor's note: *For Alsheimer's most recent predictions, see the October 2000 issue of* Deer & Deer Hunting.

Calendar of Rubbing, Scraping and Breeding Activity for Whitetails

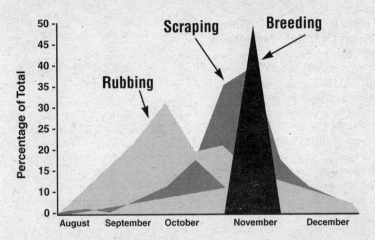

For centuries, hunters have relied on the "Hunter's Moon" — the full moon following the traditional September "Harvest Moon" — for the best indicator of peak movement of white-tailed bucks. In 2000, the "Hunter's Moon" will occur Friday, Oct. 13.

Once September has passed, things begin changing rapidly for a white-tailed buck. With October's arrival comes a greater infusion of testosterone. This not only causes a buck's attitude to change, but it also causes bucks to cover more ground. During the rut, it's common for a buck's range to encompass anywhere from 600 to 3,000 acres or more as it searches for receptive does.

Around the end of October, bucks are literally making a scrape wherever an adequate licking branch presents itself. They work the branch above the ground. Once they have left their scent on the branch, bucks then paw the ground out under the branch. Most scrapes are not revisited because the majority of them are a result of an instinctive action.

However, some of these scrapes will become prime scrapes for bucks when November arrives. Primary scrapes become almost like whitetail "bus stations" with several bucks using the same scrape.

Breeding activity varies in Southern climates, and the peak of the rut varies greatly by region within the same state. For example, in Louisiana, hunters can hunt the peak of the rut from Oct. 1 to Jan. 15, depending on which region they're in.

Northern climates have more precise rutting schedules. For example, in Wisconsin, the peak of the rut typically occurs in the 19-day window of Nov. 10 to 29.

CHAPTER 8
STATE·BY·STATE DEER HUNTING INFORMATION

Who Has the Most Whitetails?

It's hard to imagine what deer hunting was like at the beginning of the 1900s. Let's face it, today's hunters have it good. In 1900, an official United States survey estimated that less than 500,000 white-tailed deer remained in the nation. Need some perspective? In 1987, bow- and gun-hunters killed more than 504,000 whitetails in Texas alone. The second all-time single-state deer harvest record was set in 1999 when Wisconsin hunters tagged 494,116 whitetails.

This chapter celebrates the country's incredible deer management success story. Today, whitetails are abundant in more than 40 states. What few nonhunters realize is market interests, not sport hunting, pushed deer to the brink of extinction at the turn of the last century. Deer were killed in mass quantities for their meat and hides in the name of profit. That decimating trend was turned around with sound game management laws and responsible sport hunting.

The statistics found on these pages were compiled by our editorial staff through annual surveys of deer managers from each state. No two states have the same reporting systems, therefore, recent harvest figures are subject to minor changes from year to year. For example, a state that reports a 1999 overall deer harvest of 350,000 most likely submitted an estimate based on early harvest reports. Final figures would then reported in next year's *Almanac*. The same system is used for deer population, gun-hunter and bow-hunter estimates.

Annual Deer Harvests in the U.S.

(5-Year Averages from 1994 to 1999)

1.	Wisconsin	437,732
2.	Michigan	418,832
3.	Georgia	399,302
4.	Texas	393,948
5.	Pennsylvania	386,935
6.	Alabama	385,720
7.	Mississippi	321,205
8.	Louisiana	248,140
9.	New York	218,920
10.	Missouri	216,783
11.	West Virginia	209,932
12.	Virginia	198,740
13.	Minnesota	170,830
14.	N. Carolina	171,814
15.	S. Carolina	166,636
16.	Arkansas	154,507
17.	Ohio	147,148
18.	Tennessee	143,497
19.	Illinois	134,816
20.	Iowa	110,332
21.	Indiana	109,176
22.	Kentucky	106,233
23.	Florida	80,067
24.	Montana	73,561
25.	Oklahoma	72,812
26.	Maryland	69,907
27.	Kansas	67,776
28.	North Dakota	62,886
29.	New Jersey	62,287
30.	South Dakota	45,296
31.	Nebraska	39,726
32.	Idaho	34,395
33.	Maine	29,325
34.	Vermont	18,584
35.	Connecticut	11,817
36.	N. Hampshire	10,772
37.	Delaware	10,183
38.	Washington	10,126
39.	Massachusetts	9,776
40.	Arizona	4,350
41.	Rhode Island	1,850
42.	Oregon	736

In short, we strive to bring you the most up-to-date information on white-tailed deer hunting trends in your state.

Which state has the most whitetails? That's a trick question because not all states use the same methods to estimate deer herds. However, one can accurately gauge deer populations with harvest figures. For example, Michigan and Texas estimate their harvests, while Wisconsin requires mandatory registration of each deer killed during bow and gun seasons. In that event, the verifiable No. 1 state for deer hunting is probably Wisconsin, followed closely by Michigan, Texas and Alabama.

The totals on this page are five-year averages. Some state compile harvest figures at various times of the year. Some averages are from 1995 to 1999, and some are from 1994 to 1998. Although Texas held the No. 1 spot for several years, Michigan moved into the top spot in 1999 after a 1998 harvest of more than 450,000 whitetails.

Use this chart to see how your home state ranks, then flip through the chapter to learn more interesting facts on deer hunting in other parts of the country.

Editor's note — *This chapter is designed to educate all hunters on various aspects of deer hunting in the United States. Regulations are provided in general terms. Contact your game and fish department for detailed information.*

***In "Snapshot" charts on pages 126 through 170, data provided are from 1998.**

ALABAMA
Camellia State
Harvest Ranking: #6

For more information, contact:
Dept. of Wildlife and Freshwater Fisheries
64 N. Union St.
Montgomery, AL 36130
(334) 242-3469   www.dcnr.state.al.us

HISTORY OF ALABAMA'S WHITETAIL HARVEST

Year	Firearms	Bow	Total
1963-64	NA	NA	31,123
1973-74	NA	NA	121,953
1983-84	NA	NA	192,231

TEN-YEAR HISTORY

Year	Firearms	Bow	Total
1990-91	263,100	31,300	294,400
1991-92	269,500	25,500	295,000
1992-93	261,500	31,600	293,100
1993-94	305,300	45,200	350,500
1994-95	353,000	45,100	398,100
1995-96	334,200	32,600	366,800
1996-97	310,000	40,000	350,000
1997-98	367,900	55,500	423,400
1998-99	349,000	41,300	390,300

DMAP Takes Off in Alabama

The Alabama Cooperative Deer Management Assistance Program was developed in 1984 to assist those who wish to intensify deer management on their land. More than 1,900 land owners and hunting clubs covering more than 3.6 million acres are enrolled as DMAP cooperators.

Wildlife biologists are assigned to help cooperators develop deer management plans and harvest strategies. Conservation officers assist with legal aspects of the program. Cooperators collect biological information from deer taken on their land. Analysis of the data results in a status report and deer management recommendations which are provided to each cooperator before the following hunting season.

Hunter Education Required

In 1991, the Alabama Legislature passed legislation that requires all first-time hunters born on or after Aug. 1, 1977, to complete a hunter education course prior to purchasing their first hunting license. Alabama is one of 49 states that has a mandatory hunter education program.

The Alabama Division of Wildlife and Freshwater Fisheries expects approximately 13,000 students to complete the hunter education course this year alone. The goal of the program is to make Alabama hunters more responsible and more knowledgeable about wildlife conservation.

The Alabama hunter education course involves a minimum of 10 hours of instruction plus a written examination. The course is taught by Alabama Division of Wildlife and Freshwater Fisheries personnel and volunteer instructors, and is offered to interested participants 10 years old and older.

Students who successfully complete the course receive a patch and a card that is recognized by other states that require hunter education.

The course includes, but is not limited to, firearm safety and handling, responsible hunting and hunter ethics, wildlife laws, wildlife management and identification, archery, muzzleloading, first aid, survival, and game care.

ALABAMA WHITETAIL RECORDS

•**Record harvest:** 423,400 (1997-98)
•**Record low harvest:** 31,123 (1963-64)
•**Bow-hunting record:** 55,500 (1997-98)
•**Gun-hunting record:** 367,900 (1997-98)

•**Season to remember:** 1981-1982. Alabama deer hunters set state record with a harvest of 202,449 — a 55 percent increase from the previous season's harvest.

ALABAMA SNAPSHOT

Deer Population: 1.6 million, 4th in U.S.
Average Harvest: 385,720, 6th in U.S.
Gun-Hunters: 210,000
Bow-Hunters: 58,684
Forested Land: 21.97 million acres
Hunter Education: Required for persons born on or after Aug. 1, 1977. Bow-hunter education is not required.

ARIZONA
Grand Canyon State
Harvest Ranking: #40

For more information, contact:

Game & Fish Department
2221 W. Greenway Road
Phoenix, AZ 85023

(602) 942-3000   www.gfstate.az.us

HISTORY OF ARIZONA'S WHITETAIL HARVEST

Year	Firearms	Bow	Total
1958	5,096	NA	5,096
1968	2,927	NA	2,927
1978	2,287	NA	2,287
1988	4,600	108	4,708

TEN-YEAR HISTORY

Year	Firearms	Bow	Total
1990	4,449	100	4,549
1991	5,375	129	5,504
1992	5,737	95	5,832
1993	5,556	152	5,772
1994	5,363	1,315	6,678
1995	4,899	239	5,138
1996	4,126	178	4,304
1997	4,229	175	4,404
1998	4,160	204	4,364
1999 (estimated)	3,339	200	3,539

Deer are More Popular than Elk

Arizona is famous for its elk hunting, but its deer hunting is much more popular. In 1996, deer hunters accounted for 45 percent of Arizona's big-game hunters, according to statistics compiled by the U.S. Fish & Wildlife Service. Elk hunters made up 22 percent of the total.

When it comes to where people hunt deer, Arizona is much different than other states. Nearly 75 percent of the state's deer hunters hunt only on public land. In fact, of the resident hunters, 90 percent said they hunted on public land at some point during the previous season.

Arizona is home to mule deer and white-tailed deer.

ARIZONA WHITETAIL RECORDS

- **Record whitetail harvest:** 7,181 (1984)
- **Record low deer harvest:** 1,535 (1971)
- **Bow-hunting record:** 1,315 (1994)
- **Gun-hunting record:** 7,116 (1984)

- **Season to remember:** 1974. After years of a plummeting whitetail harvests, Arizona bounces back by topping the 3,000 mark. Archers had their best year in 1994.

The Ultimate Deer Hunter's Quiz
Part 8, State Records & Trends

71. Which subspecies is common in the mountains of southeastern Arizona?
A. Blacktails
B. Coues
C. Mule deer

72. As of 1993, which state had placed the most bucks into the Boone and Crockett record book?
A. Minnesota
B. Wisconsin
C. Iowa

73. Of these Southern states, which one has the most acres of forested land?
A. Louisiana
B. Florida
C. Mississippi
D. Alabama

74. In which state would a hunter have the best chance of bagging a mature white-tailed buck?
A. Michigan
B. Missouri
C. Iowa
D. Maine

Continued on Page 141.

ARIZONA SNAPSHOT

Deer Population: 182,000 (all species)
Average Harvest: 4,350, 40th in U.S.
Gun-Hunters: 44,851
Bow-Hunters: 23,306
Forested Land: 19.6 million acres
Hunter Education: Required for persons ages 10 to 14. Bow-hunter education is not required.

ARKANSAS
Land of Opportunity
Harvest Ranking: #16

For more information, contact:

Game & Fish Commission
#2 Natural Resources Drive
Little Rock, AR 72205

(800) 364-4263   www.agfc.state.ar.us

HISTORY OF ARKANSAS' WHITETAIL HARVEST

Year	Firearm	Bow	Total
1938-39	203	NA	203
1948-49	2,779	NA	2,779
1958-59	9,993	NA	9,993
1968-69	20,063	NA	20,063
1978-79	41,018	2,434	43,452
1988-89	94,193	16,014	110,207
TEN-YEAR HISTORY			
1990-91	70,498	20,412	90,910
1991-92	NA	NA	110,896
1992-93	NA	NA	110,401
1993-94	106,119	15,944	122,063
1994-95	104,061	16,433	120,494
1995-96	144,932	18,992	163,924
1996-97	133,704	18,756	152,460
1997-98	164,132	15,093	179,225
1998-99	NA	NA	156,431

Antlerless Program a Success

In 1984, the Arkansas Game and Fish Commission started its Triple Trophy Award program — a program that rewards hunters who take three deer in one season.

To qualify, hunters must take a deer with a modern firearm, muzzleloader and bow and arrow. The program not only recognizes outstanding hunting skills, it encourages the harvest of antlerless deer.

Successful hunters receive a certificate and a patch. For more information, call the AGFC at 501-223-6331.

ARKANSAS WHITETAIL RECORDS

•**Record harvest:** 179,225 (1997-98)
•**Record low harvest:** 203 (1938-39)
•**Bow-hunting record:** 21,190 (1997-98)
•**Gun-hunting record:** 146,115 (1997-98)

•**Season to remember:** 1962-63. After decades of low deer numbers and miniscule harvests, Arkansas hunters take 27,772 deer.

Arkansas Deer Managers Urge Protection of Buck Fawns

Although the Arkansas Game and Fish Commission encourages hunters to fill doe tags it also asks hunters to refrain from shooting buck fawns.

In Arkansas, deer hunting regulations are designed to better balance herd sex ratios while increasing the number of mature bucks. However, some deer hunters are disappointed when they take "nubbin' bucks" — male fawns with antlers less than 2 inches in length.

As a result, the commission drafted the "Tips for Selective Deer Harvest" and circulated it among hunters. To protect buck fawns, hunters should follow these steps while hunting:

✓Avoid long shots when trying to fill doe tags. Added distance makes positive identification more difficult.

✓Look extra close at the deer's head on cloudy days or in poor light conditions. Poor light can "hide" a fawn's sub-legal antlers.

✓Carry a pair of quality binoculars in the field and use them to carefully analyze antlerless deer before shooting.

✓Resist shooting at what appears to be a solitary doe. Buck fawns often travel by themselves, especially later in the season when they are abandoned by their mothers.

A fawn's snout is shorter and its head is smaller than that of a mature doe.

ARKANSAS SNAPSHOT

Deer Population: 1 million, 7th in U.S.

Average Harvest: 154,506, 16th in U.S.

Gun-Hunters: 164,701

Bow-Hunters: Unknown

Forested Land: 17.86 million acres

Hunter Education: Required for persons born on or after Dec. 31, 1968. Bow-hunter education not required.

COLORADO
Colorful Colorado

Harvest Ranking: Not ranked

For more information, contact:
Colorado Division of Wildlife
6060 Broadway
Denver, CO 80216

(303) 297-1192   www.state.co.us/wildlife

Governor Recognizes Hunting's Heritage

Colorado Governor Bill Owens recently addressed the importance of hunting.

"Hunting and angling are valued traditions in Colorado," Owens said. "License fees support wildlife management and protection. Hunters and anglers pump almost $2 billion dollars into Colorado's economy each year. Their spending is vital to the social and economic stability of many rural communities. But, just as important, hunting and angling bring families and friends together, foster a special understanding of our natural world and build strong community ties.

"The legal and ethical pursuit of game and fish in the wild is a powerful teacher for youth and adults," Owens continued. "I invite all Coloradans to appreciate our state's rich wildlife legacy and support our hunting and angling traditions."

States Seek Stiffer Penalties

Colorado is one of several states that is part of a consortium that seeks to crack down on poachers. Violators whose hunting and fishing licenses are revoked in one state will have those same licenses revoked in nine others states. Also participating are Arizona, Idaho, Minnesota, Montana, Nevada, Oregon, Utah, Washington and Wyoming.

The law went into effect in 2000. It is the result of an incident where a Minnesota man poached an elk in Montana. The man lost his hunting, fishing and trapping privileges in Montana, but he was still allowed to hunt in his home state. Under the new law, he would have lost the same privileges in Minnesota and the other states.

Editor's note: Colorado does not distinguish between white-tailed deer and mule deer in its harvest statistics. Biologists there estimate that about 1,000 whitetails are taken each year. Most of these deer come from the river bottoms of the eastern plains of Colorado.

Rare Disease Found in Deer, Elk in Colorado

Chronic wasting disease has been diagnosed sporadically in wild elk, mule deer and white-tailed deer in north-central Colorado since 1981. The disease damages the brains of deer and elk.

Affected animals show progressive loss of body condition, behavioral changes, excessive salivation, increased drinking and urination, depression and eventual death. Chronic wasting disease is fatal. The pathogen that causes the disease has not been identified.

The distribution of chronic wasting disease in Colorado appears to be restricted to the northeastern part of the state. The disease seems to primarily affect deer, although several elk have been diagnosed.

The disease is rare. Fewer than 200 cases, mostly in mule deer, have been documented since 1981. Neither the agent causing chronic wasting disease nor its mode of transmission have been identified. Experimental and circumstantial evidence suggests deer and elk probably transmit the disease through animal-to-animal contact.

There's no evidence that chronic wasting disease can be naturally transmitted to humans. However, it's wise to avoid contact with any wild animal that appears sick.

In the rare event that an infected deer or elk is harvested, contact the Colorado Division of Wildlife. If the animal appears to have chronic wasting disease, the hunter will be issued a duplicate carcass tag.

COLORADO SNAPSHOT

Deer Population: 516,458 (all species)

Average Harvest: 40,539 (mostly mule deer)

Gun-Hunters: 90,000

Bow-Hunters: 12,850

Forested Land:

Hunter Education: Required for persons born after Jan. 1, 1949. Bow-hunter education is not required.

CONNECTICUT
Constitution State
Harvest Ranking: #35

For more information, contact:
Dept. of Environmental Protection
391 Route 32
N. Franklin, CT 06254
(860) 424-3105   www.dep.state.ct.us

HISTORY OF CONNECTICUT'S DEER HARVEST

Year	Firearms	Bow	Total
1975	475	75	550
1985	3,817	722	4,539

TEN-YEAR HISTORY

Year	Firearms	Bow	Total
1990	NA	NA	9,896
1991	NA	NA	11,311
1992	NA	NA	12,486
1993	NA	NA	10,360
1994	NA	NA	10,438
1995	11,039	2,701	13,740
1996	9,323	2,691	12,014
1997	9,537	2,300	11,837
1998	7,958	2,186	10,144
1999	8,791	2,561	11,352

Livers Can Contain Toxin

The Connecticut Departments of Health Services and Environmental Protection advise hunters to limit their consumption of white-tailed deer liver. Analysis of livers collected from 49 hunter-killed deer in 1991 indicated that some samples had unacceptably high levels of cadmium, a toxic metal. Kidneys also concentrate cadmium, and hunters should also avoid eating them.

Hunters who eat deer liver should follow these recommendations:

✓Eat the liver of younger deer.

✓Reduce the number of meals of deer liver to no more than a few per year.

High levels of cadmium in deer livers are not unusual in the Northeast. For more information, call 860/509-7742.

Hunting is Key to Control

The Connecticut Wildlife Division recommends the use of controlled hunting to effectively reduce and maintain deer populations in balance with cultural and habitat carrying capacities.

Because white-tailed deer have a high reproductive potential and few natural predators, deer populations have the potential to increase rapidly. In the absence of significant mortality, deer populations can double in size in two years. High deer populations can significantly alter forested habitats, reducing plant diversity and habitat suitability for other wildlife species. In addition, deer can damage flower and vegetable gardens, landscape plantings, and pose a threat to motorists on Connecticut roadways. All of these scenarios have affected the Connecticut landscape to varying degrees in the past few years.

Although other control methods exist, hunting is the cheapest and most effective. Managers have tried electric fencing, woven-wire fences and repellents. Fencing is expensive and not practical. Repellents are also costly because they must be re-applied after rain. However, even in dry conditions, repellents seldom keep deer from consuming plants because areas with high deer densities typically don't have other food sources.

For information on deer hunting opportunities in Connecticut, contact the Wildlife Division at the above address.

CONNECTICUT WHITETAIL RECORDS

•Record harvest: 13,740 (1995)
•Record low harvest: 550 (1975)
•Bow-hunting record: 2,701 (1995)
•Gun-hunting record: 11,039 (1995)

•Season to remember: 1995. This year ended a 10-year span in which state bow-hunters jumped their overall harvest by more than 274 percent.

CONNECTICUT SNAPSHOT

Deer Population: 75,000, 34th in U.S.
Average Harvest: 11,817, 35th in U.S.
Gun-Hunters: 31,942
Bow-Hunters: Unknown
Forested Land: 1.8 million acres
Hunter Education: Required for first-time hunters. Bow-hunter education not required

DELAWARE
First State
Harvest Ranking: #37

For more information, contact:

Department of Natural Resources
89 Kings Hwy., Box 1401
Dover, DE 19903

(302) 739-5295   www.dnrec.state.de.us

HISTORY OF DELAWARE'S WHITETAIL HARVEST

Year	Firearms	Bow	Total
1976-77	1,475	19	1,494
1979-80	1,783	20	1,803
1981-82	2,080	31	2,111
1984-85	2,473	41	2,514
1987-88	3,420	121	3,541

TEN-YEAR HISTORY

Year	Firearms	Bow	Total
1990-91	4,814	252	5,066
1991-92	4,970	362	5,332
1992-93	6,721	524	7,245
1993-94	6,917	548	7,465
1994-95	7,151	673	7,824
1995-96	8,050	728	8,778
1996-97	9,034	786	9,820
1997-98	9,073	930	10,003
1998-99	9,386	926	10,312
1999-00 (estimated)	NA	NA	12,000

Delaware Hunting License Sales

Year	Resident	Nonresident	Total
1972	23,713	1,357	25,070
1975	27,434	2,560	29,994
1978	25,411	2,443	27,854
1981	23,811	2,600	26,411
1984	23,644	3,516	27,160
1987	23,378	4,320	27,698
1990	21,157	3,848	25,005
1991	21,674	2,995	24,669
1992	21,863	2,362	24,225
1993	21,664	2,184	23,848
1994	21,769	2,042	23,811
1995	19,518	1,945	21,463
1996	19,914	1,693	21,607
1997	20,257	1,731	21,988

Facts About the First State

Delaware might rank at the bottom of the list for deer hunting states, but it does offer some opportunities. What's more, the state is home to thousands of dedicated hunters.

About 40,000 people hunt in Delaware each year, including 24,600 deer hunters. According to a survey by the U.S. Fish & Wildlife Service, hunters spent 716,000 days afield in 1996, an average of 18 days per hunter.

Delaware hunters are big spenders. In 1996, they spent nearly $28.5 million on hunting-related items, including $20.2 million on equipment and $8.3 million on transportation. That equates to an average of $683 per hunter, or $12 per day.

Hunters spent $7 million on auxiliary equipment like tents, clothes, boats and trail bikes. The purchase of other items such as magazines, membership dues, licenses, permits, land leasing and owner-ship cost hunters $3 million — 12 percent of all hunting expenditures. They spent $5 million on food and lodging and $2 million on transportation. Other expenses, such as equipment rental, totaled $1 million.

Some state residents hunted only in another state or in another state as well as in Delaware. Altogether, 13,000 Delaware hunters, 42 percent of the total, hunted as non-residents in other states. Their 102,000 days of hunting in other states represented 15 percent of all days Delaware residents hunting in 1996.

DELAWARE WHITETAIL RECORDS

- **Record harvest:** 10,312 (1998-99)
- **Record low harvest:** 1,494 (1976)
- **Bow-hunting record:** 930 (1997-98)
- **Gun-hunting record:** 9,386 (1998-99)

- **Season to remember:** 1976-77. Nineteen lucky bow-hunters kill deer in Delaware. Bow-hunting numbers will continue to lag until 10 years later, when the harvest exceeds 100 deer.

DELAWARE SNAPSHOT

Deer Population: 30,000, 35th in U.S.

Average Harvest: 10,183, 37th in U.S.

Gun-Hunters: 16,000

Bow-Hunters: 6,500

Forested Land: 398,000 acres

Hunter Education: Required for persons born after Jan. 1, 1967. Bow-hunter education is not required.

FLORIDA
Sunshine State

Harvest Ranking: #23

For more information, contact:

Fish & Game Commission
620 S. Meridian Farris Bryant Blvd.
Tallahassee, FL 32399

(850) 488-3641   www.state.fl.us/gfc

HISTORY OF FLORIDA'S WHITETAIL HARVEST

Year	Firearms	Bow	Total
1971	NA	NA	48,900
1981	NA	NA	66,489
1989	NA	NA	85,753

TEN-YEAR HISTORY

Year	Firearms	Bow	Total
1990	NA	NA	79,170
1991	NA	NA	81,255
1992	NA	NA	81,942
1993	NA	NA	104,178
1994	NA	NA	84,408
1995	NA	NA	81,891
1996	NA	NA	78,446
1997	NA	NA	80,000
1998	NA	NA	80,000
1999 (estimated)	NA	NA	80,000

Deer Escape Wrath of Wildfires

The wildfires that ravaged public hunting areas in central Florida in 1998 affected more hunters than deer.

Mike Abbott, chief wildlife biologist for the Florida Game and Fish Commission, said that timber loss was extensive, but few deer died.

"There might be some negative effects, but for the most part, the flush of revegetation will be beneficial to deer," Abbott said.

Biologist Ray McCracken said deer are already back in the burned areas, browsing on new plant growth. However, McCracken added that the area's whitetails lost a major winter food source. "That fire did a number on our scrub oak. I'm worried about mast production this fall," he said.

— *Rollin Moseley*

FLORIDA WHITETAIL RECORDS

- **Record harvest:** 107,240 (1988)
- **Record low harvest:** 48,900 (1971)
- **Bow-hunting record:** Not available
- **Gun-hunting record:** Not available

- **Season to remember:** 1987. Florida deer hunters kill more than 100,000 whitetails for the first time. That season's harvest of 105,917 still stands as the state's second-best.

Florida's Tiny Deer Rebound

Despite massive habitat damage from Hurricane George in September 1998, Florida's Key deer are thriving.

This white-tailed deer species, which consisted of less than 50 animals in the 1940s, is making a comeback. Today, the herd consists of more than 600 deer.

Key deer are the smallest and most southern whitetail subspecies, and they are found only on the Florida Keys. Development of the islands for tourism pushed the species to the brink of extinction. However, heavy federal building and development restrictions were enacted in the early 1980s. The regulations halted the mass eradication of habitat, and the herd grew steadily.

Human encroachment is still the Key deer's No. 1 enemy. For example, a record 133 Key deer were killed in 1998, with most deaths caused by automobile collisions.

The Key deer is a diminutive subspecies of the Virginia whitetail. Does weigh between 45 and 55 pounds on the hoof, and mature bucks typically weigh 70 to 80 pounds.

It is not known how or when Key deer came to the islands, but researchers speculate the deer migrated to the area several thousand years ago and were then isolated by melting glaciers that separated the land bridge into hundreds of small islands.

Key deer were documented in 1575 by Escalante Fontaneda, a Spaniard who was held captive by Indians. The population was decimated by the late 1800s.

— *Dinny Slaughter*

FLORIDA SNAPSHOT

Deer Population: 820,000, 13th in U.S.

Average Harvest: 80,067, 23rd in U.S.

Gun-Hunters: 108,300

Bow-Hunters: 35,756

Forested Land: 16.55 million acres

Hunter Education: Required for persons born on or after June 1, 1975. Bow-hunter education is not required.

GEORGIA
Peach State
Harvest Ranking: #3

For more information, contact:

Wildlife Resources
2070 U.S. Hwy. 278 SE
Social Circle, GA 30025

(770) 414-3333   www.dnr.state.ga.us

HISTORY OF GEORGIA'S WHITETAIL HARVEST

Year	Firearm	Bow	Total
1980-81	NA	NA	135,500
1985-86	NA	NA	189,600
1989-90	NA	NA	293,167

TEN-YEAR HARVEST

Year	Firearm	Bow	Total
1990-91	NA	NA	351,652
1991-92	265,352	15,708	281,060
1992-93	284,412	21,841	306,253
1993-94	309,522	37,331	346,853
1994-95	345,869	35,687	381,556
1995-96	355,267	36,328	391,595
1996-97	351,990	49,368	401,358
1997-98	350,000	45,000	395,000
1998-99	383,000	44,000	427,000

Researchers Focus on Lyme

Researchers might have found a way to use deer to stop the spread of Lyme disease. The "Tick Licker" is a device that kills ticks as they prey on deer.

The Tick Licker works like this: When deer congregate to eat from a large, round bucket, they brush against a column in the center of the bucket that contains pesticide. That way, a deer's ears, head and nose, become covered with pesticide.

The device can be placed in a field and forgotten about. It is light, durable and inexpensive, and will not contaminate the environment. The product is far from ready for consumers. Numerous questions need to be resolved before it can be released, such as what pesticide can be used that will not contaminate venison and render it inedible for humans.

GEORGIA WHITETAIL RECORDS

•**Record harvest:** 427,000 (1998-99)
•**Record low harvest:** 134,000 (1981-82)
•**Bow-hunting record:** 49,368 (1996-97)
•**Gun-hunting record:** 383,000 (1998-99)

•**Season to remember:** 1996. Georgia's rise to prominence as one of the top deer hunting states in the nation is capped with the state's first 400,000 deer-harvest season.

How to Manage a Surplus

One of the greatest stories in modern wildlife management is the restoration of white-tailed deer populations throughout North America. Georgia's deer herd numbered only 33,000 in 1951, but today it stands at about 1 million. With the abundance of whitetails, hunters are interested in managing deer on their land. Two primary ingredients are necessary for sound deer management: regulated harvests and habitat improvement.

The most important part of the equation is harvest, particularly the doe segment. If you're interested in managing your land for deer, you must decide what you want for your hunting experience. Here are three options:

✓Maximum population. Hunters see a lot of deer, but bucks will exhibit poor antler growth. The habitat also suffers because natural vegetation becomes over-browsed.

✓Maximum harvest. Hunters see moderate numbers of deer, and they will have ample opportunities to kill does. Young bucks will exhibit good antler growth and, as a result, few will live to see old age.

✓Quality bucks. Young bucks must be passed up by hunters and harvest must include large numbers of does. This type of management balances the age structure among the herd and, therefore, increases a hunter's chance of killing a large-antlered buck.

GEORGIA SNAPSHOT

Deer Population: 1 million, 7th in U.S.
Average Harvest: 399,302, 3rd in U.S.
Gun-Hunters: 357,727
Bow-Hunters: 86,118
Forested Land: 24.1 million acres
Hunter Education: Required for persons born after Jan. 1, 1961. Bow-hunter education is not required.

IDAHO
Gem State
Harvest Ranking: #32

For more information, contact:

Fish & Game Department
Box 25
Boise, ID 83707

(208) 334-3717   www.2state.id.us

HISTORY OF IDAHO'S DEER HARVEST

Year	Firearm	Bow	Total
1980	NA	NA	45,988
1984	NA	NA	42,600
1988	NA	NA	82,200

TEN-YEAR HISTORY

Year	Firearm	Bow	Total
1990	NA	NA	72,100
1991	16,721	364	17,085
1992	NA	NA	23,633
1993	23,251	303	23,554
1994	29,760	595	30,355
1995	28,180	320	28,500
1996	NA	NA	22,600
1997	37,450	1,100	38,550
1998	38,162	880	39,042
1999	41,972	1,312	43,284

Editor's note — The figures before 1991 include white-tailed deer and mule deer.

Idaho Holds Big Whitetails

Idaho's deer population consists primarily of mule deer, but whitetails are present, including some big bucks.

Whitetails are found primarily north of the Salmon River, and they are generally hunted later in the fall than mule deer.

Whitetail seasons commonly open in mid-October and early November and close in mid- to late-November. In 1998, 49 percent of bucks harvested were 8-pointers, while 19 percent were 10-pointers or larger.

Mule deer are found mostly in the southern two-thirds of the state.

IDAHO WHITETAIL RECORDS

•**Record harvest:** 43,284 (1999)
•**Record low harvest:** 17,085 (1991)
•**Bow-hunting record:** 1,312 (1999)
•**Gun-hunting record:** 41,972 (1999)

•**Season to remember:** 1991. For the first time in state history, Idaho recognizes the white-tailed deer separately. Of the 17,085 deer killed, 97.9 percent were taken by gun-hunters.

Idaho Welcomes Hunters

Idaho deer hunting licenses can be purchased at Idaho Fish & Game offices, on the Internet, over the telephone (800/554-8685), or at any of the 400-plus license vendors statewide.

Nonresidents can add a tag for another species as long as the quota on the tag you want has not been reached. Licenses and tags for the following year go on sale Dec. 1. Another person can make the purchase for you. When you apply for licenses, be sure to include your name, mailing address, social security number, height, weight, date of birth and telephone number. If you take advantage of the convenience of ordering by the Internet or by telephone, by using a credit card.

The Fish & Game Division prints brochures explaining hunting rules. If you buy your license over the telephone, be sure to ask the operator to put you on the mailing list for the type of brochure you will need. The regulations can also be downloaded from the Web site listed at the top of this page.

Deer brochures are available March 7. The number of nonresident deer tags is limited. However, most year, nonresidents deer tags have not sold out.

Deer are found throughout Idaho. With the adoption of the A-B zone tags for elk, there is now more overlap of elk and deer seasons, and more opportunity to hunt both on the same trip.

IDAHO SNAPSHOT

Deer Population: 255,000, 24th in U.S.

Average Harvest: 34,395, 32nd in U.S.

Gun-Hunters: 112,800

Bow-Hunters: 12,436

Forested Land: 21.6 million acres

Hunter Education: Required for persons born after Jan. 1, 1975. Bow-hunter education is required for first-time bow-hunters.

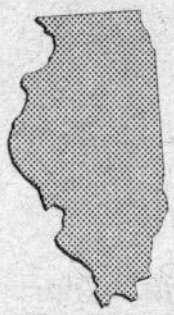

ILLINOIS

Prairie State

Harvest Ranking: #19

For more information, contact:

Department of Conservation
524 S. Second St.
Springfield, IL 62701
(217) 782-7305 www.dnr.state.il.us

HISTORY OF ILLINOIS' WHITETAIL HARVEST

Year	Firearm	Bow	Total
1957	1,709	NA	1,709
1967	6,588	NA	6,588
1977	16,231	2,810	19,041
1987	42,932	6,646	49,578

TEN-YEAR HISTORY

Year	Firearm	Bow	Total
1990	NA	NA	81,000
1991	83,191	18,099	101,290
1992	84,537	19,564	104,101
1993	92,276	23,215	115,491
1994	97,723	25,607	123,330
1995	107,742	34,491	142,233
1996	97,498	35,239	132,737
1997	96,511	36,763	133,274
1998	97,500	37,000	134,500
1999 (estimated)	93,500	37,000	130,500

Illinois Hunters Pay Dearly

Hunters 16 years old and older spent $470 million in Illinois in 1996, according to a report by the United States Fish & Wildlife Service.

Trip-related expenses such as food and lodging, transportation and other trip costs, including equipment rental fees, cost hunters $111 million, 24 percent of their total expenditures. They spent $57 million on food and lodging and $34 million on transportation. Other expenses such as equipment rental totaled $20 million for the year. The average trip-related expenditure per hunter was $256.

Hunters spent $239 million on equipment, 51 percent of all hunting expenditures.

ILLINOIS WHITETAIL RECORDS

- **Record harvest:** 142,233 (1995)
- **Record low harvest:** 1,709 (1957)
- **Bow-hunting record:** 37,000 (1998)
- **Gun-hunting record:** 107,742 (1995)

- **Season to remember:** 1980. Although Illinois bow-hunters harvested only 1,463 deer, the season marked the first of 19 consecutive seasons in which bow-hunters bettered their previous year's harvest total.

Big-Buck Program Soars

In the early 1980s, the Illinois Department of Natural Resources unveiled its Big Buck Recognition Program. The program, patterned after the standards of the Boone and Crockett Club, promotes deer hunting while recognizing hunters who take big bucks. Here's a look at some of the top bucks entered into the program:

Firearm — Typical

Hunter	Score	Date	County
Larry Shaw	188 7/8	1998	Clark
Daniel Lincoln	187 7/8	1998	Mercer
Bernard Emat	183 3/8	1996	La Salle
Stephen Smith	181 2/8	1973	Pike

Firearm — Nontypical

Hunter	Score	Date	County
William Seidel	239 1/8	1987	Unknown
John Boshears	220 1/8	1998	Iroquois
Chris Schweigert	219 3/8	1998	Fulton
Stanley Walker	218 6/8	1998	Cass

Archery — Typical

Hunter	Score	Date	County
Gary Adcock	177 0/8	1998	Hamilton
Mark Simon	176 4/8	1998	Will
Mike Foote	176 1/8	1998	Adams
Ron Wadsworth	174 6/8	1998	Menard

Archery — Nontypical

Hunter	Score	Date	County
Walter Baker	216 3/8	1998	Jersey
Ronald Okonek	205 7/8	1998	Greene
Rich Humphreys	205 3/8	1994	Macoupin
Joseph Licatesi	202 3/8	1998	Cook

Editor's note — These are Illinois BBRP listings. They do not reflect official records of the Boone and Crockett Club.

ILLINOIS SNAPSHOT

Deer Population: 700,000, 16th in U.S.

Average Harvest: 134,816, 19th in U.S.

Gun-Hunters: 205,000

Bow-Hunters: 95,000

Forested Land: 4.3 million acres

Hunter Education: Required for persons born after Jan. 1, 1980. Bow-hunter education is not required.

INDIANA
Hoosier State
Harvest Ranking: #21

For more information, contact:

Division of Wildlife
553 E. Miller Drive
Bloomington, IN 47401

(317) 232-4080   www.state.in.us/dnr

HISTORY OF INDIANA'S WHITETAIL HARVEST

Year	Firearm	Bow	Total
1951	NA	NA	1,590
1961	NA	NA	2,293
1971	NA	NA	5,099
1981	12,600	5,527	18,127

TEN-YEAR HISTORY

Year	Firearm	Bow	Total
1990	70,928	17,775	88,703
1991	77,102	21,581	98,683
1992	73,396	21,918	95,314
1993	77,226	23,988	101,214
1994	89,037	23,379	112,416
1995	92,496	25,233	117,729
1996	99,886	23,200	123,086
1997	84,637	20,300	104,937
1998	82,101	18,360	100,461
1999	67,295	32,373	99,668

Hunters Manage the Herd

In the 12-year period of 1987 to 1998, Indiana deer hunters became better deer managers.

For example, in 1987, adult does made up only 21 percent of the state's total deer harvest (51,778), while adult bucks made up 57 percent of the harvest. By 1995, hunters killed a lot more does, 32 percent of the overall harvest, and fewer bucks, 40 percent. The change likely showed a decline in the number of hunters who killed yearling bucks.

Over the last four years of the period, does, adults and fawns, comprised 40 percent to 50 percent of the state's overall deer harvest.

INDIANA WHITETAIL RECORDS

•**Record harvest:** 123,086 (1996)
•**Record low harvest:** 68 (1954)
•**Bow-hunting record:** 25,233 (1995)
•**Gun-hunting record:** 99,886 (1996)

•**Season to remember:** 1990. Indiana gun-hunters top the 70,000 deer-harvest for the first time, an amazing figure considering state gun-hunters only took 12,600 deer in 1981.

Hunters Help Motorists

Indiana hunters have been credited with reducing the number of deer/vehicle accidents in the Hoosier State.

In 1990, Indiana reported a state record 12,465 deer/vehicle accidents. Coincidentally, hunters killed a record 98,683 deer that year. In fact, hunters broke the harvest record four more times over the next eight years, knocking the herd down to a more manageable level.

The Indiana State Police reported 10,779 deer/vehicle collisions in 1998 — 13.5 percent less than in 1990. What's more, although more vehicles are on the road traveling more miles each year, the number of deer/vehicle collisions has been dropping when compared to the number of miles traveled.

In 1990, 232 deer/vehicle accidents were reported for each billion miles traveled in Indiana. That number dropped to 146 in 1997 and 152 per billion miles traveled in 1998.

The DNR's Division of Fish and Wildlife sets hunting seasons and bag limits to maintain the state's deer herd at a level that maximizes opportunities for hunting and wildlife watching, and minimizes crop damage and collisions between deer and vehicles.

Deer provide Indiana hunters with more than 6 million pounds of venison each year, and deer hunting pours $142 million into the state's economy.

INDIANA SNAPSHOT

Deer Population: 450,000, 18th in U.S.

Average Harvest: 109,176, 21st in U.S.

Gun-Hunters: 235,000

Bow-Hunters: 130,000

Forested Land: 4.4 million acres

Hunter Education: Required for persons born after Dec. 31, 1986. Bow-hunter education is not required.

IOWA
Hawkeye State

Harvest Ranking: #20

For more information, contact:

Department of Natural Resources
Wallace State Office Bldg.
Des Moines, IA 50319-0034

(515) 281-4687   www.state.ia.us

HISTORY OF IOWA'S WHITETAIL HARVEST

Year	Firearm	Bow	Total
1953	4,007	1	4,008
1963	6,612	538	7,151
1973	12,208	1,822	14,030
1983	30,375	5,244	35,619

TEN-YEAR HISTORY

Year	Firearm	Bow	Total
1990	87,856	10,146	98,002
1991	74,828	8,807	83,635
1992	68,227	8,814	77,684
1993	67,139	9,291	76,430
1994	75,191	12,040	87,231
1995	83,884	13,372	97,256
1996	90,000	16,000	106,000
1997	104,091	14,313	118,404
1998	102,000	13,000	115,000
1999 (estimated)	NA	NA	115,000

Hunt the Land of Big Bucks

Iowa is not only a top-notch place to hunt big bucks as a nonresident, it's affordable.

Iowa issues nonresident tags on a lottery basis.

Hunters cannot apply for or obtain more than one nonresident deer license in the same year.

Calls for information are accepted from 7 a.m. to 9 p.m., central time, Monday through Friday, and from 8 a.m. to 4 p.m. on Saturdays.

The license fee is $150.50. Other nominal fees apply. For more information, visit the Web site listed at the top of this page.

IOWA WHITETAIL RECORDS

•**Record harvest:** 118,404 (1997)
•**Record low harvest:** 2,423 (1954)
•**Bow-hunting record:** 16,000 (1996)
•**Gun-hunting record:** 104,091 (1997)

•**Season to remember:** 1953. Iowa records its first bow-kill in the state's modern bow-hunting era. Ironically, that was the only bow-killed deer reported that season.

State Harbors Healthy Herd

The white-tailed deer's ability to thrive in Iowa is likely the result of an abundant, reliable food source and a winter climate where snow depths rarely exceed 12 inches for prolonged periods. These factors combine to allow deer to come through winter in excellent condition. Excellent nutrition also enables deer to have high reproductive rates.

Most Iowa does have a single fawn their first year and two fawns each subsequent year. Deer in the wild can probably maintain these high reproductive rates until they are 10 years old. Research in Iowa shows that 8 percent to 12 percent of adult does have triplets.

Another reason that deer do so well in Iowa is they are highly mobile. Although some deer stay near their birth sites, many travel to new areas before establishing a core area. Core areas can change seasonally with deer shifting between wintering and breeding areas.

Careful management of deer populations by man played a crucial role in allowing deer numbers to return to the levels enjoyed today. Management consists of carefully regulating the harvest since hunting provides the only major source of mortality for deer today. Unchecked, Iowa's deer herd could grow at a rate of 20 percent to 40 percent annually, doubling the herd in as few as three years.

IOWA SNAPSHOT

Deer Population: 325,000, 22nd in U.S.

Average Harvest: 110,332, 20th in U.S.

Gun-Hunters: 165,000

Bow-Hunters: 35,000

Forested Land: 2 million acres

Hunter Education: Required for persons born after Jan. 1, 1967. Bow-hunter education is not required.

KANSAS

Sunflower State

Harvest Ranking: #27

For more information, contact:

Department of Wildlife
Box 1525
Emporia, KS 66801
(316) 672-5911 www.kdwp.state.ks.us

HISTORY OF KANSAS' WHITETAIL HARVEST

Year	Firearm	Bow	Total
1965	1,340	164	1,504
1975	4,352	1,136	5,488
1985	21,296	4,230	25,526

TEN-YEAR HISTORY

Year	Firearm	Bow	Total
1990	40,800	5,000	45,800
1991	41,803	NA	41,803
1992	31,750	NA	31,750
1993	33,590	NA	33,590
1994	36,040	7,800	43,840
1995	39,390	7,200	46,590
1996	43,550	8,500	52,050
1997	53,440	9,700	63,140
1998	73,100	8,000	81,100
1999	84,230	11,770	96,000

Program Promotes Hunting

The Kansas Department of Wildlife has taken a proactive role in promoting hunting, implementing a hunting recruitment and retention plan.

"Hunting is an important part of our state's heritage, and it is vitally important to our wildlife management programs, as well as our state economy," said Governor Bill Graves. "But perhaps most important is the value of hunting in our culture and quality of life. Hunting is a wholesome, family activity that creates special bonds, teaches youngsters responsibility and fosters a special appreciation for our natural world."

For more information on the program, call 316/672-5911 or send e-mail to mikegm@wp.state.ks.us

KANSAS WHITETAIL RECORDS

- **Record harvest:** 96,000 (1999)
- **Record low harvest:** 1,504 (1965)
- **Bow-hunting record:** 11,770 (1999)
- **Gun-hunting record:** 84,230 (1999)

•**Season to remember:** 1968. In a time when killing a deer with a bow was practically unheard of, Kansas bow-hunters took 614 deer — 27 percent of the state's total harvest.

Kansas is Home to Brutes

Kansas harbors some of the biggest white-tailed bucks in North America. To recognize these animals, and the hunters who took them, the state has its own records program, patterned after the standards of the Boone and Crockett Club. Here's a look at some of the top bucks entered into the program:

Firearm — Typical

Hunter	Score	Date	County
Dennis Finger	198 2/8	1974	Nemaha
William Mikijanis	194 7/8	1985	Leavenworth
Michael Young	191 4/8	1973	Chautauqua
Jamie Fowler	190 7/8	1992	Lyon

Firearm — Nontypical

Hunter	Score	Date	County
Joseph Waters	280 4/8	1987	Shawnee
Chris Theis	279 1/8	1992	Leavenworth
John Band	258 6/8	1965	Republic
Jamie Remmers	257 1/8	1997	Marion

Archery — Typical

Hunter	Score	Date	County
Stephen Weilert	193 2/8	1994	Woodson
Gary Freeman	187 7/8	1995	Neosho
Douge Selbe	187 2/8	1988	Sumner
Greg Hill	186 1/8	1994	Marshall

Archery — Nontypical

Hunter	Score	Date	County
Kenneth Fowler	257 0/8	1988	Reno
Clifford Pickett	249 6/8	1968	Greenwood
Richard Stahl	246 3/8	1992	Anderson
Douglas Siebert	244 1/8	1988	Chase

Editor's note — *These are Kansas Big Game Records listings. They do not reflect official records of the Boone and Crockett Club.*

KANSAS SNAPSHOT

Deer Population: 125,000, 30th in U.S.

Average Harvest: 67,776, 27th in U.S.

Gun-Hunters: 73,194

Bow-Hunters: 21,443

Forested Land: 1.36 million acres

Hunter Education: Required for persons born after July 1, 1957. Bow-hunter education is not required.

KENTUCKY
Bluegrass State

Harvest Ranking: #22

For more information, contact:

Department of Wildlife
#1 Game Farm Road
Frankfort, KY 40601

(800) 858-1549   www.state.ky.us

HISTORY OF KENTUCKY'S WHITETAIL HARVEST

Year	Firearm	Bow	Total
1976	3,476	NA	3,476
1979	7,442	620	8,062
1982	15,804	2,165	17,969
1985	26,024	4,051	30,075
1988	57,553	6,707	64,260

TEN-YEAR HISTORY

Year	Firearm	Bow	Total
1990	66,151	7,767	73,918
1991	84,918	8,016	92,934
1992	73,664	8,274	81,938
1993	64,598	8,680	73,278
1994	93,444	12,672	106,116
1995	98,033	12,900	110,933
1996	98,430	13,010	111,440
1997	NA	NA	109,496
1998	94,299	9,771	104,070
1999	83,307	11,920	95,227

The Top Counties for Deer

A six-year run of annual deer harvests exceeding 100,000 ended in 1999 in Kentucky, but hunters still managed to bag thousands of bucks.

The best counties for bucks in 1999 were Owen, 1,250; Crittenden, 1,026; Ohio, 1,009; ; Lawrence, 946; and Christian, 878.

Eight counties topped the 1,000-mark for antlerless harvest. They were: Owen, 1,563; Crittenden, 1,175; Lawrence, 1,136; Ohio, 1,118; Shelby, 1,011; Christian, 937; Henry, 905; and Hardin, 904.

Owen, Lawrence, Ohio and Crittenden were the only counties to post deer harvests exceeding 2,000.

KENTUCKY WHITETAIL RECORDS

- **Record harvest:** 111,440 (1996)
- **Record low harvest:** 3,476 (1976)
- **Bow-hunting record:** 13,010 (1996)
- **Gun-hunting record:** 98,430 (1996)

- **Season to remember:** 1991. With a bulging deer herd, Kentucky issues more permits, and the overall deer harvest jumps 25.7 percent, led by a gun-hunting harvest of 84,918.

Public Land is Plentiful

Kentucky is home to thousands of acres of public hunting land. Most of the wildlife areas open for public hunting are owned by various agencies of the state and federal government.

More than one-third of the areas listed in the state's hunting guide were bought with dollars from hunting and fishing license sales. Funding from the same sources support wildlife management programs in more than 70 percent of these areas.

The hunting guide, available by writing to the address listed at the top of this page, is designed to give fairly specific directions to these areas, most of which are not shown on standard highway maps. Maps of some of the areas are available from the Kentucky Wildlife Division by calling 502/564-4406. Information is also given on the kinds of terrain, vegetation and common species that live on these public lands. No attempt is made to list all species present or rank species in order of abundance.

Management practices on many of these areas provide food, cover and water for white-tailed deer. Food plots and farm crops left standing in the field are important food sources, and brushy areas, unmowed fields and woods provide both natural foods and places for deer to hide.

Kentucky is an attractive state to muzzleloading hunters. In 1999, muzzleloading hunters took 17,641 whitetails.

KENTUCKY SNAPSHOT

Deer Population: 611,191, 17th in U.S.

Average Harvest: 106,233, 22nd in U.S.

Gun-Hunters: 206,104

Bow-Hunters: 71,000

Forested Land: 12.7 million acres

Hunter Education: Required for persons born after Jan. 1, 1975. Bow-hunter education is also required.

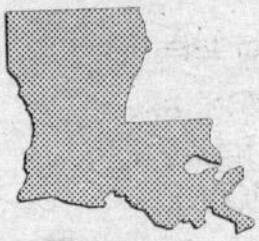

LOUISIANA

Pelican State

Harvest Ranking: #8

For more information, contact:

Department of Wildlife
Box 98000
Baton Rouge, LA 70898

(225) 765-2887 www.wlf.state.la.us

HISTORY OF LOUISIANA'S WHITETAIL HARVEST

Year	Firearm	Bow	Total
1960-61	16,500	NA	16,500
1970-71	53,500	NA	53,500
1980-81	105,500	5,000	110,500

TEN-YEAR HISTORY

Year	Firearm	Bow	Total
1990-91	176,200	18,200	194,300
1991-92	186,400	17,700	204,100
1992-93	192,300	22,600	214,900
1993-94	193,000	20,100	213,100
1994-95	210,200	27,200	237,400
1995-96	208,500	26,200	234,700
1996-97	220,000	25,000	245,000
1997-98	243,400	24,200	267,600
1998-99	222,300	21,100	243,400
1999-00 (estimated)	230,000	20,000	250,000

Louisiana State-Record Bucks

Typical Antlers

Hunter	Parish	Date	Score
Don Broadway	Madison	1943	184 5/8
Ernest McCoy	Bossier	1961	184 1/8
H.B. Womble	Franklin	1914	184 2/8
Shawn Ortego	St. Landry	1975	180 5/8
Buford Perry	Madison	1961	180 4/8

Nontypical Antlers

Hunter	Parish	Date	Score
James McMurray	Tensas	1994	281 6/8
Joseph Shields	Concordia	1948	252 2/8
Picked Up	Concordia	1969	227 7/8
W.D. Ethredge	Caddo	1988	219 6/8
Drew Ware	St. Martin	1941	218 4/8

— Louisiana Big Game Recognition Program

LOUISIANA WHITETAIL RECORDS

- **Record harvest:** 267,600 (1997-98)
- **Record low harvest:** 16,500 (1960-61)
- **Bow-hunting record:** 27,200 (1994-95)
- **Gun-hunting record:** 243,000 (1997-98)

- **Season to remember:** 1997-98. Thanks to a record-setting gun-hunting season, Louisiana hunters take 22,600 more deer than the previous season.

Louisiana is Home to Record-Class Whitetails

The above photo is of four bucks that were killed within the past few seasons in Louisiana — proof that the Pelican State can produce Boone-and-Crockett-class bucks.

The buck on the top left scored 177 5/8 points. It was killed by John King in Concordia Parish. The buck on the top right scored 168 5/8 points and is the new state record typical for deer killed with muzzleloaders. It was taken in Avoyelles Parish by Michael Wills.

The bottom two deer had not been officially scored as of press time, but they both qualify for Boone and Crockett. The buck on the bottom left was killed by Donald Riviere in Avoyelles Parish. The other buck was taken by Lee Rice in West Feliciana Parish.

LOUISIANA SNAPSHOT

Deer Population: 1 million, 7th in U.S.

Average Harvest: 248,140, 8th in U.S.

Gun-Hunters: 198,527

Bow-Hunters: 55,152

Forested Land: 13.86 million acres

Hunter Education: Required for persons born after Sept. 1, 1969. Bow-hunter education is not required.

MAINE
Pine Tree State
Harvest Ranking: #33

For more information, contact:

Department of Inland Fisheries
284 State St., State House Station 41
Augusta, ME 04333

(207) 287-2571   www.state.me.us/ifw

HISTORY OF MAINE'S DEER HARVEST

Year	Firearm	Bow	Total
1919	5,784	NA	5,784
1929	11,708	NA	11,708
1939	19,187	NA	19,187
1949	35,051	NA	35,051
1959	41,720	15	41,735
1969	30,388	21	30,409
1979	26,720	101	26,821
1989	29,844	416	30,260

TEN-YEAR HISTORY

Year	Firearm	Bow	Total
1990	25,658	319	25,977
1991	26,236	500	26,736
1992	28,126	694	28,820
1993	26,608	682	27,402
1994	23,967	716	24,683
1995	26,233	1,151	27,384
1996	27,601	774	28,375
1997	30,149	1,003	31,152
1998	26,996	1,245	28,241
1999	29,361	2,112	31,473

Maine Produces Big Bucks

Though Maine doesn't boast the white-tail numbers many states do, as home one of the largest whitetail subspecies, Maine hunters kill large bucks.

After reaching maturity, most Maine bucks reach body weights from 200 to 300 pounds and stand 36 to 40 inches tall at the shoulder. Some older bucks have weighed up to 400 pounds.

MAINE WHITETAIL RECORDS

•**Record harvest:** 41,735 (1959)
•**Record low harvest:** 5,784 (1919)
•**Bow-hunting record:** 2,112 (1999)
•**Gun-hunting record:** 41,730 (1951)

•**Season to remember:** 1919. Despite the fact that deer populations were on the brink of extinction in many states, Maine hunters were allowed a generous season, and 5,784 hunters took deer.

The Ultimate Deer Hunter's Quiz
Part 8, State Records & Trends

74. In which state would a hunter have the best chance of bagging a mature white-tailed buck?
A. Michigan
B. Missouri
C. Iowa
D. Maine

75. Which state holds the modern-day record for whitetail harvest in one season?
A. Wisconsin
B. Alabama
C. Texas

76. About 20 percent of Oklahoma is blanketed with which type of forest?
A. Oak
B. Red pine
C. Locust

77. Which state allows hunters to pursue deer with dogs?
A. California
B. Minnesota
C. New Hampshire

Continued on Page 165.

MAINE SNAPSHOT

Deer Population: 335,000, 21st in U.S.

Average Harvest: 29,325, 33rd in U.S.

Gun-Hunters: 155,600

Bow-Hunters: 9,477

Forested Land: 17.5 million acres

Hunter Education: Required for all first-time hunters. Bow-hunter education is also required.

MARYLAND
Old Line State

Harvest Ranking: #26

For more information, contact:

Division of Wildlife
4220 Steele Neck Road
Vienna, MD 21869

(410) 260-8200   www.dnr.state.md.us

HISTORY OF MARYLAND'S WHITETAIL HARVEST

Year	Firearm	Bow	Total
1983	16,239	2,181	18,420
1984	17,324	2,501	19,825
1985	17,241	2,549	19,790
1986	22,411	3,404	25,815
1987	24,846	4,216	29,062
1988	27,625	5,983	33,608
1989	38,305	7,988	46,293

TEN-YEAR HISTORY

Year	Firearm	Bow	Total
1990	37,712	8,605	46,317
1991	36,169	10,454	46,623
1992	39,858	11,240	51,098
1993	39,429	11,251	51,234
1994	39,547	11,324	50,871
1995	49,237	12,397	61,634
1996	39,048	13,588	52,636
1997	52,600	12,919	65,519
1998	57,270	16,300	93,570
1999	59,963	16,214	76,177

Contest Promotes QDM

Each year, the Maryland Bowhunters Society and the DNR co-sponsor the *Maryland Trophy Deer Contest*. This contest recognizes hunters who have killed big bucks and promotes Quality Deer Management in Maryland.

The contest is open only for deer taken legally in Maryland. A possession tag is required. Deer taken with crop damage permits and road-killed deer are not eligible.

For more information, contact the Maryland Department of Natural Resources at the address/phone number listed at the top of this page.

Sika, Whitetails Coexist in Maryland's Woodlands

Maryland's exotic sika deer (pronounced SEE-kuh), natives of western Asia, first appeared on the state's eastern shore, primarily Dorchester County, following their release on James Island in 1916.

Today, the sika deer inhabits the lower eastern shore counties with its largest populations in the marshes and wetlands of southern Dorchester County.

Initially, biologists and deer managers feared the "miniature elk-like" species would spread into the optimal upland white-tailed deer territory. This resulted in higher bag limits on sika deer. However, over the years, managers have learned that sika deer lives most of their lives in the suboptimal regions of the whitetail's habitat, lessening competition between the species. This changed the Wildlife and Heritage Division's attitude and management techniques towards sika deer.

Today, Maryland sika deer are managed as a trophy animal. The DNR's goal is to maintain this exotic species at current levels so crop damage problems are balanced with hunting opportunities.

For more information on deer hunting opportunities in Maryland, contact the Wildlife and Heritage Division with the information listed at the top of this page.

— *Doug Hotton and Dave Armentrout*

MARYLAND WHITETAIL RECORDS

•**Record harvest:** 93,570 (1998)
•**Record low harvest:** 18,420 (1983)
•**Bow-hunting record:** 16,300 (1998)
•**Gun-hunting record:** 57,270 (1998)

•**Season to remember:** 1996. Maryland bow-hunters take 13,588 deer. The total represented a whopping 25.6 percent of the state's overall harvest of 52,636.

MARYLAND SNAPSHOT

Deer Population: 247,000, 26th in U.S.

Average Harvest: 69,907, 26th in U.S.

Gun-Hunters: 78,860

Bow-Hunters: 45,581

Forested Land: 2.7 million acres

Hunter Education: Required for persons born after July 1, 1977. Bow-hunter education is not required.

MASSACHUSETTS
Bay State

Harvest Ranking: #39

For more information, contact:
Massachusetts Wildlife
Westborough, MA 01581

(617) 727-1614
www.state.ma.us/dfwele

HISTORY OF MASSACHUSETTS' DEER HARVEST

Year	Firearm	Bow	Total
1989	5,818	890	6,708
1990	5,829	1,061	6,890
1991	8,085	1,378	9,463
1992	8,470	1,570	10,040
1993	6,514	1,387	8,345
1994	7,545	1,587	9,132
1995	9,158	1,901	11,059
1996	7,029	1,687	8,714
1997	8,473	1,813	10,286
1998	7,501	1,803	9,304
1999	7,047	2,469	9,516

Bay State Spends Big Bucks on Deer Hunting

Massachusetts might be one of the smallest deer hunting states, but its hunters are serious about their pastime.

According to a survey by the U.S. Fish & Wildlife Service, the state's 76,000 deer hunters spent about 604,0000 days pursuing whitetails in 1996. That's an average of 7.9 days per hunter.

Massachusetts residents also spent considerable time traveling to other states to hunt. About 36,000 residents traveled out of the state to hunt, and they logged more than 530,000 days. That's an average of 14.7 days per hunter.

Including other types of hunting, Massachusetts hunters spent $106 million in the state in 1996. Trip-related expenses such as food and lodging, transportation and other trip costs, including equipment rental fees, cost hunter $20 million, or 19 percent of their expenditures. They spent $10 million on food and lodging and $9 million on transportation.

Hunters also spent $455 apiece on guns and rifles and $42 apiece on ammunition. The per-hunter expense for food was $122; lodging, $109; and transportation, $110.

Most Massachusetts hunters have access to private land. Only 23 percent of the hunters surveyed said they hunted exclusively on public land. Twenty-eight percent said they hunt on public and private land.

Program Helps Women Learn Outdoors Skills

In an effort to attract more women to outdoor sports, Massachusetts holds several "Becoming an Outdoor Woman" programs each year.

This program focuses on outdoor skills — skills traditionally passed from father to son — but valuable to anyone wishing to enjoy outdoor pursuits. A sampling of workshop offerings can include fishing, shooting, kayaking, orienteering, reading the woods, archery, pond and stream adventures, nature photography and game cooking. Designed primarily for women, it is an opportunity for anyone 18 or older who want an opportunity to learn outdoor skills. The program is co-sponsored by the Massachusetts Sportsmen's Council.

For more information, contact the Massachusetts Division of Wildlife at the address/phone number listed at the top of this page, or visit the Web site: www.magnet.state.ma.us

MASSACHUSETTS DEER RECORDS

•**Record harvest:** 11,059 (1995)
•**Record low harvest:** 6,708 (1989)
•**Bow-hunting record:** 2,469 (1999)
•**Gun-hunting record:** 9,158 (1995)

•**Season to remember:** 1989. Massachusetts begins keeping detailed records of its gun-hunting and bow-hunting seasons. Hunters register 6,708 deer, including 890 bow kills.

MASSACHUSETTS SNAPSHOT

Deer Population: 85,000, 32nd in U.S.

Average Harvest: 9,776, 39th in U.S.

Gun-Hunters: 65,000

Bow-Hunters: 27,495

Forested Land: 3.2 million acres

Hunter Education: Required for first-time hunters and hunters ages 15 to 18. Bow-hunter education is not required.

MICHIGAN
Wolverine State
Harvest Ranking: #2

For more information, contact:

Department of Natural Resources
Box 30028
Lansing, MI 48909

www.dnr.state.mi.us

HISTORY OF MICHIGAN'S WHITETAIL HARVEST

Year	Firearm	Bow	Total
1878	NA	NA	21,000
1899	NA	NA	12,000
1911	NA	NA	12,000
1920	NA	NA	25,000
1929	NA	NA	28,710
1939	44,770	6	44,776
1949	77,750	780	78,530
1959	115,400	1,840	117,240
1969	106,698	2,582	109,280
1979	119,790	25,640	145,430
1989	355,410	97,080	452,490

TEN-YEAR HISTORY

Year	Firearms	Bow	Total
1990	338,890	93,800	432,690
1991	318,460	115,880	434,340
1992	274,650	99,990	374,640
1993	232,820	98,160	330,980
1994	251,420	112,490	363,910
1995	346,830	132,130	478,960
1996	319,289	100,000	419,289
1997	282,000	100,000	382,000
1998	329,000	121,000	450,000

Editor's note — *These harvest totals are estimates. Firearm harvest totals before 1975 did not include muzzleloader harvest. Also, totals since 1978 do not include deer taken with camp-deer permits.*

Hunting is Big Business
As a renewable resources, hunting and fishing are important to Michigan's economy. Hunters spend more than $800 million each year, and anglers, including 334,000 nonresidents, spend nearly $1 billion annually.

MICHIGAN WHITETAIL RECORDS
•**Record harvest:** 478,960 (1995)
•**Record low harvest:** 8,000 (1916)
•**Bow-hunting record:** 132,130 (1995)
•**Gun-hunting record:** 355,410 (1989)

•**Season to remember:** 1995. Michigan hunters lead the nation with an overall harvest of 478,960. This total ranks second, all-time, to the 502,000-plus deer killed in Texas in 1987.

Market Interests Drove Michigan Whitetails to Brink of Extinction

Prior to settlement, southern Michigan had an abundant deer herd. The mixture of hardwoods, wetlands, bogs and forest openings was perfect for deer. There were few deer in the virgin forests of the north, which were inhabited mostly by elk and moose. However, as farmers and settlers moved into southern Michigan, deer were exterminated by removal of cover and by unregulated shooting. Deer were mostly gone by 1870. As the northern herd climbed to estimated 1 million deer in the 1880s, the abundance fostered a public attitude that the resource was inexhaustible.

Logging camps used venison as the primary source of meat for months at a time. Railroads that had been developed to facilitate the timber market also provided transportation of game meat to Eastern markets.

Market hunters slaughtered hundreds of thousands of deer. Usually, they only kept the hindquarters and legs (saddles) and discarded the rest. Hunting methods commonly involved the use of dog packs, jacklighting, and shooting deer while they were swimming.

Soon, sporting groups realized the need to lobby against commercial hunting interests. In 1875, the first meeting of the Michigan Sportsmen's Association was held in Detroit. The group's work helped pave the way for modern deer management.
— *Michigan Dept. of Natural Resources*

MICHIGAN SNAPSHOT
Deer Population: 1.8 million, 2nd in U.S.

Average Harvest: 418,832, 2nd in U.S.

Gun-Hunters: 765,914

Bow-Hunters: 430,049

Forested Land: 18.25 million acres

Hunter Education: Required for persons born after Jan. 1, 1969. Bow-hunter education is not required.

MINNESOTA
Gopher State
Harvest Ranking: #13

For more information, contact:
Department of Natural Resources
Box 7, 500 Lafayette Road
St. Paul, MN 55155

(651) 296-4506   www.dnr.state.mn.us

HISTORY OF MINNESOTA'S WHITETAIL HARVEST

Year	Firearm	Bow	Total
1918	9,000	NA	9,000
1928	27,300	NA	27,300
1938	44,500	NA	44,500
1948	61,600	NA	61,600
1958	75,000	403	75,403
1968	103,000	819	103,819
1978	57,800	2,608	60,408
1988	138,900	8,262	147,162

TEN-YEAR HISTORY

Year	Firearms	Bow	Total
1990	166,600	11,106	177,706
1991	206,300	12,964	219,264
1992	230,064	13,004	243,068
1993	188,109	13,722	202,928
1994	180,008	13,818	193,826
1995	200,645	14,521	215,166
1996	142,979	14,338	157,317
1997	130,069	13,258	143,327
1998	146,548	12,306	158,854
1999	166,487	13,000	179,487

Minnesota Deer Facts
✓Estimated number of deer killed annually by vehicles: 15,000.
✓Deer killed by wolves: 40,000.
✓Deer killed by coyotes, bears, bobcats and fishers: 60,000 (mostly fawns).
✓Minnesota has several metropolitan areas with high deer numbers. Some regulated hunting is allowed. Methods not allowed include trap-and-transfer and birth control. Both methods have been deemed ineffective and, in some cases, harmful to deer.

MINNESOTA WHITETAIL RECORDS

•**Record harvest:** 243,068 (1992)
•**Record low harvest:** 1,279 (1971)
•**Bow-hunting record:** 14,521 (1995)
•**Gun-hunting record:** 230,064 (1992)

•**Season to remember:** 1972. After being forced to forego a season for the deer herd's sake, Minnesota gun-hunters return to the woods and enjoy a successful season.

Minnesota Offers Millions of Acres of Public Land

Finding a great place to hunt is often as challenging as the actual hunting itself. Minnesota hunters are fortunate that the search is not nearly as difficult as it is in many states where public land is rare. Texas, for example, has only 2 percent of its total area open to public hunting. Compare that to Minnesota, where 23 percent — more than 11 million acres — is publicly owned, and almost all of that land is open to hunting.

The most commonly hunted public lands in Minnesota are state wildlife management areas, state forests, national forests and federal waterfowl production areas.

WMAs: Minnesota's 1,034 WMAs are wetlands, uplands and woods owned and managed for wildlife by the Department of Natural Resources. The DNR's *Guide to Minnesota Wildlife Lands* shows the location of each WMA, and lists the larger areas that have resident managers and maps. Get this free map by writing or calling the DNR Information Center, 500 Lafayette Road, St. Paul, MN 55155. Phone: 651-296-6157.

State forests: The 3 million acres encompassed by Minnesota's 56 state forests hold good populations of whitetails. A free map showing the location of all state forests is available by writing: Minnesota Office of Tourism, 100 Metro Square, 121 Seventh Place East, St. Paul, MN 55101-2112.

For more information, visit the DNR's Web site at www.dnr.state.mn.us

MINNESOTA SNAPSHOT

Deer Population: 1,000,000, 7th in U.S.
Average Harvest: 170,830, 13th in U.S.
Gun-Hunters: 465,000
Bow-Hunters: 71,000
Forested Land: 16.7 million acres
Hunter Education: Required for persons born after Jan. 1, 1980. Bow-hunter education is not required.

Deer Research Gets a Boost from Helicopter Crew

In January 2000, wildlife researchers from the Minnesota Department of Natural Resources enlisted a helicopter crew for four days to capture deer in the various woodlands of southeastern Minnesota.

The crew's mission was to capture does. By the end of Day 4, the crew netted, radio-collared and released 58 deer. The purpose of the study is to determine how deer die from factors other than hunting in the farmland region.

When the radio-collared deer eventually die, information on how, when and where they died will be recorded. Over time, the DNR will have much more accurate data than is currently available on deer mortality. The DNR has accurate information on hunting mortality, but it can only make "best guesses" on how many farmland deer die each year from other factors, such as auto accidents, disease and predation.

When the study is complete, wildlife managers expect to obtain information that will allow them to more precisely manage local deer populations through antlerless permits.

Biologist Chris DePerno, study coordinator, said the importance of the information will far offset any short-term trauma the deer might have experienced during the trapping project. "Both the helicopter company, which does this kind of work on big-game animals all over the country, and our staff go to great lengths to minimize any stress the animals could potentially experience," DePerno said.

The netting and collaring process is quick and methodical. First, a deer is located in a wooded area, flushed out into the open, and the helicopter zooms in. A net is propelled over the deer, and a handler immediately jumps out to hobble and blindfold the deer. The deer is then transported a short distance to where DNR researchers stand waiting.

When the deer is lowered to the ground, five biologists go to work. They take the deer's temperature, record its sex and age, draw blood, administer an antibiotic and affix an ear tag and radio collar. The workers speak, but when they do, they whisper

Minnesota DNR

Researchers work quickly and quietly to obtain information from captured deer. Here, a Minnesota biologist prepares a radio collar for a mature doe.

to avoid scaring the deer. In a few short minutes, the deer is released.

The minimal stress allows the deer to regain complete strength in moments. The information that will be gathered, however, is invaluable to the future of deer management.

— *Tom Conroy*

Minnesota Avoided Disaster

Although Minnesota has nearly 1 million whitetails today, the population was so low in the Fall 1971 the Minnesota Department of Natural Resources was forced to cancel the deer season.

It was a difficult decision, but years of severe winters, habitat loss and an over-harvest of does had decimated the deer herd to the point that it would not be able to recover from a hunting season.

Today, thanks to better logging and wildlife-management practices, Minnesotans consistently harvest more than 170,000 deer annually.

MISSISSIPPI
Magnolia State
Harvest Ranking: #7

For more information, contact:

Department of Conservation
Southport Mall, Box 451
Jackson, MS 39205

(800) 546-4868   www.mdwfp.com

HISTORY OF MISSISSIPPI'S WHITETAIL HARVEST

Year	Firearm	Bow	Total
1971	580	39	619
1976	2,529	975	3,504
1980	184,163	17,437	201,600
1984	209,574	17,815	227,389
1988	236,012	28,744	264,756

TEN-YEAR HISTORY

Year	Firearm	Bow	Total
1990	218,347	29,982	249,572
1991	243,175	33,940	277,714
1992	260,093	40,886	300,980
1993	229,425	32,971	262,409
1994	262,342	47,345	309,687
1995	286,293	48,669	334,962
1996	289,399	44,574	333,973
1997	284,190	48,119	332,309
1998	256,692	38,406	295,098

The South's Finest for Deer?

Mississippi boasts more than 800,000 acres of prime habitat for public hunting in 38 Wildlife Refuges.

Scattered over the entire state, these areas offer unspoiled woodlands, fields and marshes. Each fall, hunters from across the country come to Mississippi to hunt one of the largest white-tail deer populations in North America. Some hunters combine deer hunting trips with trips for ducks and turkeys.

Mississippi contains eight soil regions that vary in fertility and use. Forests, which cover 55 percent of the state, include stands of hardwoods, pines, mixed pine/hardwoods and pine plantations.

MISSISSIPPI WHITETAIL RECORDS

•**Record harvest:** 334,962 (1995-96)
•**Record low harvest:** 619 (1971)
•**Bow-hunting record:** 48,669 (1995-96)
•**Gun-hunting record:** 289,399 (1996-97)

•**Season to remember:** 1980. Just nine years earlier, Mississippi had few whitetails — only 619 were killed by hunters. However, in 1980, hunters took more than 200,000.

FAQs About Deer Hunting in the Magnolia State

Mississippi is one of the 10 best deer hunting states in the country. However, many nonresident hunters have questions regarding the regulations. Here's some of the most commonly asked questions.

(For complete details, use the information at the top of this page to contact the Mississippi Department of Conservation.)

✓Is it legal to hunt deer with a scoped muzzleloader?

No. Telescopic sights are prohibited during the primitive weapons season. Non-magnifying devices and red-dot sights are permitted. Scopes are legal when using a muzzleloader during the regular firearms season.

✓Is it legal to hunt deer over bait?

No. It's illegal to hunt any wild animal with the aid of bait. Normal agricultural processes, such as ryegrass patches, are exempt from this law.

✓Is it legal to hunt deer from a boat?

No. The only game that can be legally hunted from a boat are squirrels and waterfowl. Even then, special regulations apply.

✓Are there rifle and ammunition restrictions for deer hunting?

There are none except for certain Wildlife Management Areas and Federal Refuges. Check with that area for specific restrictions.

MISSISSIPPI SNAPSHOT

Deer Population: 1,750,000, 3rd in U.S.

Average Harvest: 321,205, 7th in U.S.

Gun-Hunters: 231,095

Bow-Hunters: 55,578

Forested Land: 17 million acres

Hunter Education: Required for persons born after Jan. 1, 1972. Bow-hunter education is not required.

MISSOURI
Show-Me State
Harvest Ranking: #10

For more information, contact:

Department of Conservation
Box 180
Jefferson City, MO 65102-0180

(573) 751-4115
www.conservation.state.mo.us

HISTORY OF MISSOURI'S WHITETAIL HARVEST

Year	Firearm	Bow	Total
1944	583	NA	583
1954	7,648	22	7,670
1964	20,619	316	20,935
1974	29,262	1,437	30,699
1984	71,569	5,134	76,703

TEN-YEAR HISTORY

Year	Firearm	Bow	Total
1990	161,857	11,118	172,975
1991	149,112	14,096	164,384
1992	150,873	15,029	166,929
1993	156,704	14,696	172,120
1994	164,624	17,136	181,760
1995	187,406	20,077	207,483
1996	190,770	23,566	214,336
1997	196,283	20,915	217,198
1998	207,764	20,000	227,764
1999	193,720	23,414	217,134

Order Tags Over the Telephone

In 1999, the Missouri Department of Conservation initiated a telephone permit sale system that allows hunters to order permits by telephone. The system operates 24 hours a day year-round.

"There's no need to stand in line to buy most permits now," said Carter Campbell of the MDC. "The whole process takes about five minutes. If you don't want to buy all your permits for the year, you can wait until the day before you need each permit without having to make several trips to a permit vendor."

To order permits, call 800/392-4115. Payments can be made with Visa or Mastercard.

MISSOURI WHITETAIL RECORDS

•**Record harvest:** 227,764 (1998)
•**Record low harvest:** 583 (1944)
•**Bow-hunting record:** 23,566 (1996)
•**Gun-hunting record:** 207,764 (1998)

•**Season to remember:** 1997. The state cracks the top 10 for average annual harvest. This comes only a few years after having few white-tailed deer.

Deer Harvest Yields Bounty

Missouri hunters hunt whitetails for a variety of reasons, but those who are successful share in what can be an enjoyable feast of venison.

Missouri hunters killed 193,720 deer in 1999. Considering the average deer weighs 150 pounds on the hoof and yields 75 pounds of meat, the total yield per deer is impressive. Using those figures, Missouri hunters put about 15 million pounds of venison in their freezers. All of those steaks, roasts and hamburger are a valuable contribution to the food budgets of many families.

Venison is a good buy ecologically, too. Because deer live in forests and other undeveloped land, eating their meat saves the costs associated with clearing land, plowing and fertilizing, applying pesticides to crops and raising domestic livestock. Consuming deer close to home also saves the cost of transporting food.

Many hunters are generous . It is estimated that Missouri hunters donate more than 15 tons of venison to the state's "Share the Harvest" program each year. Participation in the program increased 43 percent in 1999, and it's likely to grow in the future.

For information on a Missouri-specific cookbook by Cy Littlebee, contact the Missouri Department of Conservation Nature Shop at the address at the top of this page.

— Jim Auckley

MISSOURI SNAPSHOT

Deer Population: 850,000, 12th in U.S.

Average Harvest: 216,783, 10th in U.S.

Gun-Hunters: 445,000

Bow-Hunters: 95,751

Forested Land: 14 million acres

Hunter Education: Required for persons born after Jan. 1, 1967. Bow-hunter education is not required.

MONTANA
Treasure State
Harvest Ranking: #24

For more information, contact:

Department of Fish and Wildlife
1420 E. Sixth Ave.
Helena, MT 59620

(900) 225-5397   www.fwp.mt.gov

HISTORY OF MONTANA'S ANNUAL DEER HARVEST

Year	Firearm	Bow	Total
1984	NA	NA	56,760
1985	NA	NA	43,019
1986	NA	NA	44,733
1987	NA	NA	40,675
1988	NA	NA	43,971
1989	NA	NA	44,261

TEN-YEAR HISTORY

Year	Firearm	Bow	Total
1990	NA	NA	49,419
1991	NA	NA	56,789
1992	58,565	2,067	60,632
1993	60,369	2,038	62,407
1994	67,577	1,857	69,434
1995	60,907	1,636	62,543
1996	76,487	1,800	78,287
1997	70,000	1,600	71,600
1998	84,445	1,500	85,945

*These totals include mule deer harvest figures.

Deer are Montana's Top Draw

Montana has a reputation as a top-notch elk hunting state, but its deer hunting opportunities are what lure most hunters.

Known for record-class whitetails and mule deer, Montana attracts more than 160,000 deer hunters annually. In fact, 70 percent of all big-game hunters in Montana hunt strictly for deer.

Including elk hunters and small-game hunters, Montana hunters spend more than $215 million each year to hunt the Treasure State. That's an average of $954 per hunter.

In 1996, Montana hunters spent more than $116 million on hunting equipment, according to a survey by the United States Fish & Wildlife Service.

MONTANA WHITETAIL RECORDS

- **Record harvest:** 85,945(1998)
- **Record low harvest:** 40,675 (1987)
- **Bow-hunting record:** 2,067 (1992)
- **Gun-hunting record:** 84,445 (1998)

- **Season to remember:** 1984. In the first year of monitored whitetail hunting, Montana hunters take 56,760 deer. The first-year harvest mark stood as a state record for seven years.

NBEF Lands in Montana

The National Bowhunter Education Foundation is headed into the new millennium with a clear vision for the future and a new team of administrators.

Earlier this year, the NBEF moved its headquarters from Loveland, Colo., to Townsend, Mont. The move was made shortly after Tim Pool replaced Robert Anderson as NBEF executive director. Anderson, who was executive director for nine years, left the organization in Fall 1998 to pursue other interests.

The move also created openings for two new administrators: Cheri Tarbget, office manager, and Crystal Booth, warehouse clerk.

Pool said the move to Montana helped the NBEF streamline its operation by reducing overhead and expanding future opportunities. The headquarters includes an adjoining 3,000-square-foot warehouse, an art gallery, and a public display area of vintage archery equipment, animal mounts and hides.

"The new world headquarters will provide opportunities for anyone to visit and increase their knowledge of archery and bow-hunting," Pool said.

NBEF's offices are open 9 a.m. to 9 p.m. (Mountain time) Monday through Friday. Its Archery Hotline (800-461-2728) is staffed during the same times. The hotline is open for anyone who needs information on archery, archery equipment and archery safety courses.

— *Daniel E. Schmidt*

MONTANA SNAPSHOT

Deer Population: 250,000, 25th in U.S.

Average Harvest: 73,562, 24th in U.S.

Gun-Hunters: 140,340

Bow-Hunters: 26,311

Forested Land: 22.5 million acres

Hunter Education: Required for persons 12-17. Bow-hunter education is required for all first-time bow-hunters.

NEBRASKA
Cornhusker State

Harvest Ranking: #31

For more information, contact:

Nebraska Game and Parks
Box 508
Bassett, NE 68714-0508

(402) 471-0641　　www.ngpc.state.ne.us

HISTORY OF NEBRASKA'S WHITETAIL HARVEST

Year	Firearm	Bow	Total
1945	2	0	2
1955	189	0	189
1965	6,853	338	7,191
1975	8,404	1,155	9,559
1985	20,930	2,593	23,523

TEN-YEAR HISTORY

Year	Firearms	Bow	Total
1990	21,973	2,716	24,689
1991	20,820	2,931	23,751
1992	20,125	3,141	23,266
1993	23,377	3,282	26,683
1994	26,050	3,830	29,880
1995	26,000	4,000	34,160
1996	30,400	4,500	34,560
1997	41,700	3,900	45,600
1998	40,000	3,000	43,000
1999	37,263	4,254	41,490

Bow-Hunter Education Required in Nebraska

Since Jan. 1, 1993, Nebraska has required that anyone born on or after Jan. 1, 1977 must complete a National Bowhunter Education Foundation course before they can buy an archery permit to hunt deer, antelope, elk, and turkeys.

Prospective bow-hunters must reach their 11th birthday in the year the class is taken. There is no maximum age limit. A minimum of 10 hours of instruction is required to complete the course. The NBEF course is recognized throughout the United States and Canada as the best in bow-hunter education instruction. The course includes eight chapters of information, including two chapters designed around in-the-field lessons.

NEBRASKA WHITETAIL RECORDS

•**Record harvest:** 45,600 (1997)
•**Record low harvest:** 0 (1949)
•**Bow-hunting record:** 4,500 (1996)
•**Gun-hunting record:** 41,700 (1997)

•**Season to remember:** 1945. Nebraska holds its first season of the modern era. Once gone from the state, whitetails are reintroduced and two lucky hunters take deer with firearms.

Food Plots Keep Deer Healthy, Benefit Other Game Species

Natural plant communities such as those of a marsh or hardwood forest provide some food for wildlife species. However, many species of wildlife are associated with and dependent upon the less natural environments of cultivated crops. In Nebraska, ring-necked pheasants and bobwhite quail rely on planted food plots for cover. However, many other species, including white-tailed deer, utilize cultivated crops for food.

Many of the cultivated agricultural crops grown in Nebraska such as corn, sorghum, wheat, oats, soybeans, sunflowers and alfalfa are highly preferred and nutritious. However, modern farming practices can critically diminish their value as wildlife food. A 160-acre field of solid wheat might not have many weeds or insects, or it might be integrated with other needed cover. A milo field bordered by grass and woody draws might look good in July, but with highly efficient harvesting equipment, or post-harvest grazing or plowing, it might provide no food in December.

Man can team up with nature, however, and plant cultivated crops or leave portions of agricultural crops unharvested specifically for wildlife. To benefit deer in winter, landowners should consider planting long-growing, late producing grain plants with sturdy stalks, such as corn and milo.

For more information on planting food plots in Nebraska, refer to the contact information at the top of this page.

NEBRASKA SNAPSHOT

Deer Population: 300,000, 23rd in U.S.

Average Harvest: 39,762, 31st in U.S.

Gun-Hunters: 69,000

Bow-Hunters: 14,213

Forested Land: 462,000 acres

Hunter Education: Required for persons born after Jan. 1, 1977. Bow-hunter education is required.

NEW HAMPSHIRE
Granite State
Harvest Ranking: #36

For more information, contact:
New Hampshire Fish & Game
Region 1, Rt. 2, Box 241
Lancaster, NH 03584
(603) 271-3422
www.wildlife.state.nh.us

HISTORY OF NEW HAMPSHIRE'S DEER HARVEST

Year	Firearm	Bow	Total
1922	1,896	NA	1,896
1932	1,687	NA	1,687
1942	4,844	NA	4,844
1952	6,932	NA	6,932
1962	7,917	5	7,922
1972	6,923	20	6,943
1982	4,577	97	4,674

TEN-YEAR HISTORY

Year	Firearm	Bow	Total
1990	6,466	482	7,872
1991	8,060	732	8,792
1992	9,013	1,202	10,215
1993	9,012	877	9,889
1994	7,478	901	8,379
1995	9,627	1,580	11,207
1996	8,901	1,462	10,363
1997	10,042	1,758	11,800
1998	8,236	1,549	9,785
1999	8,722	1,981	10,703

State Sets Safety Record

Just two injuries occurred during New Hampshire's 1999 hunting season, making it the safest on record.

"This is an excellent example of how safe hunting has become," said Randy Curtis, hunter education coordinator for the New Hampshire Fish and Game Department. "We've kept hunting incident records since 1960, and this past season set a new state record for safety."

The 1999 season was the seventh consecutive season without a fatality. It was the sixth consecutive year that the total number of incidents was less than 10.

NEW HAMPSHIRE DEER RECORDS

- **Record harvest:** 14,186 (1967)
- **Record low harvest:** 1,402 (1923)
- **Bow-hunting record:** 1,981 (1999)
- **Gun-hunting record:** 14,153 (1967)

- **Season to remember:** 1992. Bow-hunting takes a huge leap in New Hampshire as state archers crack the 1,000 deer harvest mark for the first time.

Managers Rebuild Herd

Deer densities in much of New Hampshire have been declining since 1997 when a state-wide early snowfall resulted in a doe harvest that exceeded the goal set by wildlife managers. That deadly snowfall was followed by two years of high doe harvests during the muzzle-loader season.

For 2000, the managers proposed a state-wide either-sex muzzleloading season, followed by eight days of bucks-only hunting. The proposals were aimed at reducing the overall doe kill proportionally and allocating the allowable doe harvest among archery, muzzle-loader and regular firearms seasons.

Based on adult buck harvest data — an index of the overall deer population — deer numbers are below the goals set in the 1997. The downward trend in most units began in the mid-1990s as more hunters participated in the muzzleloader season.

"This year's (2000) situation is an artifact of the method New Hampshire uses to manage its deer herd," said Wildlife Division Chief Steven J. Weber. "The influence weather might have on deer kill is amplified when short either-sex seasons are used. … By the time an individual season occurrence becomes a trend, the effect on the deer herd may be pronounced."

A better system for managing deer is through the use of doe permits. Permits are typically valid throughout the deer season, so the effects of weather tend to even themselves out from year to year, and a hunter's choice of method for taking deer does not influence the overall success rates.

NEW HAMPSHIRE SNAPSHOT

Deer Population: 80,000, 33rd in U.S.

Average Harvest: 10,772, 36th in U.S.

Gun-Hunters: 62,000

Bow-Hunters: 20,919

Forested Land: 4.98 million acres

Hunter Education: Required for persons born after 1971. Bow-hunter education is not required.

NEW JERSEY
Garden State
Harvest Ranking: #29

For more information, contact:

Division of Fish & Wildlife
Box 418
Port Republic, NJ 08241

(609) 748-2044   www.state.nj.us/dep/fgw

HISTORY OF NEW JERSEY'S WHITETAIL HARVEST

Year	Firearm	Bow	Total
1909	86	NA	86
1919	353	NA	353
1929	1,331	NA	1,331
1939	2,336	NA	2,336
1949	3,618	9	3,627
1959	9,612	1,230	10,842
1969	7,121	1,356	8,477
1979	13,843	2,263	16,106
1989	34,812	13,714	48,526

TEN-YEAR HISTORY

Year	Firearm	Bow	Total
1990	34,372	13,850	48,222
1991	29,936	15,480	45,416
1992	31,257	16,418	47,675
1993	32,936	17,006	49,942
1994	32,602	18,840	51,442
1995	39,176	20,593	59,769
1996	36,709	19,995	56,704
1997	39,290	20,261	59,551
1998	39,039	20,975	60,014
1999	50,266	25,132	75,398

Awards Program Going Strong

New Jersey's "Outstanding White-Tailed Deer Program" recognizes large deer. The program was initiated in 1964 and includes categories for heaviest deer and finest antler development. Antler categories are subdivided into typical and nontypical configurations. The minimum eligible score is 125 for typical bucks, while the minimum score is 135 for nontypical entries.

For more information, send a SASE to: Outstanding Deer Program, NJ Div. of Fish, Game & Wildlife, Box 400, Trenton, NJ 08625-0400.

NEW JERSEY WHITETAIL RECORDS

•**Record harvest:** 75,398 (1999)
•**Record low harvest:** 86 (1909)
•**Bow-hunting record:** 25,132 (1999)
•**Gun-hunting record:** 50,266 (1999)

•**Season to remember:** 1999. New Jersey deer hunters shatter six state harvest records. Muzzleloading hunters killed 10,920 deer, an increase of more than 10 percent from 1998.

New Jersey Documents Health of Whitetail Herd

Every year, data on age, sex, antler beam diameter, antler points and field-dressed weights of New Jersey whitetails are collected from a representative sample of deer harvested in the various hunting seasons. This information is used to assess the health of the deer herd and the quality of the habitat throughout the state. The majority of this information is collected at deer-check stations on the opening days of the six-day firearms season.

Condition parameters are used to group deer and deer range into the following four categories: below standard, standard, above standard and substantially above standard. In general, the physical condition of New Jersey's deer is considered to be above standard. Deer from the fertile agricultural regions are at the top of the condition scale, whereas deer from zones located in the outer coastal plain (the Pinelands) are generally in less-than-ideal condition. Outer coastal plain zones are characterized by sandy, acidic soils that support vegetation of low nutritional value.

The average antler beam diameter and the number of points a yearling buck produces are good indicators of the general quality of the deer range and deer condition. Age, genetics and nutrition contribute to antler development. Statewide, yearling bucks average 4.4 points; 2½-year-old bucks average 6.3 points; 3½-year-olds average 7.3 points and 4½-year-olds average 6.9 points.

NEW JERSEY SNAPSHOT

Deer Population: 178,600, 29th in U.S.

Average Harvest: 62,287, 29th in U.S.

Gun-Hunters: 87,200

Bow-Hunters: 47,400

Forested Land: 2 million acres

Hunter Education: Required for first-time hunters. Bow-hunter education is also required.

NEW YORK
Empire State
Harvest Ranking: #9

For more information, contact:

Department of Conservation
50 Wolf Road
Albany, NY 12233

(518) 457-4480
www.dec.state.ny.us/web site/outdoors

HISTORY OF NEW YORK'S WHITETAIL HARVEST

Year	Firearm	Bow	Total
1941	18,566	NA	18,566
1951	31,049	75	31,124
1961	57,723	731	58,454
1971	47,039	1,243	48,282
1981	161,593	3,792	165,385

TEN-YEAR HISTORY

Year	Firearm	Bow	Total
1990	175,544	14,664	190,208
1991	192,812	19,008	211,820
1992	212,988	18,947	231,935
1993	200,240	20,048	220,288
1994	146,255	19,428	165,683
1995	166,430	21,854	188,284
1996	180,082	22,683	202,765
1997	194,684	22,152	216,836
1998	205,074	25,684	230,758
1999	224,524	30,435	255,959

How to Determine Season Dates

Many hunters like to know deer season dates well in advance so they can schedule vacation and other plans accordingly. You can calculate these season dates in New York by using the following formulas:

Northern zone archery: Sept. 27 through the Friday immediately preceding the next to the last Saturday in October.

Gun season: Next to last Saturday in October through the first Sunday in December.

Southern zone archery: Oct. 15 through the day immediately preceding the opening of the firearms season, and five days immediately following close of the regular firearms season. **Regular season:** First Monday after Nov. 15 through first Tuesday after Dec. 7.

NEW YORK WHITETAIL RECORDS

- **Record harvest:** 255,959 (1999)
- **Record low harvest:** 15,136 (1945)
- **Bow-hunting record:** 30,435 (1999)
- **Gun-hunting record:** 224,524 (1999)

- **Season to remember:** 1948. Despite having successful seasons in the modern era (beginning in 1941), state hunters increase the average harvest (24,246) by more than 126 percent.

New York: A Paradise for Deer and Deer Hunters

Hunting is among the most popular forms of wildlife recreation in New York State. Nearly 700,000 New Yorkers and over 50,000 nonresidents hunt in the Empire State.

About 85 percent of New York is private property and that is where most hunting occurs. Most private property is posted, but many landowners will allow access if people ask permission. Hunters should ask permission on private lands whether or not it is posted. There are also abundant state lands, such as Wildlife Management Areas and some parks, where public hunting is allowed.

Hunting supports wildlife conservation programs, through license fees and taxes on firearms and ammunition, including the successful Federal Aid in Wildlife Restoration program. It also provides substantial economic benefits to New York retailers and the tourism industry. Regulated hunting helps manage some wildlife populations to prevent crop and environmental damage.

Hunting is closely regulated by the Department of Environmental Conservation.

Hunters must complete a mandatory hunter education course to obtain a hunting license in New York. Hunters following safety rules taught in those courses have made hunting one of the safest types of recreation.

NEW YORK SNAPSHOT

Deer Population: 975,000, 8th in U.S.

Average Harvest: 218,920, 9th in U.S.

Gun-Hunters: 640,629

Bow-Hunters: 169,185

Forested Land: 18.7 million acres

Hunter Education: Required for all first-time hunters. Bow-hunter education is also required.

NORTH CAROLINA
Tar Heel State

Harvest Ranking: #14

For more information, contact:
North Carolina Wildlife
512 N. Salisburg St.
Raleigh, NC 27604-1188
(919) 733-7275
www.state.nc.us/Wildlife

HISTORY OF NORTH CAROLINA'S DEER HARVEST

Year	Firearm	Bow	Total
1949	NA	NA	14,616
1955	NA	NA	20,114
1967	NA	NA	38,688
1977	28,182	679	28,861
1987	74,767	3,498	78,265

SEVEN-YEAR HISTORY

Year	Firearm	Bow	Total
1992	NA	NA	217,743
1993	107,669	8,727	118,638
1994	116,462	8,235	124,697
1995	202,000	14,000	216,000
1996	177,500	13,500	191,000
1997	181,000	14,000	195,000
1998	110,352	8,095	132,372

* North Carolina's harvest statistics are calculated from mail-survey estimates.

Hunter Dollars Saved Deer

In 1927, North Carolina passed a law that made it illegal for hunters to kill does. The period from 1930 to 1960 was characterized by the restoration and recovery of deer herds in the state.

The Federal Aid in Wildlife Restoration Act, passed by Congress in 1937 provided funding for deer restoration programs and implementing management and research activities by state wildlife agencies. Initial deer restoration efforts began in 1937, but they were soon halted by World War II. The state's major restoration efforts began in 1944. At this time the statewide population was estimated to be 50,000 animals. This combination of improved regulations and increased protection resulted in a boom in North Carolina's deer herd.

NORTH CAROLINA DEER RECORDS

- **Record harvest:** 217,743 (1992)
- **Record low harvest:** 14,616 (1949)
- **Bow-hunting record:** 14,000 (1995, 1997)
- **Gun-hunting record:** 202,000 (1995)

- **Season to remember:** 1976. After years of record-breaking harvests, North Carolina takes a plunge. Hunters register 23,184 deer —a 57 percent drop from the previous year's harvest.

Whitetails Have Storied History in North Carolina

White-tailed deer originated in North America approximately 15 to 20 million years ago. Today their range extends from northern South America through Mexico and the United States to southern Canada. In North Carolina, the early traveler Captain Arthur Barlowe reported in 1584 to Sir Walter Raleigh on the first landing on Roanoke Island that, "This island had many goodly woods, full of Deere, Conies (rabbits), Hares, and Fowl, even in the midst of summer, in incredible abundance."

Early colonists, like the American Indians that preceded them, recognized the value of whitetails because deer were one of their primary sources of meat. Deer also served these early settlers as sources of clothing, implements, ornaments and ceremonial items. Deer were so economically important that by the end of the colonial period, North Carolina had enacted closed season laws for their protection. Bounties were established on wolves and cougars because colonists believed deer and livestock needed protection.

North Carolina enacted its first game laws in 1738, and deer were prominently mentioned. These laws were needed because deer also had become an important medium of exchange. For example, traders on the French Broad River gave one quart of inferior grade brandy for two deer skins. In 1753, more than 30,000 deerskins were exported from the colony of North Carolina.

NORTH CAROLINA SNAPSHOT

Deer Population: 900,000, 10th in U.S.

Average Harvest: 171,814, 14th in U.S.

Gun-Hunters: 189,097

Bow-Hunters: Unknown

Forested Land: 19.3 million acres

Hunter Education: Required for first-time hunters. Bow-hunter education is not required.

NORTH DAKOTA
Peace Garden State
Harvest Ranking: #28

For more information, contact:
North Dakota Game Department
100 N. Bismarck Expy.
Bismarck, ND 58501
(701) 328-6300
www.state.nd.us/gnf

HISTORY OF NORTH DAKOTA'S DEER HARVEST

Year	Firearm	Bow	Total
1941	NA	NA	2,665
1952	NA	NA	27,024
1962	NA	NA	23,429
1972	NA	NA	25,424
1982	NA	NA	31,210

TEN-YEAR HISTORY

Year	Firearm	Bow	Total
1990	42,347	2,862	45,209
1991	46,980	3,299	50,279
1992	54,144	3,996	58,142
1993	58,246	4,006	62,252
1994	56,462	3,946	60,408
1995	66,686	4,078	70,764
1996	65,303	4,861	70,164
1997	52,971	2,894	55,865
1998	55,405	3,200	58,605
1999 (estimated)	55,833	3,200	59,033

Bow-Hunt Offers Options

North Dakota offers some opportunities for top-notch bow-hunting. Although the state has thousands of acres of public land, most hunters rely on guides and outfitters for prime hunting locations.

The state's archery season opens in early September. A nonresident license costs $155. Hunters must also purchase a habitat stamp for $8 and a hunting, fishing and furbearer certificate for $2. Two types of archery licenses are available:

✓Any-deer — allows a hunter to take a mule deer or white-tailed deer.

✓White-tailed deer. The number of licenses is unlimited.

NORTH DAKOTA DEER RECORDS

•**Record harvest:** 70,764 (1995)
•**Record low harvest:** 2,665 (1941)
•**Bow-hunting record:** 4,861 (1996)
•**Gun-hunting record:** 66,686 (1995)

•**Season to remember:** 1986. North Dakota hunters shatter the state-record harvest total of 43,074 by more than 28 percent. The new record harvest of 60,122 stands for more than seven years.

The Top 5 Areas for Western Whitetails?

Hunting call maker and video producer Will Primos and the Primos Pro Staff have taken several trophy-class bucks while hunting Western drainages.

Primos said he became hooked on Western whitetails during a drainage-area hunt in 1990. When asked to list some of the most productive areas, Primos offered these five hotspots:

1. The Arkansas River in eastern Colorado.
2. The Milk River in Montana.
3. The Republican River in northeastern Colorado.
4. The Yellowstone River in western Montana.
5. The Missouri River in western North Dakota.

Primos said it isn't difficult to find good whitetail habitat in the West because drainage areas are the only places where cover is thick enough to hold deer year-round.

"These drainages provide deer the necessary cover for rutting activity and for getting out of the wind in winter," Primos said. "As you approach these times of the year, drainages can be as hot as a firecracker."

Western drainages have been producing big bucks for decades, but were often overlooked because most visiting hunters were seeking elk, antelope and mule deer. However, many whitetail hunters now travel to the West because it's not uncommon to see 140- and 150-class bucks and better during a week-long hunt.

— *Daniel E. Schmidt*

NORTH DAKOTA SNAPSHOT

Deer Population: 243,750, 27th in U.S.
Average Harvest: 62,886, 28th in U.S.
Gun-Hunters: 101,632
Bow-Hunters: 11,200
Forested Land: 722,000 acres
Hunter Education: Required for all persons born after Dec. 31, 1961. Bow-hunter education is not required.

OHIO
Buckeye State
Harvest Ranking: #17

For more information, contact:

Division of Wildlife
1840 Belcher Drive
Columbus, OH 43224

(614) 265-6300   www.dnr.state.oh.us

HISTORY OF OHIO'S WHITETAIL HARVEST

Year	Firearm	Bow	Total
1952	NA	NA	450
1962	NA	NA	2,114
1972	NA	NA	5,074
1982	NA	NA	52,885

TEN-YEAR HISTORY

Year	Firearm	Bow	Total
1990	80,109	12,087	92,196
1991	94,342	17,109	111,451
1992	97,676	19,577	117,253
1993	104,540	23,160	138,752
1994	141,137	29,390	170,527
1995	149,413	27,299	179,543
1996	130,237	26,305	158,000
1997	125,504	26,639	153,159
1998	92,722	25,548	118,270
1999	97,466	29,304	126,770

Smokepole Hunters Succeed

In December 1998, Ohio hunters killed a near-record 12,272 deer during the state's five-day muzzleloading season. The total was a decline of six percent to the record harvest of 13,030 set in 1997.

Counties reporting the highest number of deer checked during the muzzleloading season included Athens, 514; Washington, 497; Muskingum, 439; Gallia, 408; Ross, 388; Meigs, 375; Jackson, 369; Lawrence, 331; Guernsey, 350; and Jefferson, 321.

Hunters were allowed to hunt a deer of either sex with muzzleloading rifles of .38 caliber or larger, muzzleloading shotguns using a single ball, crossbows and longbows. More than 90 percent of the deer were taken by hunters using muzzleloaders.

OHIO WHITETAIL RECORDS

•**Record harvest:** 179,543 (1995)
•**Record low harvest:** 406 (1965)
•**Bow-hunting record:** 29,390 (1994)
•**Gun-hunting record:** 149,413 (1995)

•**Season to remember:** 1995. This season marked the second-straight year deer hunters exceeded the 170,000 mark for overall harvest — remarkable numbers for such a small state.

Facts on Ohio Whitetails

About 10 percent of Ohio's deer herd is found across western and northwestern parts of the state. About 25 percent of the deer population is found in the northeast. The remainder of the deer herd is concentrated in southern, southeastern and east-central counties.

While some hunters are satisfied to take their one-deer limit each season, additional deer permits are typically available in Zone C deer unit and in urban zones. Hunters looking to fill two deer tags in Zone C or an urban zone can do so in a single day provided they place a temporary deer tag on the first deer shot before hunting a second deer.

Special management antlerless deer permits that were previously sold at $40 as a double tag in combination with a regular deer permit, can now be purchased separately for $20. Urban deer permits sell for $10 each and allow hunters to take an antlerless deer within any of five urban deer zones. During recent seasons, hunters could take as many as six deer in the urban zones.

Instructions for how and where deer can be taken are printed on each deer permit. Regulations are printed in the Ohio Division of Wildlife's hunting and trapping digest, a free publication available from hunting license outlets, wildlife officers and OHDW offices.

About 75 percent of Ohio's deer harvest occurs during the gun-hunting season. The bow-hunting season begins in October and runs into January. The state also holds a muzzleloading season in late December.

OHIO SNAPSHOT

Deer Population: 400,000, 19th in U.S.
Average Harvest: 147,148, 17th in U.S.
Gun-Hunters: 354,124
Bow-Hunters: 182,500
Forested Land: 7.9 million acres
Hunter Education: Required for first-time hunters. Bow-hunter education is not required.

OKLAHOMA
Sooner State
Harvest Ranking: #25

Fore more information, contact:

Department of Wildlife
1801 N. Lincoln, Box 53465
Oklahoma City, OK 73105

(405) 521-3851   www.state.ok.us

HISTORY OF OKLAHOMA'S DEER HARVEST

Year	Firearms	Bow	Total
1964	3,368	140	3,508
1968	5,490	260	5,750
1972	7,714	508	8,222
1976	10,544	1,004	11,548
1980	12,800	1,497	14,297
1984	20,041	2,568	23,609
1988	34,436	4,414	38,850

TEN-YEAR HISTORY

Year	Firearms	Bow	Total
1990	38,545	5,525	44,070
1991	40,197	7,079	47,286
1992	42,620	7,792	50,412
1993	49,978	7,853	57,831
1994	51,145	9,054	60,199
1995	56,770	9,116	65,886
1996	52,826	11,430	64,256
1997	60,277	10,930	71,207
1998	67,788	12,220	80,008
1999	70,957	11,749	82,706

Oklahoma has Big-Buck Book

The Cy Curtis Award, named in honor of the man most responsible for the restoration of white-tailed deer in Oklahoma, was established in 1975 to recognize trophy deer taken throughout the state. All deer legally taken during the 1972 season or thereafter are eligible for scoring. Official scoring of trophies can be done any time following a 60-day drying period. Measurements must be taken by an ODWC employee or by a measurer certified by Boone & Crockett or Pope & Young.

For more information on the program, call 405/521-2739.

OKLAHOMA WHITETAIL RECORDS

•**Record harvest:** 82,706 (1999)
•**Record low harvest:** 3,508 (1964)
•**Bow-hunting record:** 12,220 (1998)
•**Gun-hunting record:** 70,957 (1999)

•**Season to remember:** 1990. Bow-hunters begin making a large impact on harvest totals. Today, Oklahoma archers account for 14.6 percent of the state's overall deer harvest.

Whitetails Fuel Economy

For thousands of Oklahoma men and women, autumn's approach is the time of year that signals the start of something they've been dreaming about for months: deer season.

In the early 1900s, seeing a white-tailed deer in Oklahoma was a rare event. In fact, sometimes a sighting would make the local newspaper! In the 1950s and '60s, the Oklahoma Department of Wildlife Conservation began to re-introduce deer with the trap-and-transplant projects. Today, Oklahoma has deer in every county and a total whitetail population of nearly 400,000.

Deer hunting is the most popular hunting season in Oklahoma. According to the DWC, deer hunting generates more than $600 million annually for the state's economy. More than 86,000 bow-hunters, 98,000 muzzleloading hunters and 183,000 gun-hunters combined to push 1998 overall deer harvest past 80,000 for the first time.

Even with this high number of deer being taken each year, biologists are looking for ways to help control this state's increasing deer population even more. In some areas, the deer numbers have reached such high levels that depredation control is necessary.

White-tailed deer consume more than 600 types of plants and plant products in Oklahoma, but mast producing trees, browse and cool season forage are considered some of the most important assets of quality deer habitat.

OKLAHOMA SNAPSHOT

Deer Population: 375,000, 20th in U.S.

Average Harvest: 72,812, 25th in U.S.

Gun-Hunters: 198,833

Bow-Hunters: 89,545

Forested Land: 7.54 million acres

Hunter Education: Required for all persons born after Jan. 1, 1972. Bow-hunter education is not required.

OREGON
Beaver State
Harvest Ranking: #42

For more information, contact:
Department of Fish and Wildlife
400 Public Service Bldg.
Salem, OR 97310

(503) 872-5268   www.dfw.state.or.us

HISTORY OF OREGON'S WHITETAIL HARVEST

Year	Firearm	Bow	Total
1992	422	NA	422
1993	594	NA	594
1994	707	NA	707
1995	667	NA	667
1996	893	NA	893
1997	800	NA	800
1998	NA	NA	611

Editor's Note — *The 1992 season was the first time Oregon Department of Wildlife officials distinguished between mule deer and white-tailed deer in its harvest totals. White-tailed deer are rare in Oregon. In fact, the 1992 season was the first time the Oregon Dept. of Wildlife distinguished between mule deer and whitetails in harvest totals. The estimated deer population in the "Oregon Snapshot" on this page includes mostly mule deer and blacktails.*

Oregon Requires Mandatory Tagging and Registration

Oregon law requires deer hunters to immediately tag deer they kill. Hunters are also required to have the deer examined by an Oregon Division of Fish and Wildlife agent. The agent checks deer to gather valuable information about the condition of the herd. Data on age, weight, sex, condition and place of kill are useful in studying deer populations and setting seasons.

Oregon's deer herd consists primarily of mule deer and black-tailed deer. The state has a small unhuntable population of the Columbian white-tailed deer. Once endangered in Oregon, the Columbian whitetail is found in two sub-populations in the state: on the islands of the lower Columbia River and in the valleys of the Umpqua River Basin.

OREGON WHITETAIL RECORDS

- **Record harvest:** 893 (1996)
- **Record low harvest:** 422 (1992)
- **Bow-hunting record:** Not available
- **Gun-hunting record:** 893 (1996)

- **Season to remember:** 1992. For the first time ever, the Oregon Department of Wildlife distinguishes white-tailed deer in its harvest totals.

Oregon Offers Variety

Oregon has limited numbers of white-tailed deer, but it does offer some fantastic hunting for other deer species.

Shotgun deer hunting is available by permit only for White Clay Creek, Brandywine Creek, Fort DuPont and Fort Delaware State Parks. Hunters should also check out the Blackbird State Forest, Ennis Tract at Woodland Beach, Cedar Swamp, Ted Harvey-Logan Lane and Buckaloo Tracts and the Assawoman Wildlife Areas. Permits are be issued through a pre-season lottery except at the Assawoman State Wildlife Area, which uses a daily lottery. Elevated stands are provided for each permittee.

Deer hunting is also allowed at Lums Pond State Park by permit only. Applications for the preseason lottery are available in the annual *Hunting Guide* published by the Division of Fish and Wildlife.

Three hunt locations at Assawoman, Ted Harvey and Woodland Beach Wildlife Areas and three locations at Cedar Swamp Wildlife Area are available for nonambulatory handicapped hunters.

Deer hunting opportunities without a permit are also available at many other state wildlife areas. Contact the Oregon Dept. of Fish and Wildlife for more information.

Free maps for all state wildlife areas can be obtained from the Division of Fish and Wildlife Office, 89 Kings Highway, Dover, DE 19901. Regulations covering each area are included.

OREGON SNAPSHOT

Deer Population: 647,600, (Includes other species)

Average Harvest: 736, 42nd in U.S.

Gun-Hunters: 227,874

Bow-Hunters: 27,934

Forested Land: 27.99 million acres

Hunter Education: Required for persons under the age of 18. Bowhunter education is not required.

PENNSYLVANIA
Keystone State
Harvest Ranking: #5

For more information, contact:

Game Commission
2001 Elmerton Ave.
Harrisburg, PA 17110

(717) 787-4250
www.pgc.state.pa.us

HISTORY OF PENNSYLVANIA'S DEER HARVEST

Year	Firearm	Bow	Total
1949	130,723	0	130,723
1959	88,845	1,327	90,172
1969	113,515	3,169	116,684
1979	110,562	4,232	114,794
1989	184,856	10,951	195,807

TEN-YEAR HISTORY

Year	Firearm	Bow	Total
1990	396,529	19,032	415,561
1991	365,267	22,748	388,015
1992	335,439	25,785	361,224
1993	359,224	49,409	408,557
1994	345,184	49,897	395,081
1995	375,961	54,622	430,583
1996	294,674	56,323	350,997
1997	342,556	54,460	397,016
1998	317,774	59,715	377,489
1999	306,521	72,071	378,592

Facts and Stats About Pennsylvania Whitetails

In Pennsylvania, the average adult buck weighs about 140 pounds on the hoof and stands 32 to 34 inches at the shoulder. The average buck is about 70 inches long from the tip of his nose to the base of his tail. Does tend to average less in weight and body length than males of the same age from the same area.

Deer weights vary considerably, depending on age, sex, diet and the time of year the weight is checked. For example, breeding-age bucks might weigh 25 to 30 percent more in September than they do in December.

PENNSYLVANIA DEER RECORDS

- **Record harvest:** 430,583 (1995)
- **Record low harvest:** 40,925 (1954)
- **Bow-hunting record:** 72,071 (1999)
- **Gun-hunting record:** 396,529 (1990)

- **Season to remember:** 1990. Pennsylvania becomes the second state (Texas) to top the 400,000 mark for deer harvest. State hunters topped the mark again in 1993 and 1995.

Pennsylvania Firsts and Notes

Pennsylvania is not only one of the top whitetail-hunting states, it has a rich modern hunting tradition, dating back to the mid-1600s. What follows is a glimpse at what has transpired in the Keystone State since those early days.

Year   Event

1643 — Swedes established the first permanent settlement within the present limits of Pennsylvania and in 1643 fixed their capital at Tinicum, Bucks County.

1681 — Charter granted by King Charles II of England to William Penn to found "Penn's Woods," a colony in the New World that was later renamed Pennsylvania. Penn passed a law that required settlers to leave at least one acre of trees for every five acres they cleared.

1683 — Hunting is permitted on all lands in Penn's Woods.

1683 — A bounty of 10 shillings is offered to anyone killing a wolf.

1721 — Penn's Woods holds its first regulated deer season, running from July 1 to Jan. 1. Hunters are fined 20 shillings for shooting a deer out of season. Another rule is enacted, making it illegal to hunt on "improved lands" without the owner's permission.

1749 — The deer season runs from Aug. 1 to Dec. 1. The poaching fine increases to 40 shillings.

1840 — Deer are vanishing from the Pennsylvania landscape. Deer hunting is only allowed in three counties: Monroe, Pike and Wayne.

1845 — A law is passed making it illegal to hunt "unwounded deer" with dogs. The fine for breaking the law is $25.

1873 — A law is passed making it illegal to hunt on Sundays.

1887 — Theodore Roosevelt founds the Boone and Crockett Club.

1895 — First game commissioners appointed.

1897 — Salt licks are prohibited for deer hunting.

1905 — Buckshot banned for deer hunting; state begins stocking deer in depleted areas. Deer shipped in from Michigan.

1907 — A law is passed making it illegal to hunt does.

PENNSYLVANIA SNAPSHOT

Deer Population: 1,264,000, 6th in U.S.

Average Harvest: 386,935, 5th in U.S.

Gun-Hunters: 1,060,728

Bow-Hunters: 311,500

Forested Land: 16.97 million acres

Hunter Education: Required for all first-time hunters. Bow-hunter education is not required.

RHODE ISLAND
Ocean State

Harvest Ranking: # 41

For more information, contact:

Department of Environ. Mgmt.
83 Park St.
Providence, RI 02903

(401) 222-6822   www.state.ri.us/dem

HISTORY OF RHODE ISLAND'S DEER HARVEST

Year	Firearm	Bow	Total
1972	93	57	150
1976	61	50	111
1980	145	72	217
1984	139	109	248
1988	323	125	448
1989	466	169	635

TEN-YEAR HISTORY

Year	Firearm	Bow	Total
1990	701	238	943
1991	857	291	1,148
1992	1,052	417	1,474
1993	945	378	1,323
1994	1,157	252	1,409
1995	1,351	415	1,766
1996	1,689	474	2,163
1997	1,542	243	1,785
1998	1,222	310	1,532
1999 (preliminary)	1,618	390	2,008

Hunting Interest Increases

Over a five-year period ending in 1996, interest in hunting in Rhode Island increased significantly, according to a survey by the United States Fish & Wildlife Service.

In 1991, the state attracted about 16,000 hunters annually. Five years later, that number rose to 22,000, an increase of more than 37 percent. The increase included 4,000 more resident hunters and 2,000 more nonresidents. Days afield also increased. In 1991, hunters logged 351,000 days afield. That increased to 502,000 days in 1996.

Spending by state residents remained about the same. Residents spent nearly $24 million on hunting-related activities in Rhode Island.

RHODE ISLAND DEER RECORDS

•**Record harvest:** 2,163 (1996)
•**Record low harvest:** 102 (1973)
•**Bow-hunting record:** 474 (1996)
•**Gun-hunting record:** 1,689 (1996)

•**Season to remember:** 1996. Rhode Island deer hunters enjoy their finest season ever. Amazingly, the record year came just 23 years after the state had a minimal hunting season.

Rhode Island is Home to Avid Deer Hunters

Rhode Island might lack ample hunting opportunities, but that doesn't prevent its residents from enjoying their favorite pastime in other states.

Each year, about 22,000 Rhode Island residents travel out of their home state to hunt, according to data compiled by the United States Fish & Wildlife Service. These hunters spend 450,000 days afield on out-of-state hunts, or 20 days per person. These hunters also spend more than $26.6 million on out-of-state hunts, or $1,181 per person.

About 26,000 people hunt in Rhode Island each year. About 8,000 people hunt white-tailed deer. Surprisingly, 69 percent of those hunters hunt primarily on public land. Deer hunting is the second biggest draw in the state. Small-game hunting is most popular with 11,000 hunters, while waterfowl ranks third with 4,000 hunters.

According to the survey, hunters spent $8.4 million on hunting equipment in 1996, including $3.6 million on shotguns and rifles and $1.2 million on ammunition.

Fishing and wildlife watching are also popular in Rhode Island. Each year, more than 160,000 people fish in Rhode Island, while 318,000 take trips to observe wildlife. Fishing generates more than $136 million, while wildlife watching generates $124 million annually.

RHODE ISLAND SNAPSHOT

Deer Population: 10,000, 36th in U.S.

Average Harvest: 1,851, 41st in U.S.

Gun-Hunters: 4,727

Bow-Hunters: 2,780

Forested Land: 401,000 acres

Hunter Education: Required for first-time hunters. Bow-hunter education is not required.

SOUTH CAROLINA
Palmetto State

Harvest Ranking: #15

For more information, contact:

Department of Natural Resources
Box 167
Columbia, SC 29202

(803) 734-3888
www.water.dnr.state.sc.us

HISTORY OF SOUTH CAROLINA'S DEER HARVEST

Year	Firearm	Bow	Total
1972	NA	NA	18,894
1976	NA	NA	33,749
1980	NA	NA	44,698
1984	NA	NA	60,182
1988	NA	NA	98,182

TEN-YEAR HISTORY

Year	Firearm	Bow	Total
1990	NA	NA	125,171
1991	NA	NA	130,848
1992	NA	NA	126,839
1993	NA	NA	142,795
1994	NA	NA	138,964
1995	NA	NA	142,527
1996	NA	NA	155,654
1997	NA	NA	165,000
1998	NA	NA	150,000
1999 (est.)	205,000	15,000	220,000

Women Benefit from BOW

South Carolina's "Becoming an Outdoors-Woman" is a program that provides opportunities for women to learn nature-related outdoor skills using a hands-on approach in a relaxed, noncompetitive, non-intimidating atmosphere. The program focuses on hunting, fishing and other nature-related activities.

The workshops are held at Clemson University. For more information, contact: SCDNR, BOW Coordinator, Box 167, Columbia, SC 29202, or call 803/734-4072.

SOUTH CAROLINA DEER RECORDS

•**Record harvest:** 220,000 (1997)
•**Record low harvest:** 18,894 (1972)
•**Bow-hunting record:** 15,000 (1999)
•**Gun-hunting record:** 205,000 (1999)

•**Season to remember:** 1989. South Carolina white-tailed deer hunters top the century mark for deer harvest for the first time, taking 107,081 deer.

State Recognizes Bucks

The South Carolina white-tailed deer *Antler Records Program* was initiated in Spring 1974. Since then, more than 3,200 sets of antlers have been entered into the program. Initially, scoring sessions were few. However, since 1987, scoring sessions have been scheduled throughout the state with about 20 sessions occurring annually.

Each year, wildlife biologists and technicians score between 400 and 600 sets of antlers. Generally, only about 25 percent of them qualify for entry into the program.

The program's purpose is two-fold. First, because of the increased interest in deer hunting in North America, it's a means of recognizing outstanding white-tailed deer taken in South Carolina. Second, it provides management information that allows biologists to identify areas that produce big bucks. When particular areas stand out, it's important to recognize the underlying characteristics that produce outstanding animals.

As deer populations have grown, it has become apparent that herd density in a given area is related to the production of large deer.

The scoring system is the same one used by the Boone and Crockett and Pope and Young clubs. Minimum scores for the South Carolina Antler Records List are 125 typical points and 145 non-typical points. All antlers must undergo a minimum 60-day drying period before they can be officially measured.

For more information, contact Antler Records, Box 167, Columbia, SC 29202.

SOUTH CAROLINA SNAPSHOT

Deer Population: 1 million, 7th in U.S.

Average Harvest: 166,636, 15th in U.S.

Gun-Hunters: 181,000

Bow-Hunters: 44,900

Forested Land: 12.3 million acres

Hunter Education: Required for all persons born after June 30, 1979. Bow-hunter education is not required.

SOUTH DAKOTA
Coyote State

Harvest Ranking: #30

For more information, contact:

Division of Wildlife
Bldg. 445 E. Capital
Pierre, SD 57501

(605) 773-5842
www.state.sd.us/gfp/index.htm

HISTORY OF SOUTH DAKOTA'S DEER HARVEST

Year	Firearm	Bow	Total
1985	43,989	2,738	46,727
1986	40,798	1,953	42,751
1987	32,018	2,456	34,474
1988	33,265	2,327	35,592
1989	42,947	3,081	46,028

TEN-YEAR HISTORY

Year	Firearm	Bow	Total
1990	38,902	2,986	41,888
1991	39,915	2,686	42,601
1992	41,959	2,964	44,923
1993	45,431	2,963	48,394
1994	47,142	2,325	49,467
1995	39,868	2,625	42,493
1996	39,936	3,107	43,043
1997	47,503	2,440	49,943
1998	43,000	2,800	45,800
1999	42,500	2,700	45,200

Hunting is Big in South Dakota

Pheasant and waterfowl hunting dominates in South Dakota, but the state is also home to good white-tailed deer hunting.

Hunters have access to nearly 4.5 million acres of public land. In fact, many deer hunters plan combination trips — hunting deer for a few days and spending the rest of the time fishing or chasing game birds.

For more information on hunting opportunities in South Dakota, contact the Division of Wildlife listed at the top of this page.

SOUTH DAKOTA DEER RECORDS

•**Record harvest:** 49,943 (1997)
•**Record low harvest:** 34,474 (1987)
•**Bow-hunting record:** 3,107 (1996)
•**Gun-hunting record:** 47,503 (1997)

•**Season to remember:** 1989. After suffering the two worst seasons in its modern deer hunting history, South Dakota rebounds with a banner year. Hunters take 46,028 deer.

Program Targets Poachers

When two elk were poached in the Black Hills in 1984, sportsmen lobbied the South Dakota Wildlife Division to crack down on poachers. The department responded by creating the "Turn in Poachers" program.

TIP plays an important role in helping stop poachers by the mere fact anyone can report a violation.

Since TIP began, 4,710 investigations have led to 1,596 arrests. The arrests have resulted in almost $500,000 in penalties since 1985. The breakdown is as follows:

✓Fines: $303,686
✓Civil penalties: $246,750
✓Jail time: 19,089 days; 17,811 days were later suspended.
✓Community service hours: 1,904
✓Rewards paid: $52,730

Among the poachers was one man who killed six deer and left them to rot. The man was arrested after a citizen phoned the TIP hotline.

Individuals can report violations anonymously. They do not have to disclose any personal information. Rewards range from $100 for fish and small-game tips to $500 for big-game tips. Higher rewards are sometimes paid in extreme cases.

To report a poaching incident, call the South Dakota Conservation Officer, Game, Fish and Parks office at 800/592-5522, or visit the Web site:
www.state.sd.us/gfp/index.htm

— Bob Schurmans, TIPs coordinator

SOUTH DAKOTA SNAPSHOT

Deer Population: 222,000, 28th in U.S.

Average Harvest: 45,296, 30th in U.S.

Gun-Hunters: 102,000

Bow-Hunters: 9,500

Forested Land: 1.7 million acres

Hunter Education: Required for all persons under age 16. Bow-hunter education is required.

TENNESSEE
Volunteer State
Harvest Ranking: #18

For more information, contact:

Tennessee Wildlife Resources
Box 407
Nashville, TN 37204

(888) 814-8972
www.state.tn.us/twra

HISTORY OF TENNESSEE WHITETAIL HARVEST

Year	Firearm	Bow	Total
1970	8,258	372	8,630
1974	12,624	685	13,309
1978	22,819	2,465	25,284
1982	35,726	4,644	40,370
1986	69,044	8,578	77,622

TEN-YEAR HISTORY

Year	Firearm	Bow	Total
1990	97,172	16,061	113,233
1991	105,832	15,764	121,596
1992	106,168	19,728	125,896
1993	118,946	19,596	138,542
1994	111,598	20,832	132,430
1995	124,179	20,953	145,132
1996	127,129	22,501	149,630
1997	126,233	24,108	150,341
1998	135,261	20,414	155,675
1999	122,497	21,000	143,497

Tennessee's WMAs Have Strict Deer Hunting Rules

Tennessee has 87 Wildlife Management Areas and refuges. Varying in size from 88 to 625,000 acres, all WMAs are available to the public for hunting, but certain regulations apply, including:

✓Alcoholic beverages are prohibited.

✓Deer taken on buck-only hunts must have antlers a minimum of three inches in length.

✓Baiting is prohibited.

Other restrictions apply. Check with a Tennessee Wildlife Resources Agency office for complete details.

TENNESSEE DEER RECORDS

•**Record harvest:** 155,675 (1998)
•**Record low harvest:** 6,567 (1971)
•**Bow-hunting record:** 24,108 (1997)
•**Gun-hunting record:** 135,261 (1998)

•**Season to remember:** 1989. Tennessee deer hunters top the 100,000 deer-harvest mark. This feat is amazing considering the state had few deer just 40 years earlier.

Public Land is Plentiful

Tennessee hunters are fortunate to have access to almost 800,000 acres of public hunting land. These areas are a cooperative effort between the Tennessee Wildlife Resources Agency and the various landholding companies. Their goal is to to provide public hunting, with the landowner setting, collecting and administering permits and the TWRA enforcing the regulations governing these areas.

Spread across the state, these lands are as varied as Tennessee and are within a short distance for every Tennessee hunter. Although all wildlife species are not found on every tract, excellent deer hunting is available throughout the state. Deer hunters can also expect to see boars, black bears, wild turkeys, waterfowl, grouse, squirrels, quail and rabbits.

People who use these public hunting areas can help ensure that these properties remain open by assuming some personal responsibility. Never litter or abuse the land. Some areas have been closed because of complaints from neighboring landowners about "slob hunters." Public lands are important to hunters and non-hunters alike, so all users should work to maintain a good relationship with the owners.

Bowater Inc., Champion International Corp., Cumberland Forest, Graham, Packaging of America (formerly Tenneco), Tackett Creek, Westvaco and Willamette Industries have entered into the public hunting area program. For specific permit locations, request the *Public Hunting Lands* brochure from the address listed at the top of this page.

TENNESSEE SNAPSHOT

Deer Population: 883,000 , 11th in U.S.

Average Harvest: 148,855, 18th in U.S.

Gun-Hunters: 158,000

Bow-Hunters: 102,000

Forested Land: 13.6 million acres

Hunter Education: Required for persons born after Jan. 1, 1969. Bow-hunter education is not required.

TEXAS
Lone Star State

Harvest Ranking: #4

For more information, contact:

Texas Parks & Wildlife
4200 Smith School Road
Austin, TX 78744

(800) 895-4248   www.tpwd.state.tx.us

HISTORY OF TEXAS' ANNUAL WHITETAIL HARVEST

Year	Firearm	Bow	Total
1980	253,993	6,390	260,383
1984	361,811	11,451	373,262
1988	458,576	16,392	474,968

TEN-YEAR HISTORY

Year	Firearm	Bow	Total
1990	413,910	15,622	429,532
1991	459,083	14,964	474,047
1992	453,361	15,532	468,893
1993	438,934	13,575	452,509
1994	408,780	12,643	421,423
1995	436,975	13,518	450,593
1996	320,819	13,000	333,819
1997	357,832	13,500	371,332
1998	NA	NA	392,573

Harvest Streak Ends, but Texas is Still a Powerhouse

Despite declining deer harvest figures, Texas is still hard to beat when it comes to fast-paced deer hunting action.

The state's deer harvest was fairly constant during the nine-year period of 1987 to 1995, with a high of 504,953 in 1987 to a low of 421,423 in 1994. The average deer harvest for that period was 461,601. That's phenomenal, considering that few states consistently break the 400,000 mark.

In the 1990s, Texas broke the 400,000 plateau six times. Michigan (five) and Wisconsin (five) were the only states that posted comparable numbers.

The estimated harvest for 1996 was 333,819 — 28 percent less than the nine-year average.

The composition of the state's deer harvest varied from 40 percent to 46 percent antlerless deer over the 10-year period of 1988 to 1997.

Texas deer hunters are serious about their activity. In 1997, 613,279 hunters spent more than 4.7 million days hunting deer. That's an average of 7.6 days per hunter, a high number considering the state attracts far more gunhunters than bow-hunters.

The South Texas Plains attract about 100,000 hunters annually, and success rates are high. In 1996, 102,627 hunters in the region killed 62,273 deer for a success rate of 60 percent.

— *Daniel E. Schmidt*

Aggressive Marketing Helps Boost License Sales in Texas

Texas was one of several states that saw huge increases in the sale of hunting licenses in 1998, a trend that has continued into the new millennium.

In 1998, Texas sold 33,584 more licenses than the previous year, according to a study by the National Shooting Sports Foundation. Officials are unsure what caused the increase. It could be a combination of factors.

For example, among other programs, Texas has taken steps to better market its hunting licenses by increasing opportunities to hunt in wildlife management areas and state parks.

TEXAS DEER RECORDS

•Record harvest:	504,953 (1987)
•Record low harvest:	260,383 (1980)
•Bow-hunting record:	16,595 (1989)
•Gun-hunting record:	489,368 (1987)

•**Season to remember:** 1987. Texas sets the all-time record for most whitetails taken in a year. In fact, no state had ever — or has since — topped the 500,000 mark for overall harvest in a year.

TEXAS SNAPSHOT

Deer Population: 3,785,000, 1st in U.S.

Average Harvest: 393,948, 4th in U.S.

Gun-Hunters: 663,279

Bow-Hunters: 41,973

Forested Land: 19.2 million acres

Hunter Education: Required for all persons born on or after Sept. 1, 1979. Bow-hunter education is not required.

VERMONT
Green Mountain State
Harvest Ranking: #34

For more information, contact:
Vermont Dept. of Fish and Wildlife
103 S. Main St.
Waterbury, VT 05671

(802) 241-3701   www.anr.state.vt.us

HISTORY OF VERMONT'S WHITETAIL HARVEST

Year	Firearm	Bow	Total
1899	90	NA	90
1909	4,597	NA	4,597
1919	4,092	NA	4,092
1929	1,438	NA	1,438
1939	2,589	NA	2,589
1949	5,983	NA	5,983
1959	11,268	232	11,500
1969	20,753	1,547	22,300
1979	14,936	1,587	16,523
1989	8,030	1,202	9,232

TEN-YEAR HISTORY

Year	Firearm	Bow	Total
1990	7,930	1,053	8,983
1991	9,993	1,591	11,584
1992	11,215	3,245	14,460
1993	10,043	2,999	13,333
1994	9,177	3,276	12,903
1995	12,769	5,046	18,116
1996	13,632	4,990	18,622
1997	14,836	5,000	19,836
1998	12,000	4,562	16,562
1999	14,487	5,296	19,783

Bow-Hunting Law Simplified

An improvement in Vermont's bow-hunting law simplifies the wording describing how deer can be taken during the October and December archery season. Under the new law, there are no sequential order requirements about how hunters use their first or second archery tags. With the two permits, hunters are allowed to kill one buck and one doe.

For details, obtain a copy of the state's hunting regulations from the Vermont Department of Fish and Wildlife. Contact information is listed at the top of this page.

VERMONT DEER RECORDS

•**Record harvest:** 25,932 (1980)
•**Record low harvest:** 90 (1899)
•**Bow-hunting record:** 5,296 (1999)
•**Gun-hunting record:** 24,675 (1980)

•**Season to remember:** 1980. Vermont hunters have best season ever, taking 25,932 deer.

The Ultimate Deer Hunter's Quiz
Part 8, State Records & Trends

78. Which of the following states does not require the use of blaze orange?
A. Michigan
B. Missouri
C. New York

79. Which state shows steady increases in the number of youth hunters?
A. Wisconsin
B. Missouri
C. Tennessee

80. In which state have car/deer accidents declined?
A. Delaware
B. Maryland
C. Rhode Island
D. Michigan

81. True or false: Most states do not allow hunters to blood-trail deer with dogs.

82. True or false: Baiting is legal for deer hunting in a majority of states.

Continued on Page 166.

VERMONT SNAPSHOT

Deer Population: 110,000 , 31st in U.S.
Average Harvest: 18,584, 34th in U.S.
Gun-Hunters: 82,450
Bow-Hunters: 30,187
Forested Land: 4.5 million acres
Hunter Education: Required for first-time hunters. Bow-hunter education required in 2001.

VIRGINIA
Old Dominion

Harvest Ranking: #12

For more information, contact:

Department of Game & Fisheries
Box 11104
Richmond, VA 23230

(804) 367-1000   www.dgif.state.va.us

HISTORY OF VIRGINIA'S WHITETAIL HARVEST

Year	Firearms	Bow	Total
1935	NA	NA	1,158
1945	NA	NA	4,545
1955	NA	NA	14,227
1965	NA	NA	27,983
1975	NA	NA	63,443
1985	NA	NA	101,425

TEN-YEAR HISTORY

Year	Firearms	Bow	Total
1990	NA	NA	160,411
1991	NA	NA	179,344
1992	NA	NA	200,446
1993	185,222	15,900	201,122
1994	190,673	18,700	209,373
1995	202,277	16,199	218,476
1996	193,134	15,974	209,108
1997	182,881	15,074	197,995
1998	164,449	14,578	179,027
1999	172,854	15,210	189,096

Editor's note — *Virginia has one of the most popular "Hunters for the Hungry" programs in the nation. For more information, contact Hunters for the Hungry, Box 304, Dept. DDH, Big Island, VA 24526.*

VIRGINIA DEER RECORDS

•**Record harvest:** 218,476 (1995)
•**Record low harvest:** 1,158 (1935)
•**Bow-hunting record:** 18,700 (1994)
•**Gun-hunting record:** 202,277 (1995)

•**Season to remember:** 1992. Virginia bow-
and gun-hunters combine to harvest more
than 200,000 whitetails for the first time.

VIRGINIA SNAPSHOT

Deer Population: 960,000 , 9th in U.S.

Average Harvest: 198,740, 12th in U.S.

Gun-Hunters: 255,900

Bow-Hunters: 60,240

Forested Land: 15.8 million acres

Hunter Education: Required for all
persons born after June 30, 1979. Bow-
hunter education is not required.

The Ultimate Deer Hunter's Quiz
Part 8, State Records & Trends

83. Which state does not require any
form of hunter education?
A. Arkansas
B. Louisiana
C. New Mexico
D. None of the above

84. Which type of oak forests are
most common in Oklahoma?
A. Post/blackjack
B. Pin
C. Live

85. What disease wreaked havoc on
the Virginia white-tailed deer herd?
A. Tuberculosis
B. Lyme
C. Epizootic Hemorrhagic

86. What drove deer to the brink of
extinction in many states at the turn of
the 20th century?
A. Tuberculosis
B. Hunting
C. Commercial/subsistence hunting
D. Wolves/coyotes

87. Which famous hunter bagged his
first deer when he was 12?
A. Larry Koller
B. Siguard Olson
C. Aldo Leopold

88. True or false: Only five states do
not offer muzzleloading seasons.

*This concludes the quiz for this chapter.
The quiz continues on Page 175.
Answers begin on Page 194.*

WASHINGTON
Evergreen State
Harvest Ranking: #38

For more information, contact:

Department of Fish & Wildlife
600 Capitol Way N.
Olympia, WA 98501

(360) 902-2200   www.wa.gov/wdfw

HISTORY OF WASHINGTON'S ANNUAL DEER HARVEST

Year	Firearms	Bow	Total
1974	49,792	808	50,600
1984	38,416	1,790	40,206

TEN-YEAR HISTORY

Year	Firearms	Bow	Total
1990	41,549	3,606	45,155
1991	52,745	4,367	57,112
1992	50,441	4,856	55,297
1993	31,892	3,789	35,681
1994	42,054	4,948	47,002
1995	34,469	3,296	37,765
1996	35,970	3,472	39,442
1997	29,775	2,366	32,141
1998	27,578	2,675	30,253

Editor's note — *Washington is one of several states that has limited numbers of white-tailed deer. The above harvest figures are for all species, including blacktails, whitetails and mule deer.*

Whitetails and Mule Deer Thrive in Evergreen State

Both mule deer and whitetail populations in southeast Washington are at high levels except for the very southern and mountainous part of the Blue Mountains. In fact, since 1992, whitetail populations have steadily increased in the Spokane area.

In 1991, the state had a record whitetail harvest of about 18,000. Since then, the harvest has leveled off at about 10,000 deer annually. That's an excellent figure considering most deer hunters target blacktails and mule deer.

WASHINGTON DEER RECORDS

•**Record harvest:** 66,000 (1979)
•**Record low harvest:** 30,253 (1998)
•**Bow-hunting record:** 4,948 (1994)
•**Gun-hunting record:** 64,888 (1979)

•**Season to remember:** 1979. Washington deer hunters harvest more than 60,000 for the third-straight year and set an all-time state record for deer harvest with firearms.

Hemorrhagic Disease a Concern in Washington

Epizootic Hemorrhagic Disease periodically affects whitetails in Washington, but the disease is not considered to be widespread.

EHD occurs in the driest part of the year when conditions are just right for biting gnats, the carriers of the disease.

Here are some facts about EHD:

✓The disease is not contagious from one animal to another, and it is not transferable to humans. It comes from a virus carried by biting gnats that live in or near water. It is transmitted to deer that congregate at watering holes during warm, dry weather.

✓The disease is usually cut short with cold, wet weather, or the first hard frost, which kills the gnats.

✓Deer with EHD might appear lethargic, disoriented, lame, or unresponsive to humans. As the disease progresses, a deer might have bloody discharge from the nose, lesions on the mouth, and swollen, blue tongues.

Since hunting season usually doesn't open until well after the first killing frost, hunters usually don't see infected animals. Hunters should avoid shooting and consuming deer that show any EHD symptoms, even though the disease cannot be transmitted to humans.

Major outbreaks have occurred from mid-August to mid-October in the northeast counties of Spokane, Stevens, Ferry and Okanogan (1999), and in the southeast counties along the Snake River (1998).
— *Washington Dept. of Fish & Wildlife*

WASHINGTON SNAPSHOT

Deer Population: 380,000 (includes other species)

Average Harvest: 10,126, 38th in U.S.

Gun-Hunters: 155,750

Bow-Hunters: 19,250

Forested Land: 20.5 million acres

Hunter Education: Required for all persons born after Jan. 1, 1972. Bow-hunter education is not required.

WEST VIRGINIA
Mountain State

Harvest Ranking: #11

For more information, contact:
W. Va. Wildlife Resources
State Capital, Bldg. 3
Charleston, WV 25305

(304) 367-2720   www.wvwildlife.com

HISTORY OF WEST VIRGINIA'S WHITETAIL HARVEST

Year	Firearms	Bow	Total
1939	897	NA	897
1949	6,466	6	6,472
1959	19,588	90	19,678
1969	13,620	470	14,090
1979	49,625	5,461	55,086
1989	129,350	16,217	145,567

TEN-YEAR HISTORY

Year	Firearms	Bow	Total
1990	148,233	21,715	169,948
1991	149,536	27,448	176,984
1992	177,265	28,659	205,924
1993	142,589	26,425	169,014
1994	120,954	24,448	145,402
1995	173,553	28,072	201,625
1996	157,275	29,637	186,912
1997	200,859	34,446	235,305
1998	166,877	28,933	195,810
1999	197,037	32,971	230,008

Deer Hunting's Roots Run Deep

Hunting in West Virginia is a time-honored tradition in which the majority of families have at least one member who participates on a regular basis. Each year more than 145,000 hunters take to West Virginia's woods in search of white-tailed deer. With this pursuit, millions of dollars are directed toward the state's economy, creating more than 5,000 jobs. In 1996, West Virginia's hunting expenditures related for food, lodging, transportation and equipment brought in more than $271 million to the state's economy.

WEST VIRGINIA DEER RECORDS

•**Record harvest:** 235,305 (1997)
•**Record low harvest:** 897 (1939)
•**Bow-hunting record:** 34,446 (1997)
•**Gun-hunting record:** 200,859 (1997)

•**Season to remember:** 1982. Bow-hunters shatter the West Virginia harvest record by taking 13,454 deer — 49.4 percent more than the previous record of 9,003 deer.

Deer Fuel State's Economy

Thanks to a bulging white-tailed deer population, West Virginia is one of the top hunting destinations in the United States.

West Virginia not only ranks in the Top 15 for deer harvest, it attracts nearly 150,000 deer hunters annually. The state's herd, estimated at 800,000 animals, ranks 14th in the United States.

General hunting statistics compiled by the United States Fish & Wildlife Service show how important hunting is to the state's economy. Each year, about 23,000 West Virginia residents travel out of their home state to hunt. These hunters spend more than 5.6 million days afield on out-of-state hunts, or 22 days per person. These hunters also spend more than $234 million on out-of-state hunts, or $912 per person.

In 1996, hunters spent $240 million in West Virginia. Trip-related expenses such as food and lodging, transportation and equipment rental fees cots hunters $68 million.

About 369,000 people hunt in West Virginia each year, with 150,000 of those hunting white-tailed deer. Unfortunately, public-land opportunities are scarce. According to the survey, two-thirds of all hunters hunt exclusively on private land. Only 19 percent of the hunters said they hunted public land at some point in 1996.

WEST VIRGINIA SNAPSHOT

Deer Population: 800,000, 14th in U.S.
Average Harvest: 209,932, 11th in U.S.
Gun-Hunters: 145,082
Bow-Hunters: Unknown
Forested Land: 12.1 million acres
Hunter Education: Required for all persons born after Jan. 1, 1975. Bow-hunter education is not required.

WISCONSIN
Badger State
Harvest Ranking: #1

For more information, contact:

Department of Natural Resources
101 S. Webster St.
Madison, WI 53707

(608) 266-2621   http://www.dnr.state.wi.us

HISTORY OF WISCONSIN'S WHITETAIL HARVEST

Year	Firearms	Bow	Total
1897	2,500	NA	2,500
1907	4,750	NA	4,750
1917	18,000	NA	18,000
1928	17,000	NA	17,000
1937	14,835	0	14,835
1947	53,520	368	53,888
1957	68,138	NA	68,138
1967	128,527	7,592	136,119
1977	131,910	16,790	148,700
1987	250,530	42,651	293,181

TEN-YEAR HISTORY

Year	Firearms	Bow	Total
1990	350,040	49,291	399,331
1991	352,328	67,005	419,333
1992	288,906	60,479	349,385
1993	217,584	53,008	270,592
1994	307,629	66,254	373,883
1995	397,942	69,158	467,100
1996	388,211	72,313	460,524
1997	292,513	66,792	359,305
1998	332,314	75,301	407,615
1999	402,179	91,937	494,116

That's a lot of Grilled Roadkill

In 1999, 44,897 deer were killed by auto-mobiles in Wisconsin. Of those, 13,419 were tagged and taken home by motorists. Conservatively, that represents about a half-million pounds of boneless venison that was not left to rot on the side of the road.

The top counties for roadkills were Waupaca, 1,909; Dane, 1,747; and Columbia, 1,512.

WISCONSIN DEER RECORDS

- **Record harvest:** 494,116 (1999)
- **Record low harvest:** 2,500 (1897)
- **Bow-hunting record:** 91,937 (1999)
- **Gun-hunting record:** 402,179 (1999)

- **Season to remember:** 1999. Wisconsin hunters shatter three records, including overall, gun-hunting and bow-hunting harvests. The overall harvest is the largest of the 1990s and second only to the 504,953 mark set in Texas in 1987.

How to Feed Whitetails

Winter feeding does little to help a regional deer herd survive winter because most of the herd — as much as 70 percent — is inaccessible to feeding. However, it can benefit individual deer if done properly. If you intend to feed, do it right or don't do it at all. Careful consideration should be given to feeding efforts prior to implementation. If done improperly, you can do more harm than good.

✓Try to feed near sheltered areas with conifers that are out of the wind.

✓Feed away from areas of high human use, dogs, cars and snowmobiles.

✓Supply feed at a rate of two pounds per deer per day.

✓Resupply feeders when 90 percent of food is eaten.

✓Put food in several places to avoid competition among deer for food.

✓Use trough or box-type feeders placed on the ground to avoid fecal contamination.

Keep feeding deer until the snow melts in spring. Be aware that feeding can attract high numbers of deer, and can result in high expenses. Feeding deer in or near your yard can attract and concentrate deer where they might browse on ornamental trees and shrubs.

Biologists recommend the use of premixed deer feeds. These feeds consist of varying amounts of corn, alfalfa, oats, soybeans, molasses, and several vitamins and minerals.

Do not feed deer a pure corn diet. It can cause high acidity in the rumen which kills microorganisms necessary for digestion.

WISCONSIN SNAPSHOT

Deer Population: 1.3 million, 5th in U.S.

Average Harvest: 437,732, 1st in U.S.

Gun-Hunters: 693,300

Bow-Hunters: 231,675

Forested Land: 15.5 million acres

Hunter Education: Required for all persons born after Jan. 1, 1973. Bow-hunter education is not required.

WYOMING
Equality State

Harvest Rating: (not ranked)

For more information, contact:
Wyoming Game and Fish
5400 Bishop Blvd.
Cheyenne, WY 82002

(900) 884-4263   www.gf.state.wy.us

HISTORY OF WYOMING'S DEER HARVEST

Year	Firearm	Bow	Total
1971	7,806	NA	7,806
1981	7,286	NA	7,286
1989	8,903	197	9,100

TEN-YEAR HISTORY

Year	Firearm	Bow	Total
1990	9,535	147	9,632
1991	10,240	139	10,379
1992	14,533	216	14,749
1993	12,623	1,322	13,945
1994	8,249	228	8,477
1995	6,959	175	7,134
1996	6,857	232	7,089
1997	6,889	200	7,089
1998	6,842	194	7,036
1999	6,883	196	7,079

Wyoming Harbors Whitetails

Wyoming is a first-class mule deer hunting state. Each year, hunters harvest nearly 30,000 mulies, and some of them are record-class bucks. Wyoming, however, also harbors good numbers of whitetails in some areas.

The state's whitetail harvest accounts for 20 percent of the overall harvest. Gun-hunters account for 96 percent of the harvest, while bow-hunters account for 2.8 percent, and muzzleloading hunters, 1.2 percent.

Whitetail-hunter success rates are high in Wyoming. Nonresidents enjoy a 45.8 percent success rate, while residents average a 30 percent rate. Nonresidents, no doubt, have a higher success rate because they rely on guides and outfitters. In 1998, it took a nonresident an average of 6.5 days to bag a whitetail. A successful resident hunter took an average of 12.5 days to fill his tag.

WYOMING DEER RECORDS

•**Record harvest:** 14,749 (1992)
•**Record low harvest:** 4,306 (1972)
•**Bow-hunting record:** 1,322 (1993)
•**Gun-hunting record:** 14,533 (1992)

•**Season to remember:** 1974. Wyoming whitetail hunters crack the 10,000 whitetail deer harvest mark for the first time.

Hunter Tags 3-Beam Buck

Bob Walker has killed several large white-tailed bucks, but none was as unusual as the one he took in 1998.

While hunting in northeastern Wyoming with guide Pat Watkins, Walker tagged a bizarre 10-pointer that sported three developed main beams.

The buck's rack consists of a symmetrical 8-point rack and an "extra" main beam with its own brow tine. The third beam grew out of the same pedicle as the right main beam, but it sprouted below it and grew parallel with the main beam.

As a result, the rack looked like the antlers from two bucks when profiled.

"We spotted this buck about 300 yards away as he was chasing a doe up the side of a hill," Walker said. "As I peeked over the top, all I saw were antlers sticking out of the bushes about 75 yards away.

"I told the guide there were two bucks right in front of us."

As luck would have it, the buck turned its head the opposite way, and Walker got a glimpse of the 4-point left antler. Thinking the "other" buck had bedded down, Walker placed the cross-hairs on the shoulder of the standing buck. One shot from his 7mm-08 dropped the deer in its tracks.

— Daniel E. Schmidt

WYOMING SNAPSHOT

Deer Population: 25,000 (includes mule deer)

Average Harvest: 7,085 (not ranked)

Gun-Hunters: 18,240

Bow-Hunters: 6,920

Forested Land: 9.97 million acres

Hunter Education: Required for all persons born after Jan. 1, 1966. Bow-hunter education is not required.

Aaron Phelan found these two dead bucks floating in an Ontario lake. The bucks' massive antlers were locked, and they likely drowned after falling through ice the previous fall.

Fishing Trip Nets Two Monster White-tailed Bucks

Day 1 of a fishing vacation in Canada turned up more than fish for the Al Phelan family of Madison, Wis.

Phelan and his son Aaron were fishing on Lake of the Woods in Ontario when Aaron noticed what looked like a dead moose floating about 60 yards away. Closer inspection revealed the partially decomposed bodies of two massive white-tailed bucks with their antlers locked together.

The bucks were found more than 100 yards from shore. Phelan said he believes the fight occurred during the previous fall's rut. The lake was frozen earlier than normal that year, and Phelan said it appeared as though the locked bucks, desperate to free themselves, pushed each other onto the thin ice. He believes the ice collapsed from the weight of the two massive animals.

"Even if one went through, I don't think the other would've been able to pull it out," he said.

It took the Phelans 45 minutes to get the deer unlocked after severing the heads. Aaron rough-scored the larger head, which also had a broken jaw, at 134 inches. "He must've been the loser of the fight," Al said.

Phelan aged the jawbones at 3½ and 4½ years old. Aaron, an avid antler collector, added the skulls to his collection, and he and his father plan to have the heads mounted with the antlers locked together.

— *Amber Paluch*

CHAPTER 9
MEAT PROCESSING INSIGHTS

How Much Meat is on One Deer?

The image is forever burned in my mind. My buddy and I stood side by side at a deer registration station waiting for a biologist to inspect our bucks.

We were just two of several hundred successful hunters who had participated in a controlled hunt at a Wisconsin military reserve. Deer were plentiful, and we had both tagged bucks on the second day of the hunt.

The biologist shot me a congratulatory smile as he lifted my buck by the legs and placed it on a pallet. The pallet was centered on a butcher's scale. I turned to my buddy and proclaimed my field-dressed 8-pointer would weigh at least 175 pounds.

After adjusting the scale's calibrator a few times, the biologist turned to his intern and read the deer's field-dressed weight aloud.

"One hundred and twelve."

My buddy and I looked at each other in disbelief, and we heard chuckles from hunters standing behind us. The biologist then loaded my buddy's 6-pointer and readjusted the scale.

"One hundred and eight."

We dragged our deer off to the side and watched as the next hunter prepared to load his mature doe onto the scale.

"I figure she's at least 140," the hunter said confidently.

The biologist had the calculation within a minute.

"Ninety-one."

I took the biology lesson home to my dad, who had butchered deer and farm animals since he was a boy in the 1940s. He sized up the buck as we hoisted it to the rafters.

"About one-fifteen," he said. "Maybe one-twenty."

For me, it was a lesson in humility, times two.

Field-Dressed Fallacies

I've learned a lot of things about deer and deer hunting since that day in 1989. It's a fact across deer country that more antlerless deer have to be killed each year to keep herds in check. However, how many of us brag about shooting a doe or, heaven forbid, a fawn? We should take pride in any deer we bring home, but hunters too often try to gloss over the facts by exaggerating the vital statistics. As we often joke about at the office, who has ever killed a small doe or a buck fawn? It's always a "big doe" or a "nubbin buck."

The typical Northern fawn, which includes "button bucks," weighs about 55 to 75 pounds field dressed, while a healthy doe fawn weighs 45 to 65 pounds field dressed. Southern fawns weigh less — sometimes less than 30 pounds field dressed.

DANIEL E. SCHMIDT

How Much Does it Weigh?

Mature white-tailed deer can be heavy, but much of their weight is distributed in non-meat areas. Here are some example of how weight is distributed in Northern deer. (Live weights in parenthesis)

✓ **Hide Factor**
Fawn: (100 pounds) 6.7 percent
Adult doe (140 pounds): 7.9 percent
Adult buck (160 pounds): 8.7 percent
Bucks more than 160 pounds: 9 percent

✓ **Bone Factor**
Fawn: (100 pounds) 13.8 percent
Adult doe: (140 pounds) 13 percent
Adult buck: (160 pounds) 12.4 percent
Bucks more than 160 pounds: 11.7 percent

✓ **Blood Factor**
Fawn: (100 pounds) 6 percent
Doe: (140 pounds) 5 percent
Buck: (160 pounds) 5 percent
Bucks more than 160 pounds: 5 percent

Using this guide as an example, a 180-pound buck would have 16.2 pounds of hide, 21.06 pounds of bones and 9 pounds of blood. Unfortunately, it's difficult to estimate the live weight of a deer if it has been field-dressed because the weight of a deer's innards varies depending on its health and diet.
— *Pennsylvania State University, Department of Animal Science and the Pennsylvania Game Commission, 1968.*

does weigh 45 to 65 pounds.

With these facts in mind, how many times has someone told you they killed a big doe? "Yep, she field dressed at about 150 pounds," they say. "Big dry doe. Got 100 pounds of meat off that deer."

Not likely.

In fact, on average, the healthiest mature Northern does weigh 105 to 120 pounds field dressed.

For decades, some hunters have relied on chest-girth charts to estimate live weights of deer. Unfortunately, such charts are often inaccurate because — among other things — they don't account for fluctuations in the body sizes of bucks before and after the rut. Most biologists put no stock in any weight estimates based on chest-girth measurements.

Charles Alsheimer, Northern field editor for *D&DH*, estimates chest-girth measurements fluctuate by as much as 20 percent on Northern bucks. "In October, a buck's organs are packed in fat," Alsheimer said. "It's different when the rut is over."

However, a hunter can obtain a ballpark estimate of his deer's live weight by multiplying its field-dressed weight by 1.28. I came up with this number after comparing it with several chest-girth charts. Granted, this estimate won't pass muster with biologists, but it should be good enough for deer-camp comparisons. For example, a yearling buck with a field-dressed weight of 125 pounds will have an estimated live weight of 160 pounds.

Misconceptions

By misjudging field-dressed weights of whitetails, hunters often have unrealistic expectations of how

The scales don't tip that much farther for field-dressed yearlings. Yearling bucks, which range from small spikes to basket-racked 10-pointers, typically weigh 105 to 125 pounds. Therefore, my yearling 8-pointer mentioned earlier was perfectly normal. Northern yearling does typically weigh 80 to 90 pounds field dressed.

Southern yearling bucks average 75 to 95 pounds field dressed, while much venison they should receive from their butcher. Many aspects combine to determine venison yields. Although a neck-shot mature buck can yield a big amount of steaks, chops, hamburger and stew meat, the amount of meat seems minuscule when compared to the meat yield of domestic animals.

In preparing this article, I surveyed meat-processing professionals across the country. Besides revealing insights into meat yields, they agreed deer hunters often have false expectations of how much venison they'll get from their deer.

"Some people assume they should get a lot (of meat) because the deer was so heavy to drag out of the woods," said one Michigan processor. "They feel they should get meat equivalent to a half of beef."

Another meat cutter echoed those comments.

"A customer wanted to watch his first deer get processed," he said. "So, we started by weighing his field-dressed doe. It was 95 pounds. We then skinned the doe and started boning out the muscles. We processed his order, freezer-wrapped the cuts — basic chops, steaks, roast with bone attached and hamburger — and weighed all of the meat. We came up with 45 pounds.

"The customer was amazed at how much waste was in the hide, bones, head and hoofs."

Dave Santkuyl, a professional butcher from Kaukauna, Wis., recalled a hunter who, after dropping off his deer, went home with great expectations. When returning to pick up the processed venison, the hunter and his buddy pulled into the parking lot with two pickup trucks. In their trucks were six empty cardboard

The Ultimate Deer Hunter's Quiz
Part 9, Meat Processing
(A total of 10 questions in this chapter. Answers are listed on Page 198)

89. The healthiest mature Northern does weigh how much, on average, when field dressed?
A. 100 to 120 pounds
B. 120 to 140 pounds
C. 140 to 150 pounds
D. About 160 pounds

90. To obtain the best-tasting venison, where should hunters strive to shoot their deer?
A. In the neck
B. In the chest
C. Through the shoulders
D. In the hind quarters

91. Which of the following statements is true?
A. Venison will get freezer burn more easily than beef.
B. Venison will keep longer than beef in a freezer.
C. Venison shanks contain more fat than beef shanks.
D. Venison cannot be frozen for more than two months.

92. Which part of a deer do many old-time hunters refer to as "the poison glands?"
A. Gall bladder
B. Tarsal glands
C. Testicles
D. Tenderloins

93. Venison from mature deer, especially bucks, must be aged before being butchered and frozen.
A. True
B. False
C. There is no perfect answer.

Continued on Page 177.

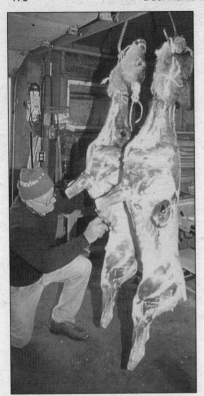

A deer's condition plays a role in how much boneless venison its carcass will yield. Shot placement is critical to ensuring maximum yield. Lung shots that enter and exit the rib cage result in minimal meat loss.

Meat Yields
(In Pounds)

Animal Meat	Weight*	Meat	Waste
Lamb** 80%	50	40	10
Hog 79%	240	189	51
Black Angus 73%	600	438	162
Holstein Steer 57%	900	513	387
Mature Buck 40%	180	72	108

*Carcass weight. Head, hide and intestines removed.

**University of Wisconsin research.

boxes from electric ovens.

The hunter must have been hugely disappointed when he realized his processed deer fit more easily into a few grocery bags!

Deer and Domestic Animals

Our survey asked meat processors to provide information on meat yields for deer, hogs, lambs, black Angus steers and Holstein steers.

The average weights from their responses follow:

Why the discrepancies? Santkuyl said it comes down to the old apples-and-oranges comparison.

"All animals are built a little different," he said. "For hogs, almost everything is used — bacon, hocks, etc. A deer has long legs with little meat on them, whereas steers have the same bone structure (but with more meat). It's the muscle and fat that make them different."

Also, the statistics for domestic animals are calculated by the manner their meats are packaged. For example, the amount of waste depends on the cutting method. Beef steaks, lamb chops and pork hams include dense bones, which increase the amount of meat volume sold to consumers. Venison, on the other hand, is often boned, thereby reducing a deer's meat yield.

I'm certain meat cutters provided "best estimates" for their meat yields, making the figures open for debate. In fact, their overall meat-yield for venison appears to be a low-ball percentage. However, their insights are remarkably accurate when compared to precise tests.

The data from two venison processors — Santkuyl and my dad, Daniel J. Schmidt — provide an equation that allows hunters to accurately gauge venison yields.

In 1996, Santkuyl meticulously butchered a buck that a gun-hunter shot in the head. His calibrated scale measured the buck's field-dressed weight at 157 pounds. After skinning the buck and cutting off its head, the carcass weighed 118 pounds. Finally, Santkuyl boned out all the meat off the carcass and ended up with 78 pounds of venison.

My dad conducted a similar experiment in 1984 on a northern Wisconsin buck. Because the mature 8-pointer had been shot in the head, nothing went to waste. Dad also knew he would get an accurate reading of the venison yield because he planned to grind all the meat for summer sausage.

The buck weighed 197 pounds field dressed, and it produced exactly 100 pounds of boneless venison. The percentage of meat obtained from this deer and three other deer we killed with head/neck shots ranged from 47.7 percent to 50.7 percent of the field-dressed weights.

Although it would be more convenient to say a deer's meat yield is equal to 50 percent of its field-dressed weight, it wouldn't be totally accurate.

A buck's condition plays a large role in how much boneless venison it will yield. For example, the 197-pound buck was killed in late November. It had the physique of a body builder. Its neck was swollen and its front shoulders were muscular, but its hips and back were nearly fat-free. The same buck might have

The Ultimate Deer Hunter's Quiz
Part 9, Meat Processing
(A total of 10 questions in this chapter. Answers are listed on Page 198)

94. Which of the following practices can cause venison to become tough?
A. Removing every ounce of fat and sinew from the carcass.
B. Cooking venison in a pressure cooker.
C. Freezing the meat less than 24 hours after the kill.
D. Aging the meat in a temperature-controlled room.

95. Boneless, fat-free venison that's properly wrapped can keep in a freezer for how long?
A. 6 months
B. 10 months
C. 1 years
D. 2 years

96. If a hunter is in a hurry and must butcher his deer by himself, he should:
A. Save only the hind quarters.
B. Save the backstraps, hind quarters and tenderloins.
C. Save the backstraps, tenderloins and ribs.
D. None of the above.

97. Which of the following deer organs are not fit for human consumption?
A. Heart
B. Liver
C. Kidneys
D. All are edible.

98. While field dressing a buck, a hunter accidentally cuts the buck's urine sack, spilling fluid on the inside of the carcass. What should he do?
A. Wash out the inside of the carcass and then hang the deer from its antlers.
B. Wipe out the cavity with paper towels.
C. Wash the cavity, wipe it thoroughly with paper towels, and then hang the deer.

CONGRATULATIONS, YOU HAVE FINISHED THE QUIZ! SEE PAGE 199 FOR THE ANSWERS.

Meat Facts

Meat consumption is not declining. United State Department of Agriculture statistics show meat consumption per person has remained relatively static the past 20 years. This can be seen in the consumption figures per person since 1970:

    1970: 136.84 pounds
    1980: 139.48 pounds
    1990: 143.88 pounds

Other facts about meat include:

✓ 99 percent of U.S. households consume meat at least once every two weeks.

✓ 93 percent of U.S. households consume meat at least twice a week.

✓ 3 percent of the U.S. population claimed to be vegetarians in 1990; that figure dropped to 2 percent in 1991.

— *Texas Beef Council*

field-dressed 10 pounds more if it had been killed in September or October.

After examining more of my dad's venison data, I realized it provided an equation that is remarkably accurate.

The Equation for Venison Yield

Hunters can learn more about their deer and how much venison it will yield by first obtaining an accurate field-dressed weight. This figure helps determine the deer's carcass weight — the deer's body weight minus its head, hide and innards. From there, it's easy to calculate how much venison is on the carcass.

Santkuyl's test showed the buck carcass was 66 percent meat and 34 percent waste, while my dad's statistics on four head/neck shot whitetails revealed a 68-32 ratio.

Combining my dad's statistics with Santkuyl's, I split the difference and devised an equation that should help hunters determine how much meat they can expect from their deer.

It's important to note that this equation assumes that no part of the deer is lost to waste from tissue damage. Obviously, a deer suffering bullet — or to a lesser extent, arrow — damage to its back, hams, shoulders or neck will yield substantially less venison. Therefore, it includes calculations for "ideal" meat yield — the maximum amount of meat on a deer with nothing being lost to waste, and a "realistic" meat yield — the amount of meat a hunter can expect to receive after subtracting the pounds of meat lost to bullet/broadhead damage.

The equation does not account for meat that must be removed after being ruined by stomach contents or overexposure to warm weather.

Remember, to use the equation, first obtain an accurate field-dressed weight:

✓ Carcass weight = Field-dressed weight divided by 1.331

✓ *Ideal* boneless venison weight = Carcass weight multiplied by .67

✓ *Realistic* venison yield = Ideal boneless weight multiplied by .70

Let's say a hunter kills a mature buck, and it weighs 165 pounds field-dressed. Using the above equation, we estimate its carcass will weigh 124 pounds, and it will ideally yield 83.08 pounds of boneless meat. The deer's realistic meat yield is about 58.15 pounds.

Because waste can vary between deer, I suggest using the "realistic" figure as a gauge. In the above example, I estimated the buck's realistic meat yield would range from 58 to 68 pounds. A 10-pound difference doesn't seem like much when dealing with a deer that large, but it is noticeable when the deer is a fawn or yearling.

For example, in 1994, our hunting party tagged five deer during a North

Woods gun-hunt: one mature doe, two fawns and two yearling bucks. The resulting meat-yields from those deer follow:

	Shot Placement	Weight (Dressed)	Meat Yield
Mature Doe	Shoulder	138 lbs.	56 lbs.
Yearling Buck	Lungs	128 lbs.	50 lbs.
Yearling Buck	Brisket	112 lbs.	38 lbs.
Buck Fawn	Lungs	88 lbs.	34 lbs.
Doe Fawn	Neck	82 lbs.	32 lbs.

These four deer showed varying degrees of lost meat from bullet damage. The doe lost 19 percent; first yearling buck, 22 percent; second yearling buck, 31 percent; buck fawn, 23 percent; and doe fawn, 22 percent.

Because of excessive waste from bloodshot meat, the brisket-shot yearling buck exceeded the 30 percent calculation for realistic meat yield, and it produced just a few pounds of scrap meat more than the fawns, which lost little meat to waste. In fact, we've processed lung-shot fawns that yielded more meat than shoulder- or spine-shot yearling does and bucks.

Another interesting fact: The 8-pointer mentioned at the beginning of this article yielded 42 pounds of meat. It was shot in the neck and the chest, and a lot of meat was wasted. Remember the guy who was in line behind me? Even though we snickered at him for "shooting a puny deer," his 91-pound doe could have yielded 46 pounds of meat — 4 pounds more than what I got from my buck!

Conclusion

In most cases, hunters will likely see little difference in meat yields between the deer they shoot. Does and bucks from similar age classes yield similar amounts of venison. In fact, don't expect to see big differences in your net venison yield unless you're comparing relatively young deer with a big, mature, deep-chested buck. Even then, you won't need pickup trucks, a forklift and refrigerator boxes to take home your venison. Remember, you're dealing with a whitetail, not a bull moose.

Editor's note: *This article originally appeared in the October 1999 issue of* Deer & Deer Hunting.

Six Steps to Tastier Venison

Many hunters work hard to put themselves in position to take whitetails with their guns and bows. Therefore, it's crucial to follow through after the deer is on the ground. Memorize these six steps to ensure none of the meat on your next deer is wasted:

1. Cool venison as quickly as possible after killing a deer. If necessary, pack the carcass with bags of ice.

2. After returning to camp, immediately remove the tenderloins found inside the deer's body cavity.

3. Trim venison of all fat, membranes and connecting tissue before freezing or cooking.

4. Freezing meat in chunks or sections, as opposed to individual steaks, helps to retain moisture. Further, well-chilled or semi-frozen meat is also easier to slice than room-temperature meat.

5. Venison should thaw slowly to prevent toughness.

6. Venison steaks, roasts and stew meat must be served hot, and the balance kept hot without burning. It prevents a waxy taste.

Venison Processing Tips

For great-tasting venison, allow your deer to hang at least 24 hours. Professional butchers agree that butchering and freezing a deer in less time usually results in "gamey" venison because all of the natural body heat was not allowed to escape the carcass.

It is not necessary to "age" venison, and, in fact, proper aging can only occur under tightly regulated conditions. Do not attempt to age a deer unless you have access to a walk-in cooler.

When processing your deer, be sure to double-wrap meat and label it with the date. Two layers of wrapping paper provide better insulation and keep the meat from getting freezer burn.

Give yourself plenty of time to process a deer. Carefully remove sinew and fat from the meat before wrapping it. Fat begins to break down once meat is frozen, and it can taint the meat. It's also wise to bone as much meat as possible. Bones not only take up space in your freezer, they too can cause off-flavor in meat if left in the freezer too long.

The well-prepared home butcher keeps a variety of quality knives in his processing tool box:
- ✓Fillet knife
- ✓Boning knife
- ✓Butcher knife
- ✓Meat cleaver
- ✓Skinning/caping knives
- ✓Meat saw (hand or electric)

Processing tasks become much easier, even fun, with quality knives. However, the best knife is useless if you don't also invest in a sharpening steel or set of stones.

Other useful items include a tape dispenser, waxed-paper dispenser, hog hooks, gambrel bar, small ax, plastic meat lug, apron with pockets and numerous pairs of disposable rubber gloves.

A homemade cutting table will save you time and sore back muscles. Make your table out of wood, and construct it at a height that allows you to perform tasks without straining your back.

It's crucial to keep all utensils and work areas clean to prevent contamination. Knives should be frequently washed with hot, soapy water. Work areas can be kept bacteria-free by wiping them down with a water-bleach solution and drying them before beginning another task.

After skinning your deer, use a slightly moistened towel to remove hair from the carcass. It's much easier to remove hair at this point rather than waiting until the carcass has been quartered. It's also wise to use a fillet knife to skin away as much fat and sinew from the hind quarters and backstraps before they are removed from the carcass.

Although the backstraps and hind quarters contain the most desirable cuts, a whitetail carcass provides equally valuable venison in the neck, ribs and front legs/shoulders. Spend the time to bone out each section. These often-overlooked scraps make great additions to stew, chili, burger and sausage. Most butchershops will gladly make sausage for a reasonable charge if you supply them with clean, boned venison.

— *Daniel E. Schmidt*

CHAPTER 10
RECIPES, REFERENCES & CAMP FUN

What's for Dinner?

It has satisfied the taste buds of Medieval royalty and sustained the stomachs of Colonial American families. It has carried families through the Great Depression and been the highlight of the feast for hundreds of years. It has been canned, marinated, barbequed, slow-cooked, roasted, grilled, fried, baked and sauteed. It is lean, healthy and widely adaptable in thousands of recipes. And now, in this health-crazed society of the 21st century, venison has made its comeback as one of the healthiest meats available.

The term *venison* is derived from the the Latin word *venari*, which means "to hunt." It technically defines a variety of large-antlered animals, but the term most acceptably refers to deer.

Because the meat has little intramuscular fat, it quickly dries out without the addition of some type of moisture. This is why slow-cooking is the most complementary method of preparation. When frying, venison should be cooked quickly over high heat to sear in moisture. The outside will be browned and the inside will remain a medium or medium-rare.

As with any cut of meat, the muscles that are used the least will be the most tender. Venison chops cut from the back will be more delicate than the tougher muscles of the neck.

The methods of preparation for venison are endless. What's listed in this chapter is merely a springing board for further ideas. Experiment. Use venison as a substitute for other red meats. Find recipes that will make venison a meat that not only sustains the body, but also pleases the tongue.

Nutrient Values for 3-Ounce Portions

Source	Calories	Fat (grams)	Saturated Fat (grams)	Cholesterol (milligrams)
Deer	134	3	1	95
Elk	124	2	1	62
Moose	114	1	Trace	66
Caribou	142	4	1	93
Antelope	127	2	1	107
Beef	259	18	7	75
Pork	214	13	5	73

Source: U.S.D.A. Nutrient Data Laboratory

Foiled Venison Burgers

1 pound ground venison	2 small onions, sliced
4 large carrots, sliced	salt, pepper, garlic salt
3 medium potatoes, sliced	4 tablespoons melted butter

Form four patties out of ground meat. Sprinkle each with salt, pepper and garlic salt. Tear four pieces of aluminum foil large enough to wrap each patty generously. Brush foil with melted butter. Put burgers on foil and layer with potatoes, onions and carrots. Salt and pepper vegetables. Drizzle remaining butter over everything. Seal each packet and grill over open coals for 10 to 20 minutes on each side.

Ruth & Jerry's Venison Burgers

1 pound ground venison	⅓ package onion soup mix
salt, pepper, garlic salt	⅓ package beef soup mix
¾ c. oatmeal	

Mix ground venison with salt, pepper and garlic salt to taste. Add soup mixes and oatmeal. Form into patties. Fry in 4 tablespoons oil and 3 table-spoons butter.

— *Ruth and Jerry Pillath, Pound, Wis.*

Stir-Fry Venison and Mushrooms

1 pound venison steaks	¼ teaspoon garlic powder
1 tablespoon soy sauce	⅛ teaspoon salt
2 tablespoons sweet red wine	1 large onion
2 teaspoons cornstarch	1 cup peas
¼ teaspoon ginger powder	1 cup rice

Cut venison into ½-inch cubes. In medium bowl, mix venison, soy sauce, wine, cornstarch, ginger, salt and garlic powder. Set aside.

Thinly slice mushrooms and onions. Cook mushrooms and onions in large skillet over medium heat, stirring quickly and frequently until mushrooms are tender. Remove the mixture to a bowl.

In same skillet, over high heat, cook venison in 3 more tablespoons of butter. Stir quickly and frequently until tender. Return mushroom mixture to skillet, add peas, heat through. Serve with rice. Makes 4 servings.

Venison Macaroni Salad

1 c. elbow macaroni	1 green pepper, diced
1 pound ground venison	2 tsps. Worcestershire sauce
1 tablespoon butter	1½ c. shredded sharp cheddar
½ c. minced onion	2 c. shredded iceberg lettuce
1 tablespoon flour	½ c. chili sauce or catsup
½ c. red cooking wine	1 tomato, sliced

Cook macaroni in boiling water until tender.

In a frying pan, brown meat in butter. Add onion, salt and flour. Blend in wine. Stir in chili sauce, green pepper and Worcestershire sauce. Bring to a boil over medium heat. Remove from heat and toss with cooked hot macaroni. Fold in cheese.

To serve, line a platter with shredded lettuce. Mound hot mixture and top with whole lettuce leaves and sliced tomatoes.

Cajun Venison Sauce-Piquante

3 pounds venison steak
1 medium bell pepper, chopped
1 large onion, chopped
3 stalks green onions, chopped
2 garlic cloves, minced
1 can tomatoes
1 12-ounce can tomato sauce

2 tablespoons flour
½ teaspoon garlic powder
2-3 pinches cayenne pepper
black pepper to taste
seasoned salt
oil

Cut venison into 2-inch strips and season with seasoned salt and garlic powder. Brown venison in oil, enough to cover bottom of pot. If available, use black iron pot. Take meat out and put aside. Drain.

Add bell pepper, onion and garlic. Brown well. Take vegetables out and put aside in bowl.

Add flour and brown in pan. Add venison and tomatoes, can of tomato sauce and about 2 cups water, black pepper and cayenne pepper. Cook 45 minutes. Then add browned vegetables and cook for 30 minutes.

Add green onion and cook another 30 minutes. Caution: Spicy but delicious. Serves 4.

— *Rebecca Pizzalato, Krotz Springs, La.*

Spaghetti Sauce

1 18-ounce can tomato sauce
1 medium onion, chopped
½ c. green pepper, chopped
2 tablespoons oil
1½ pounds ground venison
1½ teaspoons Italian seasoning

1½ teaspoon garlic salt
2 teaspoons barbecue seasoning
1 teaspoon salt
½ teaspoon pepper
1 tablespoon sugar

Dilute tomato paste with 2½ cans water. Add garlic salt, Italian seasoning, barbecue seasoning, salt, pepper and sugar. Bring to boil, stirring occasionally.

Meanwhile, saute onion and pepper in oil until tender. Add to sauce. When it comes to boil, lower heat to simmer.

Brown ground venison and add to sauce. Simmer 2 to 2½ hours or until thick. Stir occasionally. Serves 4-6.

Barbara J. Stang, St. Michaels, Md.

Venison Stroganoff

2 pounds of venison roast	2 tablespoons Worcestershire
4 tablespoons margarine	1 tablespoons Teriyaki sauce

1 small can sliced mushrooms	6 tablespoons flour
1 medium onion	1 c. sour cream
1½ c. beef broth	4 c. hot cooked egg noodles
1 can cream of mushroom soup	

Dice onion and saute with can of drained mushrooms in 2 tablespoons margarine. Remove from pan. Slice venison into ½ by 2-inch strips. Add remaining margarine to pan with the venison strips and brown. Remove venison from pan. To the pan, add the flour, beef broth, cream of mushroom soup, Worcestershire sauce and Teriyaki sauce. Cover and let simmer for 15 minutes. Return onions, mushrooms and venison to pan and let simmer for about 1½ hours, or until venison is tender. Stir in sour cream just before serving. Pour over hot egg noodles and stir.

— Ralph Lane, Jr., Des Moines, Iowa

Venison Lasagna

1 pound ground venison	1 16-ounce can tomatoes
1 tablespoon oil	1 8-ounce can tomato paste
⅓ c. onion diced	1 tablespoon vinegar
salt & pepper	1 teaspoon sugar
1 garlic clove, diced	1 package lasagna noodles
½ teaspoon thyme	1½ c. cottage cheese
1 pound sliced mozzarella	1 c. Romano or Parmesan

Saute onions in oil, add garlic and meat, brown. Add vinegar, sugar, thyme, tomato paste, tomato, salt and pepper. Simmer 20 minutes.

Cook lasagna noodles until done. Rinse and cover with cold water. In shallow pan layer lasagna noodles, layer of cottage cheese, meat sauce, Parmesan cheese and Mozzarella cheese. Repeat layers, with last layer as meat sauce, and cover with remaining cheese.

Bake in 350-degree oven for 45 minutes. Let cool 10 minutes.

— Oliver Bugelli, Westville, Ill.

Venison Camp Chili

2 pounds ground venison	1-2 teaspoons chili powder
1 large onion, diced	1 c. diced celery
1 16-ounce can white beans	3 16-ounce cans stewed tomatoes
1 16-ounce can kidney beans	dash sugar
dash Tabasco sauce	1 chili pepper

Brown venison and onions in a large kettle. Add Tabasco, chili pepper, celery, stewed tomatoes and sugar. Simmer for 1 hour in large kettle.

Add beans and chili powder and cook at low heat for 10 minutes.

Pepper Steak Supreme

2 pounds of steak	3 green peppers
⅓ c. oil	4 tomatoes, quartered or
dash of garlic powder	1 qt. canned tomatoes
1 teaspoon salt	3 tablespoons sugar
dash of pepper	1 can bean sprouts, drained
¼ teaspoon ginger	2 tablespoons cornstarch
¼ c. soy sauce	½ c. water
1 onion, thinly sliced	

Cut steak across grain into thin strips. Brown with oil, garlic, salt, pepper and ginger. Reduce heat and simmer for 30 minutes.

Add soy sauce, onion and green pepper cut in 1-inch squares. Cover, cook about 5 minutes. Add tomatoes and sugar. Cover, cook another 5 minutes.

Add bean sprouts. Blend cornstarch with water, add to meat mixture, stirring well. Cook until thickened, about 3 minutes. Serve with rice.

— *James Chapell, McFarland, Wis.*

Autumn Soup

1 pound ground venison	salt to flavor
6 cups water	1 tspn. brown Bouquet sauce
1 c. cubed carrots	2 bay leaves
1 c. cubed celery	½ teaspoon basil
1 c. chopped onions	1 qt. whole canned tomatoes
3 c. cubed potatoes	

Brown venison with salt, pepper and garlic salt to taste. Saute celery and onions in butter. Combine all ingredients except tomatoes. Bring to a boil. Cook over medium heat for about 20 minutes until vegetables are tender. Add tomatoes. Cover and simmer for 10 more minutes.

— *Ruth Pillath, Pound, Wis.*

Wellington Loaf

2 pounds ground venison	1 teaspoon salt
1 6-ounce can of mushrooms	¼ teaspoon pepper
2 eggs, slightly beaten	1 c. biscuit mix
½ c. chopped onions	¼ c. mushroom liquid
2 tablespoons chopped green pepper	⅛ teaspoon poultry seasoning

(Directions on next page)

Form a meat loaf with meat, mushrooms, eggs, onions, green pepper, salt, pepper and 2 tablespoons of mushroom liquid. Put into a shallow pan. Mix biscuit mix, remaining mushroom liquid and poultry seasoning to form a soft dough. Roll onto a sheet 12 by 8 inches and put over the top and sides of the loaf. Bake at 375 degrees for 45 minutes.

Venison Burger Soup

1-2 pounds ground venison
32-ounce can of tomatoes
2 medium onions, chopped
2 stalks celery, chopped
⅓ c. pearl barley
¼ c. ketchup

1 tablespoon bouillon
2 teaspoons seasoned salt
1 teaspoon dried basil
2-3 c. shredded cabbage
5 c. water

In a large saucepan, brown venison and drain off fat. Stir in remaining ingredients. Bring to a boil. Reduce heat, cover and simmer for 1 hour. Season to taste with salt and pepper.
— *Charles Barker, Eagle, Mich.*

Wild Rice and Venison

1½ pounds ground venison
1½ c. cooked wild rice
1 can cream of mushroom soup
1 can cream of chicken soup
1 cup sliced celery

1 c. sliced mushrooms
1 c. water
1 chopped onion
3 teaspoons soy sauce

Brown venison in skillet. Add remaining ingredients and mix well. Pour into two-quart casserole dish, cover and bake in 350-degree oven for 30 minutes. Uncover and bake for 30 more minutes.

Sausage Casserole

4 slices bread
1 pound venison sausage
1 c. cheddar cheese, grated
4 eggs
2 c. milk

1 teaspoons salt
1 4-ounce can mushrooms
1 tablespoon butter
dash of pepper

Brown sausage. Tear bread in pieces and put into 1½-quart baking dish. Spread browned sausage over bread and sprinkle with cheese. Beat eggs, milk, salt and pepper. Add drained mushrooms. Pour over sausage and bread. Bake in 350-degree oven for 35 minutes. Serves 6. This makes a great breakfast casserole.

Marinated Venison Roast

3- to 4-pound rump or roast
1 c. red wine
1 c. chopped tomatoes
¼ teaspoon basil
¼ teaspoon oregano
¼ teaspoon tarragon

2 bay leaves
2 tablespoons flour
1 c. sour cream
1 teaspoon paprika
1 tablespoon chopped parsley

Put the wine, tomatoes, basil, oregano, tarragon and bay leaves in a saucepan and bring to boil. Turn the heat down and simmer 10 minutes. Cool to room temperature.

Place the roast in a non-metal bowl or dish and pour the cooled marinade over it. Cover and refrigerate for 48 hours, turning the roast every 12 hours.

Remove the roast from marinade, dry with paper towels, and put in a roasting pan. Place in a preheated 450-degree oven for 20 minutes.

Remove bay leaves from marinade, then pour it in a saucepan. Heat and sprinkle with flour while stirring. Add sour cream and paprika and stir well.

After 20 minutes, remove roast from the oven and turn heat down to 350 degrees. Pour the hot marinade mixture over roast and return it to the oven for 40 minutes (3 lb. roast) or 60 minutes (4 lb. roast), until a meat thermometer registers 130 degrees for medium rare.

Serve meat on a heated platter and the sauce in a heated gravy boat to be ladled over thin slices of meat. Sprinkle sauce with parsley. Serves 4 to 6.

Venison Sausage-Vegetable Chowder

2 tablespoons butter
2 tablespoons flour
1 teaspoon salt
1 teaspoon onion powder
¼ dried dill weed
4 cups milk

1 large package frozen
   vegetables, partially thawed
1 16-ounce can kernel corn
   drained
½ pound venison sausage,
   sliced

In a large saucepan, melt butter over low heat. Blend in flour, salt, onion powder, dill weed and pepper. Add milk all at once. Cook over medium heat, stirring constantly until thickened and bubbly. Stir the vegetables, corn and sausage into the soup. Cover and simmer for 10-15 minutes or until vegetables are done. Makes 6 servings.

Easy Venison Stir Fry

1 to 2 pounds venison steak,
cut into bite-size pieces
2 tablespoons butter
Olive oil
1 teaspoon salt
1 teaspoon seasoned salt

1 large package frozen
vegetables, partially thawed
1 tsp. Cajun powder seasoning,
or seasoning from stir fry pkg.

Place burner on medium-high heat. In a large Teflon-coated frying pan or wok, spread 1 tablespoon of olive oil. Blend in seasoned salt. When oil pops, add cubed venison. Stir quickly, browning pieces evenly. Be careful not to overcook. Remove venison from pan and place in oven-safe glass bowl or dish. Place venison in warm oven. Return frying pan to stovetop on medium heat. Add butter and melt. Add vegetables. Allow vegetables to fry about 1 minute. Add Cajun seasoning or seasoning from stir fry package. Add salt. Increase heat slightly, constantly stirring vegetables. When vegetables are thawed, return venison to pan and place heat on medium. Keep stirring until meal is hot, about 5 minutes. Makes four large servings.

Mexican Style Venison

1 pound venison steak
16-ounce can tomato sauce
1 can chopped green chili
peppers

1 cup grated Monterey Jack
cheese
½ teaspoon salt
½ teaspoon minced garlic
½ teaspoon pepper

Preheat oven to 350 degrees.

Put ½ can of tomato sauce in bottom of a casserole dish. Lay steak in sauce. Sprinkle with salt, pepper and garlic. Place chili peppers over steak. Pour remaining tomato sauce over all and cover tightly with foil. Cook for 45 minutes in 350-degree oven. Remove foil and sprinkle grated cheese over the steaks. Return to oven until cheese melts. Serve venison steaks over rice.

— *Gayle Forbes, Greer S.C.*

Venison Salami

3 pounds ground venison
3 tablespoons curing salt
1 teaspoon garlic powder
2 teaspoons liquid smoke

¼ teaspoon onion powder
1 tablespoon mustard seed
1 cup water (optional)
Pepper

In bowl, mix venison with seasoning. Add pepper for desired hotness. Make mixture into 2-by-8-by-10-inch rolls. If mixture is too dry to roll, add water. Wrap rolls in foil and refrigerate 24 hours. Poke holes in foil with a fork. Put rolls in roaster. Cover with cold water and boil for 1 hour.

— *Charles Barker, Eagle, Mich.*

Deer Sausage

6 pounds venison (boned, no fat)
3 pork sausages
6 teaspoons salt
2 teaspoons black pepper

2 teaspoons red pepper
2 teaspoons brown sugar
3 teaspoons Allspice
4 teaspoons sage

Combine all ingredients and run through a meat grinder. Wrap in plastic and freezer paper. Freeze for future use.

— *Ron Tate, Bartlesville, Okla.*

Oven Sausage

15 pounds ground venison
   mixed with beef fat
3 tablespoons black pepper
1¼ teaspoon mace
1⅛ teaspoon dry mustard
1 teaspoon accent
1 teaspoon seasoned salt

1 teaspoon garlic powder
1 tablespoon Lawry's
   hickory smoked salt
⅔ cup brown sugar
1 cup Morton Tender Quick cure
4 ounces liquid smoke

Mix all ingredients well and refrigerate covered tightly for 24 hours. Pack the mixture into unbleached white muslin sleeves, measuring 4- by 12-inches long. Pack meat tightly and tie ends together. Place bags of meat on broiler pans and bake 5 hours at 225 degrees. Turn over when half done. When complete, take rolls out of oven, or be sure to leave door open until rolls cool.

— *Ronnie Sours, Front Royal, Va.*

Things You Should Know Before Booking a Deer Hunting Trip to Canada

It's no secret that Canada offers some of the best deer hunting opportunities in North America. From British Columbia to Quebec, hunters can not only find huge whitetails, they can hunt pristine wilderness areas with little or no competition from other hunters.

What's more, most Canadian deer hunts are relatively inexpensive, considering many outfitters offer fantastic accommodations and top-notch guide services. However, it's unwise to book any hunt without doing a lot of homework. Although most outfitters offer hunting packages, many details are left to the hunter.

The following items are just a few that you should investigate before booking a Canadian hunt. For more information, contact the bureaus and information centers listed within this article.

Tax-Refund Policy

Before writing a check for what seems like an affordable hunt package, double-check to see what taxes you still owe. In many cases, package hunts are quoted on price, but they do not include the applicable federal and provincial taxes.

Nonresidents are eligible for a reimbursement of 50 percent of the taxes paid on a package. An outfitter who sells a package directly to non-residents can request this reimbursement on their behalf and deduct it from the price of the package.

For more information, contact your outfitter or call Revenue Canada at (613) 991-3346.

Trip Cancellation

Whether you are dealing with an outfitter or an intermediary, make sure to inquire about cancellation policies. These conditions should appear in the agency's guidelines or the outfitter's brochure.

Responsibilities of Agencies and Outfitters

Canadian hunting agencies serve as intermediaries between travellers and travel service organizations. Because they do not exercise any control over suppliers, agencies cannot be held responsible if the suppliers fail to provide services.

Neither intermediaries nor outfitters can be held responsible for any damage, loss, delay, illness, or injury or inconvenience arising from:

✓errors, negligence, or omissions on the part of other suppliers such as carriers, hotels, etc.

✓strikes, mechanical failures, a quarantine or other restrictive government action, meteorological conditions, or other factors beyond human control such as forest fires.

✓failure on the part of the customer to carry necessary travel documents.

✓any airport delays on the customer's day of departure, for whatever reason.

✓material damage, loss of property or theft.

Patrick Durkin

When returning to the United States from Canada, U.S. hunters must register their kill when going through the U.S. Customs Service check station.

✓illness, injury and/or death.

Insurance

Most agencies offer trip cancellation, medical, and baggage insurance. For information on such policies, please contact the fishing and hunting agency of your choice.

Terms of Payment

If the trip has not been completely paid for before your departure and you do not intend to settle the bill with cash, you should verify whether the outfitter accepts personal checks, traveller's checks and/or credit cards.

Baggage

Before departure, check if the airline has weight limits and baggage allowance. Most airlines tightly monitor baggage regulations.

Climatic Conditions

While every effort is made to comply with published timetables, irregularities in flight operations can occur in some regions due to poor weather. Such conditions can also affect the schedule of activities at an outfitter's camp. There is no refund for adjustments to activities resulting from such irregularities.

Permits and Quotas

Hunters must purchase provincial hunting licenses, generally available at sporting goods stores in most cities and towns from a number of outfitters.

Nonresidents are not obliged to produce a hunter's safety certificate to purchase a hunting license.

Deer Hunting

Non-residents are limited to

purchasing particular hunting licenses and frequenting specific hunting zones or areas according to the species hunted.

For white-tailed deer, nonresidents can hunt in all zones where hunting is allowed. However, nonresidents cannot participate in computer drawings to obtain a hunting license for antlerless deer during the firearm season.

Deer Registration

When returning to the United States from Canada, U.S. hunters must register their kill when going through the U.S. Customs Service check station.

Transporting Game

All successful deer hunters must immediately detach the appropriate transportation tag from his or her license and affix it to their deer. The tag must remain affixed throughout the registration process and until the animal has been dressed and stored.

Safety Regulations

All hunters must wear blaze-orange material of at least 400 square inches — covering their back, shoulders and chest — while gun-hunting fro deer. The clothing must be visible from all angles at all times.

In addition, a life jacket must be provided for each person using any kind of boat. All boats must be equipped with a bailer, a sound-signaling device and a pair of oars.

Money

It's wise to change your currency into Canadian dollars before leaving the U.S. Traveller's checks and major credit cards are accepted in most establishments, but it's advisable to check with your outfitter in advance.

Where to Write

Alberta
Department of Forestry,
Lands and Wildlife
Main Floor North Tower
Petroleum Plaza
9045 108th St.
Edmonton, Alberta CAN T5K 2G6

British Columbia
Ministry of Environment,
Fish and Wildlife
780 Blanchard St.
Victoria, British Columbia
CAN V8V 1X5

Manitoba
Dept. of Natural Resources
Wildlife Branch
1495 St. James Court
Winnipeg, Manitoba
CAN R3H 0W9

New Brunswick
Bureau of Natural Resources
Fish and Wildlife Branch
Box 6000
Fredricton, N.B. CAN E3B4X5

Newfoundland
Dept. of Culture, Wildlife Division
Box 8750
St. Johns, N.F. CAN A1C 5 7

Nova Scotia
Dept. of Lands and Forests
136 Exhibition St.
Kentville, N.S. CAN B4N 4E5

Ontario
Ministry of Natural Resources
Room 1-73, macDonald Block
900 Bay St.
Toronto, Ontario CAN M7A 2C3

Quebec
Dept. of Recreation, Hunting
Box 2200, 150 E. St. Cyrille
Quebec City, Quebec, CAN G1R 4Y1

Saskatchewan
Parks and Renewable Resources
3211 Albert St.
Regina, Saskatchewan
CAN S4S 5W6

The Ultimate Deer Hunter's Quiz Answers

CHAPTER 1: DEER AND DEER HUNTING

1. **C.** The commercial tripod stand. For more information see the October 1999 issue of *D&DH*.

2. **B.** The Audubon Society, since its origin at the turn of the 20th century, has never been opposed to the hunting of game species. The Humane Society, Friends of Animals and PETA are all strongly opposed to hunting of any living creature.

3. **B.** According to scientist Valerius Geist, white-tailed deer, or something very similar, appeared in North America more than 3 million years ago.

4. **C.** According to Geist, mule deer arose twice from white-tailed deer during the early Pleistocene period, first as black-tailed deer then as the mule deer we know today. That occurred, he believes, about 9,000 to 11,000 years ago.

5. **C.** According to Leonard Lee Rue, well-fed does drop fawns in the 6- to 8-pound range, while those on a starvation diet give birth to fawns weighing about 4 pounds.

6. **B.** The average length of a white-tailed deer's ear is 7 inches. The average width is 3 inches.

7. **A.** The preorbital gland is a trench-like depression in front of the eye.

8. **D.** Unlike other herbivores, the white-tailed deer does not have a gall bladder.

9. **B.** An adult buck can reach up about 7 feet. An adult doe can reach up about 6 feet, while a 7-month-old fawn can reach up about 5 feet.

10. **B.** Research shows that a 112-pound deer at rest needs 1,323 calories for each 24-hour period.

11. **D.** Although bucks typically stay in a home range of two to five square miles, research shows that some bucks cover 10 to 12 square miles when searching for does.

12. **A.** Two years.

13. **A.** The black oak acorn provides 4.3 percent crude protein. The blue oak provides 3.5 percent, while the water oak provides 3.1 percent and the scrub oak, 2.6 percent.

14. **C.** Running at a speed of 35 mph, a deer could potentially run 3,850 feet (1,283 yards) in 80 seconds. Although it is not likely a heart-shot deer would live that long, the potential exists.

15. **B.** The oldest captive whitetail lived to be 22 years old. The doe was born in captivity June 8, 1932, and died Dec. 7, 1951.

16. **D.** According to Leonard Lee Rue III, all deer can leave drag marks in the snow when there is more than half-inch of snow on the ground.

CHAPTER 2: BOW-HUNTING

17. **B.** A deer must lose at least 35 percent of its blood before it will fall. The better the hit, the quicker blood loss occurs.

18. **B.** Contrary to popular belief, a deer's chest cavity does not contain a large dead space. While it's possible to zip a broadhead-tipped arrow through a deer's chest without killing the animal, a bow-hunter probably has a better chance of winning the lottery. As a result, a broadhead that punctures a deer's chest cavity

will almost always kill the animal. For a lethal shot, the chest cavity is the best place to aim.

19. **C**. The four-year Camp Ripley study showed a "loss rate" average of 13 percent. The "loss rate" is the number of deer that researchers could not account for at the end of the study. These deer might have died, suffered a flesh wound, or represented two or more hits. In other words, bow-hunters are extremely efficient hunters and they wound few deer that die without being recovered.

20. **C**.

21. **D**. All of the statements are true. In fact, they are P&Y's top three priorities.

22. **B**. When shooting at a deer with a bow and arrow, aim for the heart region. If the deer "jumps the string" by dropping sharply before bounding away, the arrow will still hit the lungs.

23. **D**. Vitamin K1 and K2, abundant in green, leafy vegetation, are often found in high levels in deer in early fall. Vitamin K is an antihemorrhagic agent, which greatly aids blood clotting.

24. **B**. For archers, the quartering-away shot offer the best chances for success. Even if the arrow hit a bit too far back, it can angle forward into the chest cavity for a quick kill. When taking this shot, the point of aim should be through the deer to the opposite shoulder.

25. **C**. Michigan

26. **D**. H.W. Allen applied for a patent for "Archery Bow with Force Multiplying Attachments."

27. **D**. Georgia.

28. **B**. Although bow-hunting is practically as old as mankind, Wisconsin held the first structured, state-sanctioned season in 1940. The first known bow-kill of Wisconsin's modern era is credited to Roy Case of Racine, Wis., who used a stick bow to kill a buck in 1930.

29. **C**. Today's manufacturers suggest hunters shoot draw weights of at least 60 pounds when using mechanical broadheads. Lower-poundage bows sometimes do not provide enough energy to properly deploy mechanical heads.

30. **C**. Ishi was a primitive Yana Indian who was captured Aug. 29, 1911, in Oroville, Calif. Dr. Saxton Pope was assigned to conduct a physical exam of Ishi. They later became good friends and hunting companions.

CHAPTER 3: GUN-HUNTING
31. **A**. The Winchester 1894 Sporting Rifle is the champion deer rifle. More than 7 million of these rifles are in circulation.

32. **B**. The Remington Model 700 became so popular that Remington has unveiled more than 25 variations over the years.

33. **D**. The .300 Weatherby Magnum was introduced in 1944. It was followed by the .338 Winchester Magnum, 1958; the 7mm Rem. Mag, 1962; and the .300 Win. Mag., 1963.

34. **C**. The .30-06 is undoubtedly the most flexible, useful, all-around big-game cartridge. In fact, it has been the standard by which all other big-game cartridges have been measured.

35. **A**. Michigan has more than 170,000 muzzleloading hunters. Ohio is second with 105,000.

36. **B**. In 1998, Pennsylvania had 1,066,032 gun-hunters for its deer season. Texas attracted 975,943 gun-hunters, while Michigan had 957,264 and Wisconsin had 742,669.

CHAPTER 4: MUZZLELOADING

37. **B**. Michigan attracts more than 210,000 muzzleloading hunters each year.

38. **D**. Arkansas muzzleloading hunters kill about 40,000 deer annually. Louisiana and Kentucky rank second and third with harvest totals of 25,000 and 24,000, respectively, while Michigan is fourth with 23,000.

39. **D**. Oregon has a 65-day muzzleloading season. Second place goes to South Dakota, 55 days, while third goes to California, 51 days.

40. **D**. If you study the answers, you will realize this was a trick question. However, "D" is the only correct statement. Many hunters like Pyrodex pellets because they increase velocities. Other hunters like them because they burn consistently and are cleaner than black powder. Pyrodex pellets come in 30- and 50-grain charges.

41. **C**. A safety, breech plug and receiver are on modern in-line muzzleloaders.

42. **B**.

CHAPTER 5: BIG BUCKS
43. **A**. Milo Hanson.

44. **F**. All of the above.

45. **D**. The other methods, in some instances and where legal, do not necessarily prevent a hunter from registering a buck with Pope and Young.

46. **B**. Iowa.

47. **False**. In fact, the Pope and Young record book includes numerous bucks with 13- and 14-inch spreads.

48. **False**. Boone and Crockett prints numerous specialty record books. For entry into those books, a buck must score at least 160 inches as a typical or 185 inches as a nontypical. For entry into the all-time book, however, a buck must meet the 170/195 minimums.

CHAPTER 6: QUALITY DEER MANAGEMENT
49. **D**. According to research conducted at Michigan's Cusino enclosure, the field-dressed weights of mature bucks averaged 199 pounds, while mature does weighed 128 pounds.

50. **B**. Bucks typically grow their largest set of antlers at ages 5½ and 6½.

51. **D**. According to researcher John Ozoga, bucks take longer to achieve full growth. While does achieve 80 percent of their mature weight as yearling, bucks don't reach mature weight until they're at least 2½ years old.

52. **B**. A buck needs about 10 percent to 15 percent protein to reach maximum antler growth. The rest is up to genetics. However, bucks need 22 percent protein to reach ideal body weights.

53. **C**.

54. **True**.

55. **C**. Small-bodied fawns have certain physical laws working against them in winter. They have short legs, which hinders travel through snow, and they lose more heat from each square meter of surface than does a large deer.

56. **B**. In 1975, Al Brothers co-authored the book *Producing Quality Whitetails*. The ideas he and Murphy Ray put forward are considered the foundation of today's QDM movement.

57. **E**. Across much of the whitetail's range, all of these problems often occur. With a vast array of hunters

and expanding human popuations, it's difficult to meet everyone's expectations for deer and deer hunting.

58. **A.** Conservatively, 35 acres could support more than 70 deer. A 100-acre field could support at least 125 deer.

59. **True.**

60. **A.** An adult deer needs 5 to 10 pounds of food each day.

61. **B.** An adult deer eats about 1 to 2 tons of food per year. Therefore, the land would have to produce 40 to 80 tons per square mile to support 40 deer.

62. **False.** QDM encourages the harvest of does to produce a well-balanced sex and age structure in the herd. In fact, adult does typically weigh more than yearling bucks. If hunters merely want venison, they can target does and let small bucks walk.

63. **C.** In general QDM promotes the idea of balancing the deer herd with the land's carrying capacity to produce quality year-round forage.

64. **B.**

65. **C.** Highly nutritious food doesn't help a buck grow to maximum size unless it's available year-round.

CHAPTER 7: THE LUNAR INFLUENCE
66. **D.** When adult does greatly outnumber adult bucks, rutting activity is slower and spread out over a longer period.

67. **A.** Northern. The rut is more varied in the Southern United States.

68. **D.** Feeding, seeking, chasing, tending, resting.

69. **B.** Tree stands.

70. **E.** High hunting pressure sends deer into hiding faster than any natural occurrence.

CHAPTER 8: STATE TRENDS AND RECORDS
71. **B.** The Coues deer is found in Arizona's southeastern mountains, but range up to edge of the Mogollon Rim and into the White Mountains.

72. **A.** Through B&C's 1993 update, Minnesota had placed 587 bucks into the B&C record book. Iowa was second with 563, while Illinois was third with 480.

73. **D.** Alabama has 21.97 million acres. Mississippi is second with 17 million acres.

74. **D.** Although the chances of getting a buck in Maine are relatively low, the chances of it being a trophy buck are higher. In 1997, 23 percent of the antlered buck harvest consisted of bucks from 4½ to 5½ years old.

75. **C.** In 1997, Texas whitetail hunters killed more than 502,000 deer.

76. **A.** Oak.

77. **A.** California allows hunters to use dogs for deer hunting. *(Check your local regulations before hunting)*

78. **C.** *New York does not require the use of blaze orange, but about 85 percent of its deer hunters*

wear blaze-orange. (Check your local regulations before hunting)

79. **A**. Wisconsin. The other states listed have shown steady decreases in the number of youth hunters.

80. **B**. Maryland. Accidents have increased in the other states.

81. **True**. Only 14 states allow the use of trailing dogs.

82. **True**. Of the states with whitetails, 24 allow baiting, while 22 do not.

83. **D**. All states require some form of hunter education. Age requirements vary.

84. **A**. Post/blackjack oak forests are the most common in Oklahoma. They are most abundant in the central part of the state.

85. **C**. Spread by biting insects, Epizootic Hemorrhagic Disease occurs between late summer and fall. In 1998, it devastated Virginia's whitetail herd.

86. **C**. Contrary to popular belief, recreational hunting did not cause the rapid decline in deer numbers in the late 1800s. The marketing of deer meat and hides, or the slaughter of whitetails for profit and subsistence, was the biggest contributor to the decline. In fact, recreational hunting, through revenue raised by license sales, is what brought deer and many other game species back from the brink of extinction.

87. **B**. Although all of three men were avid deer hunters, Olson was the one who shot his first deer at age 12 in northern Wisconsin.

88. **True**. Five states — Wyoming, Montana, Georgia, Arizona and Alabama do not offer special muzzleloading seasons. However, muzzleloaders can be used during the regular firearms seasons in those states.

CHAPTER 9: MEAT PROCESSING

89. **A**. The largest Northern does are not as heavy as most hunters want to believe. Research shows field-dressed weights for mature does usually average 105 to 120 pounds.

90. **B**. The chest shot — a bullet or arrow through the vitals — causes the most bleeding and allows hunters to rid the carcass of the most blood.

91. **A**. Venison has less fat than beef. Therefore, it will get freezer burned more easily unless it is wrapped well.

92. **D**. Many old-timers "acquired" extra helpings of the savory inside tenderloins by tricking first-time hunters into believing these delicious pieces of meat contained "poison" that was unfit for human consumption.

93. **B**. False. Although some hunters prefer to let their deer hang for several days, this practice does not allow proper aging unless the deer is free of blood, moisture and dirt, and is hung in a temperature-controlled room.

94. **C**. Meat should be allowed to cool at least 24 hours before freezing.

95. **D**. Game laws in many states require that venison be consumed within one year, but properly wrapped boneless and fat-free venison can keep for several years in a freezer. Hunters should discard fatty meats such as hamburger if they are not used within one year.

96. **D**. No hunter should cut corners when butchering deer. Doing so is disrespectful to the deer and to

the sport. If rushed, a hunter should take the carcass to a meat processor and pay to have it butchered and wrapped. Otherwise, a hunter should cancel other plans and take the time to ensure every portion of the carcass is used.

97. D. A deer's heart, liver and kidneys are not only edible, they are delicious when prepared properly. Hunters should eat these organ meats whenever possible.

98. C. Cool water can be used to clean the inside of a deer's cavity, but hunters should thoroughly wipe the cavity of all moisture before hanging the carcass to cool.

The Scoring System

90 to 98: Master deer hunter. You eat, sleep and dream about deer and deer hunting!

80 to 90: Seasoned veteran. You are the hunter everyone aspires to be.

70 to 80: Crack shot. You don't miss much, especially when you're in the woods!

60 to 70: Up-and-comer. With a little more experience, you will soon join the class of deer hunters who tag deer annually.

Less than 60: You might want to study this book and your past issues of *Deer & Deer Hunting* before heading to the woods this fall!

ANSWER KEYS FOR WORD SEARCH & CROSSWORD PUZZLES

Deer Hunting Super Word Search

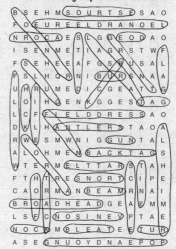

Crossword Puzzle #1

Crossword Puzzle #2

Kids' Corner:
Deer Hunting Super Word Search

```
B S E H M S U O R T S E S A O
F O E U R E E L D R A N O E L
N R O C A E S L G G E O D A O
I S E N M E T I A G R S T W F
F S E H E E A F G S B U S A L
F S L H Q R N I B U R S N A A
U H R U M E D I C G E A T T G
L O I H G E N K G G E S T A G
L C F F I E L D D R E S S A O
D K L H A N T L E R S T A O A
R W E S M W N I G G U N T A L
A L O H M E N B A C K T A G S
W T E R M E L T T A R S T A H
F T H T R E S N O R T C I P E
C A O R M A N B E A M R N A I
B R O A D H E A D G E A E M M
L S F C N O S I N E V P T A E
N O C K M B L E A T E E T U R
A S E G N U O Y D N A E P O P
```

ACORN	HOCK
ALSHEIMER	HOOF
ANTLERS	LEONARD LEE RUE
ARROW	NOCK
BACKTAG	POPE AND YOUNG
BEAM	RATTLE
BLEAT	RIFLE
BOONER	RUB
BROADHEAD	RUT
BUCK	SCRAPE
DOE	SLUG
ESTROUS	SNORT
FAWN	STAND
FIELD DRESS	TAG
FLAG	TARSAL
FULL DRAW	TINE
GRUNT	TRACK
GUN	VENISON

Puzzle Key on Page 199

Deer Hunter's Crossword Puzzle #1

Created by Daniel E. Schmidt

ACROSS

1. Helps keep bow strings and cams working properly.
3. One method of removing urban deer.
5. A doe that attracts rutting bucks.
7. Acronym for disease found in Michigan whitetails.
9. Hunters will _____ benefits in years to come by passing up small bucks.
11. She's an expert deer hunter and photographer whose last name is now Randle-Jolly.
13. Group of manufacturers dedicated to safety.
15. Woodland cow.
17. What Texans do to mature 7-pointers.
19. Set your sights.
21. First name of famed deer researcher Geist.
23. A yearling's third premolar has three of these.
25. Misalignment of this can cause poor arrow flight.
27. Large member of the deer family.
29. Abbreviation for southeastern Canadian province where deer hunting pressure is light.
31. Blood highway.
33. Water source.
35. Afternoon hunt.
37. Artery in a deer's neck.
39. What a buck does when he cross-checks deer trails.
41. This holds 13 percent of a deer's blood supply.
43. Hastens blood loss.
45. The first of the whitetail's four stomachs.

DOWN

1. White oak found in lowland areas.
2. Revolutionary product that traps human odor.
3. Chemoreceptors in a deer's nose and tongue allow them to do this.
6. Origin word for the word "rut."
4. A shot through these hits few, if any, veins.
8. The rut's timing is closely related to this.
10. If a bullet breaks this, a deer will almost always die immediately.
12. Bill Jordan's top selling camouflage pattern.
14. Staple food of whitetails in northeastern Canada.
16. You can't hunt without one of these.
18. Vertebrae found in a deer's neck.
20. Connecticut town where deadly insect disease originated.
22. Food that helps Northern whitetails make it through winter.
24. Long-time *Deer & Deer Hunting* contributor.
26. What a drop tine is considered on the score sheet of a nontypical buck.
35. Red oak found in upland areas.

Puzzle Key on Page 199

Hunter's Crossword Puzzle #2

Created by Wib Lundeen

ACROSS

1. A bow maker
4. A brand of sight
9. Part of a caribou bull's rack
10. Takes a well-placed arrow to down him.
12. Color wear for hunter's safety.
13. A type of arrow point.
15. Excuses a game bird from being shot at.
17. A deer's resting place.
19. Garbage is good bait for this animal.
20. Estimating how old game tracks are.
21. A whitetail species of the North.
23. Female deer.
25. A female turkey.
28. A lure to bring game to the hunter.
30. These types of hunts are the best for whitetails.
31. The male deer.
33. Whitetails are creatures of this.
34. What you do to a deer after field-dressing it.
36. Antlers do this annually.
37. Wood used for arrow shafts.
39. Another wood used in arrow making.
41. A game trail.
42. A game bird.

DOWN

1. A brush _____ keeps bow free of brush.
2. A trait of the whitetail.
3. A female bighorn.
4. Wood used for arrow shafts.
5. Hound trained to hunt deer.
6. Wood for making arrows.
7. A beginner in the art of bow-hunting.
8. A brand of camouflage.
11. The Pope and _____ Club.
14. Platform for hunting from trees.
16. Brand of quiver, Golden

_____.
17. These tines grow best on whitetails.
18. A species of sheep.
19. To place string in bow nocks.
21. A wounded deer will seek this.
22. Wind blowing toward game.
24. A bow-hunting animal native to Hawaii.
25. A deer's behavior pattern.
26. The bow-string fits here.
27. The whitetail can run up to _____ mph.
29. A game runway.
32. A side of the bow.
34. A deer does this to cross a river.
35. A buck's feeding time.
38. Causes the string to fray and break.
39. A loop in the bowstring.
40. Bow-hunter's aid in strange areas.

Puzzle Key on Page 199

Deer Harvest Records

Record this year's successful hunts here, and
save this book to remember each year's hunt!

Year _____   Name of Camp _____

Month & Day	Time of Day	Hunter Name	Buck (points)	Doe	Dressed Weight	Bow or Gun	Shot Distance	Tracking Distance

National Hunting Organizations

**American Shooting Sports
Council**
101 D. Street SE
Washington, DC 20003
202-544-1610
202-543-5865 fax

**Archery Manufacturers
Organization** (AMO)
4131 NW 28th Lane, Suite 7
Gainesville, FL 32606
904-377-8262
904-375-3961 fax

Archery Hall of Fame
1555 S. 150 West
Angola, IN 46703

**Archery Range
and Retailers Organization**
156 N. Main St., Suite D
Oregon, WI 53575
800-234-7499

Archery Shooters Association
Box 399
Kennesaw, GA 30144
770-795-0232

**Becoming
an Outdoors-Woman**
UW-Stevens Point
College of Natural Resources
Stevens Point, WI 54481-3897
715-228-2070

Boone & Crockett Club
The Old Milwaukee Depot
250 Station Drive
Missoula, MT 59801
406-542-1888

**Christian Bowhunters
of America**
3460 W. 13th St.
Cadillac, MI 49601
616-775-7744

**Christian Deer Hunters
Association**
Box 432
Silver Lake, MN 55381
320-327-2266

**Congressional
Sportsman's Foundation**
303 Pennsylvania Ave. SE
Washington, DC 20003
202-543-6850

Ducks Unlimited
1 Waterfowl Way
Memphis, TN 38120
901-758-3718

Hunter Education Association
Box 490
Wellington, CO 80549
970-568-7954
970-568-7955 fax

**International Association
of Fish & Wildlife Agencies**
Hall of the States
444 N. Capitol St. NW, Suite 544
Washington, DC 20001
202-624-7890

**International Bowhunters
Organization**
3409 E. Liberty, Box 398
Vermilion, OH 44089
216-967-2137

**International Sportsmen's
Expositions**
Box 2569
Vancouver, WA 98668-2569
800-545-6100
360-693-3352 fax

**Izaak Walton League of
America**
707 Conservation Lane
Gaithersburg, MD 20878-2983
301-548-0150
301-548-0146 fax

**National Association
of Sporting Goods
Wholesalers**
400 E. Randolph St., Suite 700
Chicago, IL 60601
312-565-0233
312-565-2654 fax

**National Bowhunter
Education Foundation**
101½ North Front St.
Townsend, MT 59644
406-266-3237

**National Crossbow Hunters
Organization**
Box 506, Verona, OH 45378
937-884-5017

**National Field Archery
Association**
31407 Outer I-10
Redlands, CA 92373
909-794-2133
909-794-8512 fax

**National Muzzleloading
Rifle Association**
Box 67, Friendship, IN 47021
812-667-5131
812-667-5137 fax

National Rifle Association
11250 Waples Mill Road
Fairfax, VA 22030-7400
703-267-1000

**National Shooting Sports
Foundation**
Flintlock Ridge Office Center
11 Mile Hill Road
Newton, CT 06470-2359
203-426-1320
203-426-1087 fax

**National Wild Turkey
Federation**
770 Augusta Road, Box 530
Edgefield, SC 29824-0530
803-637-3106
803-637-0034 fax

**Outdoor Writers
Association of America**
27 Fort Missoula Road, Suite 1
Missoula, MT 59804
406-728-7445

**Physically Challenged
Bowhunters of America**
Box 57, Gorham, KS 67640
785-637-5421

Pope & Young Club
15 E. 2nd St., Box 548
Chatfield, MN 55923
507-867-4144

Safari Club International
4800 W. Gates Pass Road
Tucson, AZ 85745
520-620-1220
520-622-1205 fax

U.S. Fish & Wildlife Service
1849 C St. NW
Washington, DC 20240
202-208-4131
202-208-7407

**Wildlife Legislative Fund
of America**
801 Kingsmill Parkway
Columbus, OH 43229-1137
614-888-4868

Wildlife Management Institute
1101 14th St. NW
Suite 801
Washington, DC 20005
202-371-1808

**Women's Shooting Sports
Foundation**
4620 Edison Ave., Suite C
Colorado Springs, CO 80915
719-638-1299